THE FIRST AMENDMENT
FREEDOM OF
THE PRESS

BILL OF RIGHTS SERIES

Series Editor:
David B. Oppenheimer, *Associate Dean*
Golden Gate University School of Law

Advisory Committee

THE FIRST AMENDMENT
FREEDOM OF
THE PRESS

Its Constitutional History and the Contemporary Debate

EDITED BY GARRETT EPPS

BILL OF RIGHTS SERIES

David B. Oppenheimer, Series Editor
Associate Dean
Golden Gate University School of Law

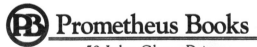 Prometheus Books

59 John Glenn Drive
Amherst, New York 14228-2119

Published 2008 by Prometheus Books

Inquiries should be addressed to
Prometheus Books
59 John Glenn Drive
Amherst, New York 14228–2119
VOICE: 716–691–0133, ext. 210
FAX: 716–691–0137
WWW.PROMETHEUSBOOKS.COM

12 11 10 09 08   5 4 3 2 1

Library of Congress Cataloging-in-Publication Data

Epps, Garrett.
    The First Amendment, freedom of the press : its constitutional history and the contemporary debate / Garrett Epps. — 1st American pbk. ed.
        p. cm.
    Includes bibliographical references.
    ISBN 978–1–59102–563–4
    1. Freedom of the press—United States. 2. Freedom of the press—United States—History. I. Epps, Garrett.

KF4774.F57 2008
342.7308'53—dc22

2007051796

Printed in the United States of America on acid-free paper

To Dan,

best of colleagues,

and Maggie,

best of readers

CONTENTS

PART II: EXPANSION THROUGH CASE LAW

PART III: CONTEMPORARY THOUGHTS

APPENDICES

BILL OF RIGHTS
SERIES EDITOR'S PREFACE

Abortion; the death penalty; school prayer; the pledge of allegiance; torture; surveillance; tort reform; jury trials; preventative detention; firearm registration; censorship; privacy; police misconduct; birth control; school vouchers; prison crowding; taking property by public domain. These issues, torn from the headlines, cover many, if not most, of the major public disputes arising today, in the dawn of the twenty-first century. Yet they are resolved by our courts based on a document fewer than 500 words long, drafted in the eighteenth century, and regarded by many at the time of its drafting as unnecessary. The Bill of Rights, the name we give the first ten amendments to the United States Constitution, is our basic source of law for resolving these issues. This series of books, of which this is volume 3, is intended to help us improve our understanding of the debates that gave rise to these rights, and of the continuing controversy about their meaning today.

When our Constitution was drafted, the framers were concerned with defining the structure and powers of our new federal government, and balancing its three branches. They didn't initially focus on the question of individual rights. The drafters organized the Constitution into seven sections, termed "Articles," each concerned with a specific area of federal authority. Article I sets forth the legislative powers of the Congress; Article II the executive powers of the President; Article III the judicial power of the federal courts. Article V governs the process for amending the Constitution. Article VI declares the supremacy of federal law on those subjects under federal jurisdiction, while Article VII provides the process for ratification. Only Article IV is concerned with individual rights, and only in a single sentence requiring states to give citizens of other states the same rights they provide to their own citizens. (Article IV also provides for the return of runaway slaves, a provision repealed in 1865 by the Thirteenth Amendment.)

When the Constitutional convention completed its work, in 1787, it sent the Constitution to the states for adoption. The opponents of ratification, known as the "Anti-Federalists" because they opposed the strong federal government envisioned in the Constitution, argued that without a Bill of Rights the federal government would be a danger to liberty. The "Federalists," principally Alexander Hamilton, James Madison and John Jay, responded in a series of anonymous newspaper articles now known as the "Federalist Papers." The Federalists initially argued that there was no need for a federal Bill of Rights, because most states (seven) had a state Bill of Rights, and because the proposed Constitution limited the power of the federal government to only those areas specifically enumerated, leaving all remaining powers to the States or the people. But in time, Madison would become the great proponent and drafter of the Bill of Rights.

The proposed Constitution was sent to the States for ratification on September 17, 1787. Delaware was the first State to assent, followed rapidly by Pennsylvania, New Jersey, Georgia and Connecticut. But when the Massachusetts Legislature met in January 1788 to debate ratification, several vocal members took up the objection that without a Bill of Rights the proposed Constitution endangered individual liberty. A compromise was brokered, with the Federalists agreeing to support amending the Constitution to add a Bill of Rights following ratification. The Anti-Federalists, led by John Adams and John Hancock, agreed, and Massachusetts ratified. When Maryland, South Carolina and New Hampshire followed, the requisite nine States had singed on. Virginia and New York quickly followed, with North Carolina ratifying in 1789, and Rhode Island in 1790. In addition to Massachusetts, New Hampshire, Virginia and New York's ratifying conventions conditioned their acceptance on the understanding that a Bill of Rights would be added.

The first Congress met in New York in March 1789, and among its first acts began debating and drafting the Bill of Rights. Federalist Congressman James Madison took responsibility for drafting the bill, having by then concluded that it would strengthen the legitimacy of the new government. He relied heavily on the state constitutions, especially the Virginia Declaration of Rights, in setting out those individual rights that should be protected from federal interference.

Madison steered seventeen proposed amendments through the House, of which the Senate agreed to twelve. On September 2, 1789 President Washington sent them to the States for ratification. Of the twelve, two, concerning Congressional representation and Congressional pay, failed to achieve ratification by over three quarters of the states; (the Congressional pay Amendment was finally ratified in 1992). The remaining ten were ratified, and with the vote of Virginia, on December 15, 1791 became the first ten amendments to the Constitution, the "Bill of Rights."

The Bill of Rights as originally adopted only applied to the federal government. Its purpose was to restrict Congress from interfering with rights reserved to the people. Thus, under the First Amendment the Congress could not establish a national religion, but the States could establish State support for selected religions, as seven States to some extent did (Connecticut, Georgia, Maryland, Massachusetts, New Hampshire, South Carolina and Vermont). Madison had proposed that the States also be bound by the Bill of Rights, and the House agreed, but the Senate rejected the proposal.

Although the Declaration of Independence provided that "We hold these truths to be self-evident — that all men are created equal" the Constitution and Bill of Rights are conspicuously silent on the question of equality, because the agreement that made the Constitution possible was the North/South compromise permitting the continuation of slavery. Thus, today's issues like affirmative action, race and sex discrimination, school segregation, and same-sex marriage cannot be resolved through application of the Bill of Rights. This omission of a guaranty of equality led to the Civil War, and in turn to the post-Civil War Fourteenth Amendment that made the newly-freed slaves US and State citizens, and prohibited the States from denying equal protection of the laws or due process of law to any citizen. In light of this Amendment, the Supreme Court began developing the "incorporation doctrine," holding that the Fourteenth Amendment extended the Bill of Rights so that they applied to all government action. By applying the Bill of Rights so expansively, the legal and social landscape of America was fundamentally changed.

In the aftermath of the Civil War, as the Supreme Court slowly began applying the Bill of Rights to the States and local government through the

Fourteenth Amendment, the debates of 1787-91 became more and more important to modern life. Could a high school principal begin a graduation ceremony by asking a minister (or a student leader) to say a prayer? Could a State require a girl under 16 to secure her parent's permission to have an abortion? Could a prison warden deny a pain medication to a prisoner between midnight and 7:00 AM? Could a college president censor an article in a student newspaper? These questions required the courts to examine the debates of the eighteenth century to determine what the framers intended when they drafted the Bill of Rights, (and raised the related question, hotly disputed, of whether the intent of the framers was even relevant, or whether a "living" Constitution required solely contemporary, not historical, analysis).

Hence this series. Our intent is to select the very best essays, from law and history, and the most important judicial opinions, and to edit them so that the leading views of what the framers intended, and of how we should interpret the Bill of Rights today, are made accessible to today's reader. If you find yourself passionately agreeing with some of the views expressed, angrily disagreeing with others, and appreciating how the essays selected have examined these questions with depth and lucidity, we will have succeeded.

David B. Oppenheimer
Professor of Law & Associate Dean for Faculty Development
Golden Gate University School of Law
San Francisco

ACKNOWLEDGMENTS

I want to thank Robert Post and David Oppenheimer for the opportunity to take on this project; I hope the product gives them no reason to regret their decision. And I must prominently thank my First Amendment professor, William Van Alstyne, who strove as a teacher and now strives as a colleague to disabuse me of my persistent errors. I am fortunate that repeated failure has not discouraged him. The book itself is the product of many hands. Robert Kinney initially spent hours in archives tracing sources and imagining what such a book should contain. After Robert moved on, I was assisted in the execution by a remarkable team of research assistants: Rachel Black-Meier, Samantha Evans, Steve Glista, Tori Klein, Darci Van Duzer, and, finally, Adam Lynn. Their work was always professional and prompt, a claim I myself cannot make about my own. My staff assistant, Jill Forcier, was the soul of the project and brooked no delay or excuse in completion of each stage. Without her, there would be no book. The team has, however, formally voted to forgive her son Oliver for being born and interrupting our work—especially as his expression at two hours old was precisely the same as his mother's when she is asking, "Have you finished that edit that was due today?" Debby Warren, who had worked with me before on a book and knew what she was getting into, stepped in for Jill and did not lose a beat.

Thanks to my children, Daniel and Maggie, who ignored all my complaints.

I want to acknowledge how much I learned from three great editors: the late Larry Stern of the *Washington Post*; Raymond H. Boone of the *Richmond Afro-American* and now the *Richmond Free Press*; and Katherine Fulton of the *Independent*. And here's a toast to four brilliant journalists who continue to adorn the profession I left: Lynn Darling, who has always written like an angel; James M. Fallows, who continues to separate the unconscionable from the merely outrageous; David Ignatius, the best reporter I have ever known; and Walter Shapiro, the Homer of American politics. Here's to us and those like us, old friends.

INTRODUCTION
Garrett Epps

The American law of press freedom is an international and historical anomaly. Even today, during a protracted and frightening state of war, the press in this country remains freer than any press in the world, or virtually any in history. Almost alone among legal systems in democratic nations, American courts give strong legal protection to "hate speech" such as Holocaust denial (banned in most countries and arguably illegal under international human rights norms), to scurrilous denunciations of public officials, and to un-censored publication of news that the government claims to find an imme-diate and serious threat to national security.

After a complex historical evolution over the past two hundred years, America has taken the English common-law concept of "the freedom of the press," which meant almost solely freedom from prior restraint, and trans-formed it into a set of institutional protections that gives critics of society and government extraordinary freedom to disseminate views that are unpopular, subversive and even just plain hateful. Though support for the institutional media waxes and wanes, most Americans seem reasonably content to allow them to function freely.

How did we get here? What are the historical roots of "the freedom of the press"? What were the key legal events in its transformation from "publish at your peril" to "uninhibited, robust, and wide-open"? What role did journalists themselves play in this process, and how important was the contribution of courts and lawyers? Does American press freedom serve as an example to the world?

These questions interest me at two levels, both of which I have tried to address in the anthology that follows. In my current life, I am a legal scholar who frequently writes on First Amendment and press-freedom topics for a professional audience. But before that, I was for more than fifteen years a working journalist. As a reporter, a feature writer, an opinion columnist, and an editor, I have grappled firsthand with many of the problems addressed by the cases and essays in this book: When should a newspaper publish material it believes to be true but cannot conclusively prove? What parts of a public figure's private life are relevant and suitable for publication, and what should remain private? How far is too far in an opinion writer's game of attack and caricature? When must a promise of confidentiality be honored, even at the cost of legal jeopardy, and when must it be broken, on the grounds that the source to whom it was made has misused the reporter-source relationship to spread false and scurrilous rumors? What should a reporter do when government secrets—such as the identity of an American intelligence agent—fall accidentally into his or her hands?

As a result of this dual consciousness, I have tried to create a volume that will be useful to editors, reporters, and ordinary citizens with an interest in these topics, while still retaining interest for specialists in the field. When in doubt, I thought of myself not as the slow-moving, polysyllabic scholar I have become but as the harried editor I used to be. As a result, I have made a couple of editorial decisions. Most of the cases and excerpts herein have been sharply edited to exclude procedural niceties, the details of lower-court adjudication and summaries of the now-obsolete state of case law at the time they were written. In addition (and this victory of the journalist over the scholar has made both of us positively giddy), there is not a single footnote in this volume. Interrupting the complex exposition of ideas with footnotes has always struck me as an obstacle both to pleasure and to comprehension; in the past century, both legal scholars and jurists have fallen prey far too often to the agreeable temptation to chat on and on in tiny type about ideas that could and should be more succinctly stated in the text itself. Citations to the original sources are included, of course, and readers who want to read more are welcome to turn to them.

In addition, I have included a few essays on the question of free speech generally, for the use of readers not grounded in the broad theory of free speech and of the American First Amendment generally. Freedom of speech and freedom of the press in American constitutional law share an uneasy relationship. Neither judges nor scholars can quite agree whether there is something called "the freedom of the press" that is separate from "the freedom of speech" that every resident of our country, by virtue of the First and Fourteenth Amendments, enjoys. Any American may speak; any American may publish a newspaper. But by publishing a newspaper, does our ordinary American become a favorite child of the First Amendment? And if so, what does that say about democracy, given that owning your own newspaper is at best a dream for all but a tiny segment of the population? "Freedom of the press," wrote the great press critic A. J. Liebling in a 1960 *New Yorker* essay, "is guaranteed only to those who own one." Are media owners simply members of a favored industry, or do they, by design, serve as surrogates for the public, to whom they owe reciprocal duties of fidelity and truthfulness?

Justice Potter Stewart, in his essay "Or of the Press," suggests that the text provides the answer. "The press" (what we today would call "the media") is, he notes, the only industry singled out by the Constitution for special protection. Stewart's argument is that "the press" as an institution provides a vital checking function on the doings of government and thus enjoys a place in the constitutional structure comparable to that of the actual institutions set up by the Constitution.

This argument boasts a distinguished pedigree. The colonial publicist James Alexander, writing in John-Peter Zenger's *New York Weekly Journal*, told American colonists that in a limited monarchy, a free press, by applying "the lash of satyr" to the malfeasance of criminal ministers, was not only "consistent with, but a necessary Part of, the Constitution itself." In the crisis of 1798, when the Federalist Party used its dominance of the new government to pass the Sedition Act and jail dissenting editors, James Madison warned that the First Amendment had been meant to entirely disable the federal government from regulating the press and thereby "binding the channel which alone can give efficacy to [the government's] responsibility to its constituents." In 1936, well before anyone could reasonably perceive the Supreme Court as "liberal," the conservative Justice Owen Sutherland analyzed a tax on newspapers as a revival of the eighteenth-century "taxes on knowledge," which were designed "to prevent, or curtail the opportunity for, the acquisition of knowledge by the people in respect of their governmental affairs." Since the Warren Court, justices (increasingly, in recent years, in dissent) often insist that a right asserted by a news outlet—the right to access a criminal trial, for example, or to publish truthful information from government records—is not a privilege sought by self-interested private actors, but a laudable function that the media exercise as constitutional surrogates for the public.

But at the same time, the Court—if not the public—has been reluctant ever to recognize this "structural" role of the press by awarding institutional media any specific prerogative not available to any citizen. Thus, while the federal courts sometimes discuss the possibility of a "reporter's privilege" to withhold the names of confidential sources, it is almost always a case of "jam yesterday and jam tomorrow, but never jam today"—a rhetorical route toward holding that such a mythical privilege, if it applies anywhere, does *not* apply to the specific case at bar. (Interestingly enough, a majority of states have enacted statutory "shield laws," without notably bad results; Congress, even in the days when the press was popular, has refused to follow suit.) News organizations that seek access to closed governmental areas or proceedings tend to win or lose depending not on how effectively such access will make them surrogates for the public but instead on how historically available the access they seek may have been for the ordinary citizen.

This theoretical difference between the clauses occupies a good deal of space in the third section of the book. The historical sources in the first section, interestingly enough, proceed on the implicit assumption that printing and publishing (at that time the only mass medium available) are fundamentally different from speaking and writing. Printing, to these authors, is, in some ways, a public utility, which later thinkers might have characterized as being "affected with a public interest"; at the same time, it is a private business to be conducted for profit. On the one hand, printers should be free to publish what they sense the market wants; at the same time, they should be careful what they choose, because printed matter is fraught with danger.

These contradictions go back to Milton's *Areopagitica*, the basic document of press freedom in the Anglo-American tradition. Books are magical, Milton asserts—and dangerous: "as lively, and as vigorously productive, as those fabulous dragon's teeth: and being sown up and down, may chance to spring up armed men. And yet, on the other hand, . . . he who destroys a good book, kills reason itself, kills the image of God, as it were, in the eye."

For this reason, he argues, no state censor could possibly have the wisdom to decide which new books should be born and which should be stifled in the womb. That decision must be made after publication, and its safety will be guaranteed by the mystical power of Truth to win over its readers. Milton's hymn to the power of truth has been quoted innumerable times since *Areopagitica* was written: "For who knows not that Truth is strong, next to the Almighty; she needs no policies, nor stratagems, nor licensings to make her victorious, those are the shifts and the defences that error uses against her power: give her but room, and do not bind her when she sleeps?" Few modern writers who quote these words also note that, for all Milton's faith in Truth, he almost offhandedly concedes that certain errors must be kept out of print: "I mean not tolerated popery, and open superstition, which as it extirpates all religions and civil supremacies, so itself should be extirpate ... ; that also which is impious or evil absolutely either against faith or manners no law can possibly permit." The broad freedom Milton foresees in fact extends only to "those neighbouring differences, or rather indifferences, ... whether in some point of doctrine or of discipline, which though they may be many, yet need not interrupt 'the unity of Spirit,' if we could but find among us 'the bond of peace.'"

Similarly, Benjamin Franklin, in his "Apology for the Printers," pleads for a public that will tolerate whatever he chooses to print for his customers, while at the same time insisting that he will set suitable limits over what those customers may print: "I my self have constantly refused to print anything that might countenance Vice, or promote Immorality; tho' by complying in such Cases with the corrupt Taste of the Majority I might have got much Money. I have also always refus'd to print such things as might do real Injury to any Person, how much soever I have been solicited, and tempted with Offers of Great Pay....I have hitherto fallen under the Resentment of large Bodies of Men, for refusing absolutely to print any of their Party or Personal Reflections."

This latter theme—that there is a special danger in the printed (or, more recently, the broadcast or recorded) word appears over and over in the pages that follow. An unbroken line of judicial anxiety stretches between Justice Holmes's conclusion that "it is impossible to say that it might not have been found that the circulation of [an antiwar] paper was in quarters where a little breath would be enough to kindle a flame" to District Judge Robert Warren's warning that allowing the *Progressive* to publish "The H-Bomb Secret" "could pave the way for thermonuclear annihilation for us all." A similar line of official authoritarianism unites New York Attorney General Richard Bradley's warning to defense counsel Andrew Hamilton in the Zenger trial in 1735— "Mr. Hamilton, have a Care what you say"—to White House spokesman Ari Fleischer's warning in 2001 to comedian Bill Maher in the wake of 9/11— "Americans...need to watch what they say, watch what they do."

Milton's assurance that the state can certainly censor anything "absolutely either against faith or manners" echoes in the arguments of contemporary scholars that certain types of "pornography" must be suppressed because they will impede society's march toward sexual equality. Throughout history, both libertarians and would-be censors agree that some things must not be printed. The only debate is, first, over how many there are, and, second, whether the publication at issue in a given case is one of them.

The first selection, *Areopagitica*, sets out these themes and many more besides; Franklin's "Apology" brings these concerns into the New World context, decades before the American Revolution or the First Amendment. Blackstone's "Libels" shows the legal result of the fight against licensing in seventeenth-century England: the doctrine that while prior restraint of publication is not permitted, subsequent punishment for any grounds Parliament chooses is. Three other documents from the pre-Revolutionary period—the essays on press freedom by "Cato" and Andrew Bradford, and the summary of Andrew Hamilton's argument to the jury on behalf of John Peter Zenger—stem from the long struggle of the American colonists for the right to criticize their colonial governors.

After the Revolution, Alexander Hamilton in "Federalist No. 84" urges ratification of the Constitution (which at that time contained no protections for speech or press); the new government, he soothingly writes a decade before the Sedition Act, would *never* have any power or desire to restrain the press. Hamilton's ally, Noah Webster, in his "Reply to the Pennsylvania Minority," urges ratification on the grounds that a firm government is needed to restrain press, lest "a man...should publish a treatise to *prove his maker a knave.*" Thomas Jefferson, in his "Letter to Edward Carrington," famously chooses newspapers without government over the reverse condition—with the qualification that it requires a public that will read and comprehend what is printed. James Madison, the legislative force behind the First Amendment, lays out the case against John Adams's Sedition Act and the doctrine of "seditious libel" in his "Virginia Report of 1799." Finally, writing three decades later, Alexis de Tocqueville gives a comforting picture of press freedom in the new nation—many newspapers, diverse ownership, little agreement, few readers.

The second section includes prominent cases on press-freedom issues decided over the past century. The choice of cases for inclusion was difficult, and some significant decisions have had to be omitted in order to keep the volume at a manageable size. Two decisions by Justice Oliver Wendell Holmes

Jr. show that brilliant jurist in his early, non-libertarian phase, enunciating with characteristic self-confidence two doctrines that time has decidedly repudiated. In *Patterson v. Colorado*, he says that courts may punish any published criticism of their proceedings while the cases are pending; in *Frohwerk v. United States*, he approves the jailing of a German-language editor who opposed America's entry into World War II. Two subsequent cases from the 1930s illustrate, however, that the doctrines of press freedom do not stem exclusively from the flowering of judicial liberalism that emerged from the New Deal. *Near v. Minnesota* writes a wide rule against prior restraint into First Amendment case law; *Grosjean v. American Press* finds in the amendment protection of the press from unfriendly taxation.

The most sweeping protections of freedom of the press, of course, come from the era of the Warren and Burger Courts in the 1960s and '70s. In his masterful opinion in *New York Times v. Sullivan*, Justice Brennan drives a stake through the heart of seditious libel. Nearly thirty years later, in *Hustler Magazine v. Falwell*, the far more conservative Rehnquist Court extends the protection of *New York Times v. Sullivan* even to a scabrous advertising parody designed to ridicule and humiliate a television evangelist. In *New York Times v. United States*, a divided Court denies the government an injunction against publication of classified government material it insists will harm national security in a time of war. Fifteen years later, however, a federal district judge in *United States v. Progressive* does enjoin publication of an article, pieced together solely from public sources, that purports to give step-by-step instructions on how to build a thermonuclear bomb.

Miller v. California puts the law of obscenity, after a long period of uncertainty, on certain (and very narrow) footing. *American Booksellers Association, Inc. v. Hudnut* demonstrates those limits. Despite impassioned arguments by feminist thinkers, the Seventh Circuit holds that states may not penalize certain kinds of violent and hateful pornography on the grounds that they harm women by encouraging men to view them as objects. "This," writes Judge Frank Easterbrook, "is thought control."

In *Branzburg v. Hayes*, the Court hints at the existence of a "reporter's privilege" but does not find it to apply to the cases of reporters with confidential sources among drug growers or Black Panthers. *Cohen v. Cowles Media*, twenty years later, holds that while the federal courts will not respect a reporter's promise of confidentiality to a source, states may, if they wish, enforce those same promises by permitting contract actions by the source to whom such a promise has been broken. Two cases consider the so-called right of reply for figures criticized in newspapers and on broadcast media: *Miami Herald v. Tornillo* makes clear that government cannot impose such a requirement on print media; *Red Lion Broadcasting v. Federal Communications Commission* finds that the special nature of broadcasting permits the federal government, if it chooses, to require such a right—as well as an obligation of general "fairness"—of holders of radio and television licenses.

In *Nebraska Press Association v. Stuart*, the Court rebukes a trial judge who sought to guarantee a fair trial by issuing a sweeping "gag order" to the media; *Richmond Newspapers v. Virginia* makes clear that judges cannot achieve the same end by simply closing the trial to everyone. *Landmark Communications v. Virginia* holds that the confidentiality of judicial discipline, while desirable, cannot be protected by criminal penalties against the media.

Finally, *Reno v. American Civil Liberties Union* throws a broad First Amendment cloak over "the vast democratic fora of the Internet"—a new arena for speech and press freedom where "any person with a phone line can become a town crier with a voice that resonates farther than it could from any soapbox."

In the section of contemporary commentary, the first three selections provide an abbreviated framework for modern legal thought about free expression generally. Justice Hugo Black's "absolutist" view—"Congress shall make no law," he argues, means "no law at all"—has never commanded a majority of the Court, but its textual emphasis has exercised a lasting gravitational pull on First Amendment jurisprudence. Thomas I. Emerson argues that free expression is not a set of isolated doctrines but a system of public values and institutional practices, in which all the parts must work together to secure a genuine, not merely nominal, freedom of speech to society. Finally, conservative jurist Robert Bork makes a contrary argument that the First Amendment should be read narrowly, allowing government a broad role in regulating and punishing speech.

The final selections focus more closely on the Press Clause and the unique problems posed by free-press practicalities. Justice Potter Stewart enunciates clearly the view that the institutional media have a role to play in safeguarding self-government analogous to those played by the actual three branches of government. Professor C. Edwin Baker attempts to imagine what the media world should look like if it is in fact to serve the purposes outlined by Justice Stewart. Leonard Levy, his generation's premier constitutional historian, looks back at the controversy sparked by his early view that the First

Amendment was not intended to void the law of seditious libel and offers a more nuanced view of the prehistory and framing of the Press Clause. Dean John C. Jeffries Jr. examines the press-specific doctrine created by the Court—the presumption against "prior restraints"—and concludes that it is incoherent. Finally, in "Or of the [Blog]," Professor Paul Horwitz attempts to apply Justice Stewart's vision of the Press Clause to a world in which anyone with an Internet connection can become a blogger and can then claim to be not only a reporter but also a publisher.

Though there are common themes in this history, the concept of freedom of the press must be viewed within a history that stretches from Milton's time—when a printing press was an exotic, expensive, high-tech device—to our own—in which printing services are available in any well-equipped office, wide publication is instantly available on the Internet, but access to a wide broadcast audience is still rare, expensive, and dominated by risk-averse corporations on the one hand and a highly restrictive government on the other. The liberty of publishers meant one thing in the days of hand-set type and John Peter Zenger, and means something else in the era of broadband and Rupert Murdoch.

Perhaps the main constant in these materials is the terror governments feel at the prospect that ordinary citizens can be heard without official approval; that "dangerous" blasphemies—against official religion, official racism, official military policy, and official morality—may be uttered in circumstances "where a little breath would be enough to kindle a flame." The well-meaning enthusiasm of the censor is undimmed from the days of Star Chamber to that of Robert Bork. And while the history of press freedom suggests that the censors rarely win in the long run, it is clear they often may delay or impede publication of news the government fears; and it is impossible to conclude that the censors never win. Sometimes they do.

Part I

HISTORICAL FOUNDATIONS

AREOPAGITICA

John Milton

Areopagitica is the mother document of Anglo-American free-press theory. The name comes from a hill near Athens that was reputed to have been the site of democratic tribunals during the height of the Athenian democratic city-state. The essay was inspired by the seventeenth-century struggle between the Crown and Parliament, which led eventually to the English Civil War and the beheading of Charles I. Ironically, the essay was not an attack on royal censorship but a response to the Licensing Act of 1643, in which Parliament attempted to replace the king as censor of all printed works in the kingdom.

The author, John Milton, was not only a prominent Puritan and supporter of Parliament, but was also a poet and essayist considered by many in Europe to be the most educated man alive. His most famous work is the epic poem *Paradise Lost*, which depicts the struggle between God and Satan for the souls of humankind and has influenced virtually every depiction of Heaven and Hell written since. But Milton was also a prolific pamphleteer, espousing, among other causes, republicanism, divorce, and freedom of the press from prior restraint.

Milton was born in 1608 in London to a well-educated and financially

---

Areopagitica, with a Commentary by Sir Richard C. Jebb and with Supplementary Material (Cambridge: Cambridge University Press, 1918).

prosperous family. His formal education began with private tutoring at home and ended with Milton graduating cum laude with a Master of Arts degree from Cambridge. He continued to educate himself by traveling Western Europe and conferring with scholars and theologians.

In 1639 Milton returned home to a developing civil war. Milton, a prolific pamphleteer, later outlined his support for the people's power to dispose of a tyrannical king in *The Tenure of Kings and Magistrates* (1649). With the execution of Charles I that year and the establishment of a Commonwealth, Milton became Secretary of Foreign Tongues, charged with defending the new government in pellucid Latin tracts admired across Europe.

Areopagitica protested a new statute that required all printers to obtain specific licenses for any new works they printed. Though opposing this sort of censorship, Milton made no objection to the legal doctrines that provided for subsequent punishment for printed material that was libelous or blasphemous; his target was simply the effrontery of a government that assumed the power and wisdom to suppress books and tracts before they could be read. And despite his rhapsodic description of Truth winning its free competition against error, Milton made clear that some publications—especially Catholic ones—remained beyond the protection of his vision of a free press.

This is true Liberty when free born men
Having to advise the public may speak free,
Which he who can, and will, deserves high praise,
Who neither can nor will, may hold his peace
What can be juster in a State than this?

Euripid. Hicetid.

...I know not what should withhold me from presenting ye with a fit instance wherein to shew both that love of truth which ye eminently profess, and that uprightness of your judgment which is not wont to be partial to yourselves; by judging over again that order which ye have ordained "to regulate printing: that no book, pamphlet, or paper shall be henceforth printed, unless the same be first approved and licensed by such," or at least one of such, as shall be thereto appointed. For that part which preserves justly every man's copy to himself; or provides for the poor, I touch not; only wish they be not made pretences to abuse and persecute honest and painful men, who offend not in either of these particulars. But that other clause of licensing books, which we thought had died with his brother quadragesimal and matrimonial when the prelates expired, I shall now attend with such a homily, as shall lay before ye, first, the inventors of it to be those whom ye will be loath to own; next, what is to be thought in general of reading, whatever sort the books be; and that this order avails nothing to the suppressing of scandalous, seditious, and libellous books, which were mainly intended to be suppressed. Last, that it will be primely to the discouragement of all learning, and the stop of truth, not only by disexercising and blunting our abilities, in what we know already, but by hindering and cropping the discovery that might be yet further made, both in religious and civil wisdom.

I deny not, but that it is of greatest concernment in the church and commonwealth, to have a vigilant eye how books demean themselves, as well as men; and thereafter to confine, imprison, and do sharpest justice on them as malefactors; for books are not absolutely dead things, but do contain a potency of life in them to be as active as that soul was whose progeny they are; nay, they do preserve as in a vial the purest efficacy and extraction of that living intellect that bred them. I know they are as lively, and as vigorously productive, as those fabulous dragon's teeth: and being sown up and down, may chance to spring up armed men. And yet, on the other hand, unless wariness be used, as good almost kill a man as kill a good book: who kills a man kills a reasonable creature, God's image; but he who destroys a good book, kills reason itself, kills the image of God, as it were, in the eye. Many a man lives a burden to the earth; but a good book is the precious life-blood of a master-spirit, embalmed and treasured up on purpose to a life beyond life. It is true, no age can restore a life, whereof, perhaps, there is no great loss; and revolutions of ages do not oft recover the loss of a rejected truth, for the want of which whole nations fare the worse. We should be wary, therefore, what persecution we raise against the living labours of public men, how we spill that seasoned life of man preserved and stored up in books, since we see a kind of homicide may be thus committed, sometimes a martyrdom; and if it extend to the whole impression, a kind of massacre, whereof the execution ends not in the slaying of an elemental life, but strikes at that ethereal and fifth essence, the breath of reason itself, slays an immortality rather than a life....

...For books are as meats and viands are; some of good, some of evil substance; and yet God in that unapocryphal vision said without exception, "Rise, Peter, kill and eat"; leaving the choice to each man's discretion. Wholesome meats to a vitiated stomach differ little or nothing from unwholesome; and best books to a naughty mind are not unapplicable to occasions of evil. Bad meats will scarce breed good nourishment in the healthiest concoction; but herein the difference is of bad books, that they to a discreet and judicious reader serve in many respects to discover, to confute, to forewarn, and to illustrate.... I conceive, therefore, that when God did enlarge the universal diet of man's body, saving ever the rules of temperance, he then also, as before, left arbitrary the dieting and repasting of our minds; as wherein every mature man might have to exercise his own leading capacity. How great a virtue is temperance, how much of moment through the whole life of man! Yet God commits the managing so great a trust, without particular law or prescription, wholly to the demeanour of every grown man.... Good and evil we know in the field of this world grow up together almost inseparably; and the knowledge of good is so involved and inter-woven with the knowledge of evil, and in so many cunning resemblances hardly to be discerned, that those confused seeds which were imposed upon Psyche as an incessant labour to cull out, and sort asunder, were not more intermixed. It was from out the rind of one apple tasted, that the knowledge of good and evil, as two twins cleaving together, leaped forth into the world. And perhaps this is that doom which Adam fell into of knowing good and evil; that is to say, of knowing good by evil. As therefore the state of man now is; what wisdom can there be to choose, what continence to forbear, without the knowledge of evil? He that can apprehend and consider vice with all her baits and seeming pleasures, and yet abstain, and yet distinguish, and yet prefer that which is truly better, he is the true wayfaring Christian. I cannot praise a fugitive and cloistered virtue unexercised and unbreathed, that never sallies out and seeks her adversary, but slinks out of the race, where that immortal garland is to be run for, not without dust and heat.... Since therefore the knowledge and survey of vice is in this world so necessary to the constituting of human virtue, and the scanning of error to the confirmation of truth, how can we more safely, and with less danger, scout into the regions of sin and falsity than by reading all manner of tractates, and hearing all manner of reason? And this is the benefit which may be had of books promiscuously read.... Seeing therefore that those books, and those in great abundance, which are likeliest to taint both life and doctrine, cannot be suppressed without the fall of learning, and of all ability in disputation, and that these books of either sort are most and soonest catching to the learned, from whom to the common people whatever is heretical or dissolute may quickly be conveyed, and that evil manners are as perfectly learnt without books a thousand other ways which cannot be stopped, and evil doctrine not with books can propagate, except a teacher guide, which he might also do without writing, and so beyond prohibiting, I am not able to unfold, how this cautelous enterprise of licensing can be exempted from the number of vain and impossible attempts. And he who were pleasantly disposed, could not well avoid to liken it to the exploit of that gallant man who thought to pound up the crows by shutting his park gate. Besides another inconvenience, if learned men be the first receivers out of books, and dispreaders both of vice and error, how shall the licensers themselves be confided in, unless we can confer upon them, or they assume to themselves, above all others in the land, the grace of infallibility and uncorruptedness? And again, if it be true, that a wise man, like a good refiner, can gather gold out of the drossiest volume, and that a fool will be a fool with the best book, yea, or without book; there is no reason that we should deprive a wise man of any advantage to his wisdom, while we seek to restrain from a fool that which being restrained will be no hindrance to his folly.... See the ingenuity of Truth, who, when she gets a free and willing hand, opens herself faster than the pace of method and discourse can over-take her. It was the task which I began with, to shew that no nation, or well instituted state, if they valued books at all, did ever use this way of licensing; and it might be answered, that this is a piece of prudence lately discovered. To which I return, that as it was a thing slight and obvious to think on, so if it had been difficult to find out, there wanted not among them long since, who suggested such a course; which they not following, leave us a pattern of their judgment that it was not the not knowing, but the not approving, which was the cause of their not using it. Plato, a man of high authority indeed, but least of all for his Commonwealth, in the book of his laws, which no city ever yet received, fed his fancy with making many edicts to his airy burgomasters, which they who otherwise admire him, wish had been rather buried and excused in the genial cups of an academic night sitting. By which laws he seems to tolerate no kind of learning, but by unalterable decree, consisting most of practical traditions, to the attainment whereof a library of smaller bulk than his own dialogues would be abundant. And there also enacts, that no poet should so much as read to any private man what he had written, until the judges and law keepers had seen it, and allowed it; but that Plato meant this law peculiarly to that commonwealth which he had imagined, and to no other, is evident. Why was he not else a lawgiver to himself, but a transgressor, and to be expelled by his own magistrates, both for the wanton epigrams and dialogues which he made, and his perpetual reading of Sophron Mimus and Aristophanes, books of grossest infamy; and also for commending the latter of them, though he were the malicious libeller of his chief friends, to be read by the tyrant Dionysius, who had little need of such trash to spend his time on? But that he knew this licensing of poems had reference and dependence to many other provisoes there set down in his fancied republic, which in this world could have no place; and so neither he himself, nor any magistrate or city, ever imitated that course, which, taken apart from those other collateral injunctions, must needs be vain and fruitless. For if they fell upon one kind of strictness, unless their care were equal to regulate all other things of like apt- ness to corrupt the mind, that single endeavour they knew would be but a fond labour; to shut and fortify one gate against corruption, and be necessitated to leave others round about wide open.... To sequester out of the world into Atlantic and Eutopian polities, which never can be drawn into use, will not mend our condition; but to ordain wisely as in this world of evil, in the midst whereof God hath placed us unavoidably. Nor is it Plato's licensing of books will do this, which necessarily pulls along with it so many other kinds of licensing, as will make us all both ridiculous and weary, and yet frustrate; but those unwritten, or at least unconstraining laws of virtuous education, reli- gious and civil nurture, which Plato there mentions, as the bonds and liga- ments of the commonwealth, the pillars and the sustainers of every written statute; these they be, which will bear chief sway in such matters as these, when all licensing will be easily eluded. Impunity and remissness for certain are the bane of a commonwealth; but here the great art lies, to discern in what the law is to bid restraint and punishment, and in what things persuasion only is to work.... If then the order shall not be vain and frustrate, behold a new labour, lords and commons, ye must repeal and proscribe all scandalous and unlicensed books already printed and divulged; after ye have drawn them up into a list, that all may know which are condemned, and which not; and ordain that no foreign books be delivered out of custody, till they have been read over. This office will require the whole time of not a few overseers, and those no vulgar men. There be also books which are partly useful and excellent, partly culpable and pernicious; this work will ask as many more officials, to make expurgations and expunctions, that the commonwealth of learning be not damnified. In fine, when the multitude of books increase upon their hands, ye must be fain to catalogue all those printers who are found frequently offending, and forbid the importation of their whole suspected typography....

Another reason, whereby to make it plain that this order will miss the end it seeks, consider by the quality which ought to be in every licenser. It cannot be denied but that he who is made judge to sit upon the birth or death of books, whether they may be wafted into this world or not, had need to be a man above the common measure, both studious, learned, and judicious; there may be else no mean mistakes in the censure of what is passable or not; which is also no mean injury. If he be of such worth as behoves him, there cannot be a more tedious and unpleasing journeywork, a greater loss of time levied upon his head, than to be made the perpetual reader of unchosen books and pamphlets, ofttimes huge volumes. There is no book that is acceptable unless at certain seasons; but to be enjoined the reading of that at all times, and in a hand scarce legible, whereof three pages would not down at any time in the fairest print, is an imposition which I cannot believe how he that values time, and his own studies, or is but of a sensible nostril, should be able to endure....

I lastly proceed from the no good it can do, to the manifest hurt it causes, in being first the greatest discouragement and affront that can be offered to learning and to learned men.... He who is not trusted with his own actions, his drift not being known to be evil, and standing to the hazard of law and penalty, has no great argument to think himself reputed in the commonwealth wherein he was born for other than a fool or a foreigner. When a man writes to the world, he summons up all his reason and deliberation to assist him; he searches, meditates, is industrious, and likely consults and confers with his judicious friends; after all which done, he takes himself to be informed in what he writes, as well as any that wrote before him; if in this, the most consummate act of his fidelity and ripeness, no years, no industry, no former proof of his abilities, can bring him to that state of maturity, as not to be still mistrusted and suspected, unless he carry all his considerate diligence, all his midnight watchings, and expense of Palladian oil, to the hasty view of an un-leisured licenser, perhaps much his younger, perhaps far his inferior in judgment, perhaps one who never knew the labour of bookwriting; and if he be not re-pulsed, or slighted, must appear in print like a punie with his guardian, and his censor's hand on the back of his title to be his bail and surety, that he is no idiot or seducer, it cannot be but a dishonour and derogation to the author, to the book, to the privilege and dignity of learning....

... Truth and understanding are not such wares as to be monopolized and traded in by tickets, and statutes, and standards. We must not think to make a staple commodity of all the knowledge in the land, to mark and license it like our broad-cloth and our woolpacks. What is it but a servitude like that imposed by the Philistines, not to be allowed the sharpening of our own axes and coulters, but we must repair from all quarters to twenty licensing forges? Had any one written and divulged erroneous things and scandalous to honest life, misusing and forfeiting the esteem had of his reason among men, if after conviction this only censure were adjudged him, that he should never hence-forth write, but what were first examined by an appointed officer, whose hand should be annexed to pass his credit for him, that now he might be safely read, it could not be apprehended less than a disgraceful punishment. Whence to include the whole nation, and those that never yet thus offended, under such a diffident and suspectful prohibition, may plainly be understood what a dis-paragement it is. . . .

And in conclusion it reflects to the disrepute of our ministers also, of whose labours we should hope better, and of the proficiency which their flock reaps by them, than that after all this light of the gospel which is, and is to be, and all this continual preaching, they should be still frequented with such an unprincipled, unedified, and laic rabble, as that the whiff of every new pam-phlet should stagger them out of their catechism and Christian walking. This may have much reason to discourage the ministers when such a low conceit is had of all their exhortations, and the benefiting of their hearers, as that they are not thought fit to be turned loose to three sheets of paper without a licenser; that all the sermons, all the lectures preached, printed, vended in such numbers, and such volumes, as have now well-nigh made all other books unsaleable, should not be armour enough against one single Enchiridion, without the castle of St Angelo of an imprimatur.

And lest some should persuade ye, lords and commons, that these argu-ments of learned men's discouragement at this your order are mere flourishes, and not real, I could recount what I have seen and heard in other countries, where this kind of inquisition tyrannizes; when I have sat among their learned men, for that honour I had, and been counted happy to be born in such a place of philosophic freedom, as they supposed England was, while themselves did nothing but bemoan the servile condition into which learning amongst them was brought; that this was it which had damped the glory of Italian wits; that nothing had been there written now these many years but flattery and fustian. There it was that I found and visited the famous Galileo, grown old, a prisoner to the Inquisition, for thinking in astronomy otherwise than the Franciscan and Dominican licensers thought. And though I knew that England then was groaning loudest under the prelatical yoke, nevertheless I took it as a pledge of future happiness, that other nations were so persuaded of her liberty....

Well knows he who uses to consider, that our faith and knowledge thrives by exercise, as well as our limbs and complexion. Truth is compared in scripture to a streaming fountain; if her waters flow not in a perpetual progression, they sicken into a muddy pool of conformity and tradition....

...And though all the winds of doctrine were let loose to play upon the earth, so Truth be in the field, we do injuriously by licensing and prohibiting to misdoubt her strength. Let her and Falsehood grapple; who ever knew Truth put to the worse, in a free and open encounter? Her confuting is the best and surest suppressing. He who hears what praying there is for light and clearer knowledge to be sent down among us, would think of other matters to be constituted beyond the discipline of Geneva, framed and fabricated already to our hands. Yet when the new light which we beg for shines in upon us, there be who envy and oppose, if it come not first in at their casements. What a collusion is this, whenas we are exhorted by the wise man to use diligence, "to seek for wisdom as for hidden treasures" early and late, that another order shall enjoin us to know nothing but by statute. When a man hath been labouring the hardest labour in the deep mines of knowledge, hath furnished out his findings in all their equipage, drawn forth his reasons as it were a battle ranged, scattered and defeated all objections in his way, calls out his adversary into the plain, offers him the advantage of wind and sun, if he please, only that he may try the matter by dint of argument, for his opponents then to skulk, to lay ambushments, to keep a narrow bridge of licensing where the challenger should pass, though it be valour enough in soldiership, is but weakness and cowardice in the wars of Truth. For who knows not that Truth is strong, next to the Almighty; she needs no policies, nor stratagems, nor licensings to make her victorious, those are the shifts and the defences that error uses against her power: give her but room, and do not bind her when she sleeps, for then she speaks not true, as the old Proteus did, who spake oracles only when he was caught and bound, but then rather she turns herself into all shapes except her own, and perhaps tunes her voice according to the time, as Micaiah did before Ahab, until she be adjured into her own likeness. Yet is it not impossible that she may have more shapes than one? What else is all that rank of things indifferent, wherein Truth may be on this side, or on the other, without being unlike herself? What but a vain shadow else is the abolition of "those ordinances, that hand-writing nailed to the cross"? What great purchase is this

Christian liberty which Paul so often boasts of? His doctrine is, that he who eats or eats not, regards a day or regards it not, may do either to the Lord. How many other things might be tolerated in peace, and left to conscience, had we but charity, and were it not the chief stronghold of our hypocrisy to be ever judging one another. I fear yet this iron yoke of outward conformity hath left a slavish print upon our necks; the ghost of a linen decency yet haunts us. We stumble, and are impatient at the least dividing of one visible congregation from another, though it be not in fundamentals; and through our forwardness to suppress, and our backwardness to recover, any enthralled piece of truth out of the gripe of custom, we care not to keep truth separated from truth, which is the fiercest rent and disunion of all. We do not see that while we still affect by all means a rigid external formality, we may as soon fall again into a gross conforming stupidity, a stark and dead congealment of "wood and hay and stubble" forced and frozen together, which is more to the sudden degen-erating of a church than many subdichotomies of petty schisms. Not that I can think well of every light separation; or that all in a church is to be expected "gold and silver, and precious stones:" it is not possible for man to sever the wheat from the tares, the good fish from the other fry; that must be the angels' ministry at the end of mortal things. Yet if all cannot be of one mind, as who looks they should be? this doubtless is more wholesome, more prudent, and more Christian that many be tolerated rather than all compelled. I mean not tolerated popery, and open superstition, which as it extirpates all religions and civil supremacies, so itself should be extirpate, provided first that all charitable and compassionate means be used to win and regain the weak and the misled: that also which is impious or evil absolutely either against faith or manners no law can possibly permit, that intends not to unlaw itself: but those neighbouring differences, or rather indifferences, are what I speak of, whether in some point of doctrine or of discipline, which though they may be many, yet need not interrupt 'the unity of Spirit,' if we could but find among us 'the bond of peace.' In the meanwhile, if any one would write, and bring his helpful hand to the slow-moving reformation which we labour under, if Truth have spoken to him before others, or but seemed at least to speak, who hath so bejesuited us that we should trouble that man with asking licence to do so worthy a deed? . . .

And as for regulating the press, let no man think to have the honour of advising ye better than yourselves have done in that order published next before this: "That no book be printed, unless the printer's and the author's name, or at least the printer's be registered." Those which otherwise come forth, if they be found mischievous and libellous, the fire and the executioner will be the timeliest and the most effectual remedy that man's prevention can use. For this authentic Spanish policy of licensing books, if I have said aught, will prove the most unlicensed book itself within a short while; and was the immediate image of a star-chamber decree to that purpose made in those very times when that court did the rest of those her pious works, for which she is now fallen from the stars with Lucifer....

"AN APOLOGY FOR THE PRINTERS"

Benjamin Franklin

Benjamin Franklin is known today for his dazzling success as a scientist, diplomat, and statesman. But the foundation of his fortunes, and the mold of his sensibilities, was his lifelong involvement with the printing trade. Long before the idea of independence had occurred to him or almost anyone else, Franklin was pleading for government and popular toleration for printers, whose role he saw as something like that of a public utility. The "Apology for the Printers" lays out the rationale for a free press and combines it with sound business sense.

Franklin was born in Boston in 1706. A the age of fifteen, he became an apprentice printer to his brother James's paper, the *New England Courant*. Prohibited by his brother from writing for the *Courant*, Franklin submitted articles signed "Mrs. Silence Dogood." Eventually Mrs. Dogood's identity was revealed, and James's displeasure created a rift in their relationship. Before long, Franklin ran away from home and became an apprentice printer in Philadelphia. It was not until 1729, when he and a friend purchased the *Pennsylvania Gazette*, that Benjamin Franklin achieved his dream of becoming a printer. He replied to his critics in "An Apology for the Printers." Though he

Pennsylvania Gazette (Philadelphia), June 10, 1731. Reprinted in Albert Henry Smyth, ed., *The Writings of Benjamin Franklin*, 10 vols. (New York: Macmillan, 1905–1907), 2: 172–79.

became internationally known for his scientific discoveries, and served as American minister to France and later as a member of the Philadelphia Convention of 1787, he never lost sight of his origins in the composing room and sometimes signed his letters, "B. Franklin, printer."

Being frequently censur'd and condemn'd by different Persons for printing Things which they say ought not to be printed, I have sometimes thought it might be necessary to make a standing Apology for my self, and publish it once a Year, to be read upon all Occasions of that Nature. Much Business has hitherto hindered the execution of this Design; but having very lately given extraordinary Offence by printing an Advertisement with a certain N.B. at the End of it, I find an Apology more particularly requisite at this Juncture, tho' it happens when I have not yet Leisure to write such a Thing in the proper Form, and can only in a loose manner throw those Considerations together which should have been the Substance of it.

I request all who are angry with me on the Account of printing things they don't like, calmly to consider these following Particulars.

1. That the Opinions of Men are almost as various as their Faces; an Observation general enough to become a common proverb, *So many Men so many Minds*.

2. That the Business of Printing has chiefly to do with Mens opinions; most things that are printed tending to promote some, or oppose others.

3. That hence arises the peculiar Unhappiness of that Business, which other Callings are no way liable to; they who follow Printing being scarce able to do any thing in their way of getting a Living, which shall not probably give Offence to some, and perhaps to many; whereas the Smith, the Shoemaker, the Carpenter, or the Man of any other Trade, may work indifferently for People of all Persuasions, without offending any of them: and the Merchant may buy and sell with Jews, Turks, Hereticks and Infidels of all sorts, and get Money by every one of them, without giving Offence to the most orthodox, of any sort; or suffering the least Censure or Ill will on the Account from any Man whatever.

4. That it is as unreasonable in any one Man or Set of Men to expect to be pleas'd with every thing that is printed, as to think that nobody ought to be pleas'd but themselves.

5. Printers are educated in the Belief, that when Men differ in Opinion, both Sides ought equally to have the Advantage of being heard by the Pub-

lick; and that when Truth and Error have fair Play, the former is always an overmatch for the latter: Hence they chearfully serve all contending Writers that pay them well, without regarding on which side they are of the Question in Dispute.

6. Being thus continually employ'd in serving both Parties, Printers naturally acquire a vast Unconcernedness as to the right or wrong Opinions contain'd in what they print; regarding it only as the Matter of their daily labour: They print things full of Spleen and Animosity, with the utmost Calmness and Indifference, and without the least Ill-will to the Persons reflected on; who nevertheless unjustly think the Printer as much their Enemy as the Author, and join both together in their Resentment.

7. That it is unreasonable to imagine Printers approve of every thing they print, and to censure them on any particular thing accordingly; since in the way of their Business they print such great variety of things opposite and contradictory. It is likewise as unreasonable what some assert, "That Printers ought not to print any Thing but what they approve;" since if all of that Business should make such a Resolution, and abide by it, an End would thereby be put to Free Writing, and the World would afterwards have nothing to read but what happen'd to be the Opinions of Printers.

8. That if all Printers were determin'd not to print any thing till they were sure it would offend no body, there would be very little printed.

9. That if they sometimes print vicious or silly things not worth reading, it may not be because they approve such things themselves, but because the People are so viciously and corruptly educated that good things are not encouraged. I have known a very numerous Impression of Robin Hood's Songs go off in this Province at 2s. per Book, in less than a Twelve-month; when a small Quantity of David's Psalms (an excellent Version) have lain upon my Hands above twice the Time.

10. That notwithstanding what might be urg'd in behalf of a Man's being allow'd to do in the Way of his Business whatever he is paid for, yet Printers do continually discourage the Printing of great Numbers of bad things, and stifle them in the Birth. I my self have constantly refused to print anything that might countenance Vice, or promote Immorality; tho' by complying in such Cases with the corrupt Taste of the Majority I might have got much Money. I have also always refus'd to print such things as might do real Injury to any Person, how much soever I have been solicited, and tempted with Offers of Great Pay; and how much soever I have by refusing got the Ill-will of those

who would have employ'd me. I have hitherto fallen under the Resentment of large Bodies of Men, for refusing absolutely to print any of their Party or Personal Reflections. In this Manner I have made my self many Enemies, and the constant Fatigue of denying is almost insupportable. But the Publick being unacquainted with all this, whenever the poor Printer happens either through Ignorance or much Persuasion, to do any thing that is generally thought worthy of Blame, he meets with no more Friendship or Favour on the above Account, than if there were no Merit in't at all. Thus, as Waller says,

> Poets lose half the Praise they would have got
> Were it but known what they discretely blot;

Yet are censur'd for every bad Line found in their Works with the utmost Severity.

I come now to the Particular Case of the N.B. above mention'd, about which there has been more Clamour against me, than ever before on any other Account. —In the Hurry of other Business an Advertisement was brought to me to be printed; it signified that such a Ship lying at such a Wharff, would sail for Barbadoes in such a Time, and that Freighters and Passengers might agree with the Captain at such a Place; so far is what's common: But at the Bottom this odd Thing was added, "N.B. No Sea Hens nor Black Gowns will be admitted on any Terms." I printed it, and receiv'd my Money; and the Advertisement was stuck up round the Town as usual. I had not so much Curiosity at that time as to enquire the Meaning of it, nor did I in the least imagine it would give so much Offence. Several good Men are very angry with me on this Occasion; they are pleas'd to say I have too much Sense to do such things ignorantly; that if they were Printers they would not have done such a thing on any Consideration; that it could proceed from nothing but my abundant Malice against Religion and the Clergy. They therefore declare they will not take any more of my Papers, nor have any farther Dealings with me; but will hinder me of all the Custom they can. All this is very hard!

I believe it had been better if I had refused to print the said Advertisement. However, 'tis done, and cannot be revok'd. I have only the following few Particulars to offer, some of them in my behalf, by way of Mitigation, and some not much to the Purpose; but I desire none of them may be read when the Reader is not in a very good Humour.

1. That I really did it without the least Malice, and imagin'd the N.B. was

plac'd there only to make the Advertisement star'd at, and more generally read.

2. That I never saw the Word Sea-Hens before in my Life; nor have I yet ask'd the meaning of it; and tho' I had certainly known that Black Gowns in that place signified the Clergy of the Church of England, yet I have that confidence in the generous good Temper of such of them as I know, as to be well satisfied such a trifling mention of their Habit gives them no Disturbance.

3. That most of the Clergy in this and the neighbouring Provinces, are my Customers, and some of them my very good Friends; and I must be very malicious indeed, or very stupid, to print this thing for a small Profit, if I had thought it would have given them just Cause of Offence.

4. That if I had much Malice against the Clergy, and withal much Sense; 'tis strange I never write or talk against the Clergy myself. Some have observed that 'tis a fruitful Topic, and the easiest to be witty upon of all others; yet I appeal to the Publick that I am never guilty this way, and to all my Acquaintances as to my Conversation.

5. That if a Man of Sense had Malice enough to desire to injure the Clergy, this is the foolishest Thing he could possibly contrive for that Purpose.

6. That I got Five Shillings by it.

7. That none who are angry with me would have given me so much to let it alone.

8. That if all the People of different Opinions in this Province would engage to give me as much for not printing things they don't like, as I can get by printing them, I should probably live a very easy Life; and if all Printers were everywhere so dealt by, there would be very little printed.

9. That I am oblig'd to all who take my Paper, and am willing to think they do it out of meer Friendship. I only desire they would think the same when I deal with them. I thank those who leave off, that they have taken it so long. But I beg they would not endeavour to dissuade others, for that will look like Malice.

10. That 'tis impossible any Man should know what he would do if he was a Printer.

11. That notwithstanding the Rashness and Inexperience of Youth, which is most likely to be prevail'd with to do things that ought not to be done; yet I have avoided printing such Things as usually give Offence either to Church or State, more than any Printer that has followed the Business in this Province before.

12. And lastly, That I have printed above a Thousand Advertisements which made not the least mention of *Sea-Hens* or *Black Gowns*; and this being the first Offence, I have the more Reason to expect Forgiveness.

I take leave to conclude with an old Fable, which some of my Readers have heard before, and some have not.

"A certain well-meaning Man and his Son, were travelling towards a Market Town, with an Ass which they had to sell. The Road was bad; and the old Man therefore rid, but the Son went a-foot. The first Passenger they met, asked the Father if he was not ashamed to ride by himself, and suffer the poor Lad to wade along thro' the Mire; this induced him to take up his Son behind him: He had not travelled far, when he met others, who said, they are two unmerciful Lubbers to get both on the Back of that poor Ass, in such a deep Road. Upon this the old Man gets off, and let his Son ride alone. The next they met called the Lad a graceless, rascally young Jackanapes, to ride in that Manner thro' the Dirt, while his aged Father trudged along on Foot; and they said the old Man was a Fool, for suffering it. He then bid his Son come down, and walk with him, and they travell'd on leading the Ass by the Halter; 'till they met another Company, who called them a Couple of senseless Block-heads, for going both on Foot in such a dirty Way, when they had an empty Ass with them, which they might ride upon. The old Man could bear no longer; My Son, said he, it grieves me much that we cannot please all these People. Let me throw the Ass over the next Bridge, and be no further troubled with him."

Had the old Man been seen acting this last Resolution, he would probably have been called a Fool for troubling himself about the different Opinions of all that were pleas'd to find Fault with him: Therefore, tho' I have a Temper almost as complying as his, I intend not to imitate him in this last Particular. I consider the Variety of Humors among Men, and despair of pleasing every Body; yet I shall not therefore leave off Printing. I shall continue my Business. I shall not burn my Press and melt my Letters.

"AN AMERICAN 'CATO' DEFENDS CRITICISM OF THE GOVERNMENT"

"Cato"

The years leading up to the American Revolution were a wellspring of progressive ideology constructing what would become the dominant values of the fledgling nation. Two inadvertent contributors were the Englishmen John Trenchard and Thomas Gordon, who wrote essays critical of the British monarchy under the pseudonym of Cato, a name honoring the Roman Cato the Younger for his republican vision. These essays were later used as the foundation for many of the American colonial beliefs that would become the driving force behind the revolutionary movement. Such famous precepts as "Freedom of speech is the great bulwark of liberty; they prosper and die together" and "general liberty...is certainly the right of all mankind" achieved near-religious significance. It was these essays that formed the basis for the American John Alexander's famous essays, published in the first openly partisan newspaper, the *New York Weekly Journal.* The *Weekly Journal* achieved great fame as the subject of the first trial involving freedom of the press in this country. A German immigrant and apprentice to printer William Bradford, *Journal* publisher John Peter Zenger wound up as the unlikely hero in the first great fight against censorship of political commentary. Zenger not only

New York Weekly Journal, November 12 and 19, 1733. Reprinted in Leonard W. Levy, ed., *Freedom of the Press from Zenger to Jefferson: Early American Libertarian Theories* (Indianapolis, IN: Bobbs-Merrill, 1966).

46

refused to cease printing articles that scathingly criticized government administrators, but also refused to identify the author of the offending essays, a decision that earned him eight months in prison. The *Journal* essays, for which author Alexander provocatively used the pseudonym Cato, and the Zenger trial thus represent integral building blocks of not only First Amendment theory but the cherished tradition of a free press in this country.

Mr. Zenger.

Incert the following in your next, and you'll oblige your Friend,

CATO.

The Liberty of the Press is a Subject of the greatest Importance, and in which every Individual is as much concern'd as he is in any other Part of Liberty: Therefore it will not be improper to communicate to the publick the Sentiments of a late excellent Writer upon this Point. Such is the Elegance and Perspicuity of his Writings, such the inimitable Force of his Reasoning, that it will be difficult to say any Thing new that he has not said, or not to say that much worse which he has said.

There are two Sorts of Monarchies, an absolute and a limited one. In the first, the Liberty of the Press can never be maintained, it is inconsistent with it; for what absolute Monarch would suffer any Subject to animadvert on his Actions when it is in his Power to declare the Crime and to nominate the Punishment? This would make it very dangerous to exercise such a Liberty. Besides the Object against which those Pens must be directed is their Sovereign, the sole Supream Magistrate; for there being no Law in those Monarchies but the Will of the Prince, it makes it necessary for his Ministers to consult his Pleasure before any Thing can be undertaken: He is therefore properly chargeable with the Grievances of his Subjects, and what the Minister there acts being in Obedience to the Prince, he ought not to incur the Hatred of the People; for it would be hard to impute that to him for a Crime which is the Fruit of his Allegiance, and for refusing which he might incur the Penalties of Treason. Besides, in an absolute Monarchy, the Will of the Prince being the Law, a Liberty of the Press to complain of Grievances would be complaining against the Law and the Constitution, to which they have submitted or have been obliged to submit; and therefore, in one Sense, may be said to deserve Punishment; so that under an absolute Monarchy, I say, such a

Liberty is inconsistent with the Constitution, having no proper Subject to Politics on which it might be exercis'd, and if exercis'd would Incur a certain Penalty.

But in a limited Monarchy, as *England* is, our Laws are known, fixed, and established. They are the streight Rule and sure Guide to direct the King, the Ministers, and other his Subjects: And therefore an Offense against the Laws is such an Offense against the Constitution as ought to receive a proper adequate Punishment; the several Constituents of the Government, the Ministry, and all subordinate Magistrates, having their certain, known, and limited Sphere in which they move; one part may certainly err, misbehave, and become criminal, without involving the rest or any of them in the Crime or Punishment.

But some of these may be criminal, yet above Punishment, which surely cannot be denied, since most Reigns have furnished us with too many instances of powerful and wicked Ministers, some of whom by their Power have absolutely escaped Punishment, and the Rest, who met their Fate, are likewise Instances of this Power as much to the Purpose; for it was manifest in them that their Power had long protected them, their Crimes having often long preceded their much desired and deserved Punishment and Reward.

That *Might over comes Right,* or which is the same Thing, that Might preserves and defends Men from Punishment, is a Proverb established and confirmed by Time and Experience, the surest Discoverers of Truth and Certainty. It is this therefore which makes the Liberty of the Press in a limited Monarchy and in all its Colonies and Plantations proper, convenient, and necessary, or indeed it is rather incorporated and interwoven with our very Constitution; for if such an over grown Criminal, or an impudent Monster in Iniquity, cannot immediately be come at by ordinary Justice, let him yet receive the Lash of satyr, let the glaring Truths of his ill Administration, if possible, awaken his Conscience, and if he has no Conscience, rouse his Fear by Shewing him his Deserts, sting him with the Dread of Punishment, cover him with Shame, and render his Actions odious to all honest Minds. These Methods may in Time, and by watching and exposing his Actions, make him at least more Cautious, and perhaps at last bring down the great haughty and secure Criminal within the Reach and Grasp of ordinary Justice. This Advantage therefore of Exposing the exorbitant Crimes of wicked Ministers under a limited Monarchy makes the Liberty of the Press not only consistent with, but a necessary Part of, the Constitution itself.

It is indeed urged, that the Liberty of the Press ought to be restrained, because not only the Actions of evil Ministers may be exposed, but the Character of good ones traduced. Admit it in the strongest Light that Calumny and Lyes would prevail, and blast the Character of a great and good Minister; yet that is a less Evil than the Advantages we reap from the Liberty of the Press, as it is a Curb, a Bridle, a Terror, a Shame, and Restraint to evil Ministers; and it may be the only punishment, especially for a Time. But when did Calumnies and Lyes ever destroy the Character of one good Minister? Their benign Influences are known, tasted, and felt by every body: Or if their Characters have been clouded for a Time, yet they have generally shined forth in greater Luster: Truth will always prevail over Falsehood.

The Facts exposed are not to be believed, because said or published; but it draws People's Attention, directs their View, and fixes the Eye in a proper Position that everyone may judge for himself whether those Facts are true or not. People will recollect, enquire and search, before they condemn; and therefore very few good Ministers can be hurt by Falsehood, but many wicked Ones by seasonable Truth: But however the Mischief that a few may possibly, but improbably, suffer by the Freedom of the Press is not to be put in Competition with the Danger which the KING and the *people* may suffer by a shameful, cowardly Silence under the Tyranny of an insolent, rapacious, infamous Minister.

The Remainder of the Letter, concerning the Liberty of the Press, begun in our last. Inconveniences are rather to be endured than that we should suffer an entire and total Destruction. Who would not lose a Leg to save his Neck? And who would not endanger his Hand to Guard his heart? The Loss of Liberty in general would soon follow the Suppression of the Liberty of the Press; for as it is an essential Branch of Liberty, so perhaps it is the best Preservation of the whole. Even a Restraint of the Press would have a fatal Influence. No Nation Antient or Modern ever lost the Liberty of freely Speaking, Writing, or Publishing their Sentiments, but forthwith lost their Liberty in general and became Slaves. LIBERTY and SLAVERY! how amiable is one! how odious and abominable the other! Liberty is universal Redemption, Joy, and Happiness; but Servitude is absolute Reprobation and everlasting Perdition in Politics.

All the venal Supporters of wicked Ministers are aware of the great use of the Liberty of the Press in a limited free Monarchy: They know how vain it would be to attack it openly, and therefore endeavor to puzzle the Case with

Words, Inconsistencies, and Nonsense; but if the Opinion of the most numerous, unprejudiced and impartial Part of Mankind is an Argument of Truth, the Liberty of the Press has that as well as Reason on its Side. I believe every honest *Britton* of whatever Denomination, who loves his Country, if left to his own free and unbyassed Judgment, is a Friend to the Liberty of the Press, and an Enemy to any Restraint upon it. Surely all the independent Whiggs, to a man, are of this Opinion. By an *Independent Whigg* I mean one whose principles lead him to be firmly attached to the present happy Establishment, both in Church and State, and whose Fidelity to the Royal Family is so staunch and rivetted as not to be called in Question, tho' his Mind is not overswayed, or rather necessitated, by the extraordinary Weight of lucrative Posts or Pensions. The Dread of Infamy hath certainly been of great Use to the Cause of Virtue, and is a stronger Curb upon the Passions and Appetites of some Men, than any other Consideration Moral or Religious. Whenever, therefore, the Talent of Satyr is made use of to restrain Men by the Fear of Shame from immoral Actions, which either do or do not fall under the Cognizance of the Law, it is properly, and justly, and commendably applied: On the contrary, to condemn all Satyr is in Effect the same Thing as countenancing Vice, by screening it from Reproach and the just Indignation of Mankind. The Use of Satyr was of great service to the patriot Whiggs in the reign of King *Charles* and King *James* the second, as well as in that of Queen *Anne*. They asserted the Freedom of Writing against wicked Ministers; and tho' they knew it would signify nothing to accuse them publicly whilst they were in the Zenith of their Power, they made use of Satyr to prepare the Way and alarm the People against their Designs. If Men in Power were always Men of Integrity, we might venture to trust them with the Direction of the Press, and there would be no Occasion to plead against the Restraint of it; but as they have Vices like their Fellows, so it very often happens that the best intended and the most valuable Writings are the Objects of their Resentment, because opposite to their own Tempers or Designs. In short, I think, every Man of common Sense will judge that he is an Enemy to his King and Country who pleads for any Restraint upon the Press; but by the Press, when Nonsense, Inconsistencies, or personal Reflections are writ, if despised, they die of Course; if Truth, solid Arguments, and elegant, just Sentiments are published, they should meet with Applause rather than Censure; if Sense and Nonsense are blended, then, by the free Use of the Press, which is open to all, the Inconsistencies of the Writer may be made apparent; but to grant a Liberty only for

Praise, Flattery, and Panegyric, with a Restraint on every Thing which happens to be offensive and disagreeable to those who are at any Time in Power, is absurd, servile, and rediculous; upon which, I beg Leave to quote one Observation of the ingenious Mr. *Gordon*, in his excellent Discourses upon *Tacitus*. "In truth," says he, "where no Liberty is allowed to speak of Governours besides that of praising them, their praises will be little believed; their Tenderness and Aversion to have their Conduct examined will be apt to prompt people to think their conduct guilty or weak, to suspect their Management and Designs to be worse perhaps than they are, and to become turbulent and seditious, rather than be forced to be silent."

"SENTIMENTS ON THE LIBERTY OF THE PRESS"

Andrew Bradford

Andrew Bradford was a prominent Philadelphia printer and publisher of the *American Weekly Mercury* during the era of the Zenger trial. Though a personal and professional enemy of Zenger, he argued strongly for freedom of the press in colonial society. In his seminal book *Freedom of the Press from Zenger to Jefferson: Early American Libertarian Theories*, Professor Leonard Levy singles out "Sentiments on the Liberty of the Press" as "one of the very few well-reasoned statements on the liberty of the press made by an American of the colonial period." Note, however, that like Milton and Franklin, Bradford is quite clear that freedom of the press does not mean "that unwarrantable License, which some People of so much fire, but little judgment have taken of endeavouring to subvert the Fundamental Points of Religion or Morality."

Mr. Bradford,

In *a former Paper, I promised you my Sentiments on the Liberty of the Press.* . . .

American Weekly Mercury (Philadelphia), April 25, 1734. Reprinted in Leonard W. Levy, ed., *Freedom of the Press from Zenger to Jefferson: Early American Libertarian Theories* (Indianapolis, IN: Bobbs-Merrill, 1966).

In this as in all other Cases where the Subject of Liberty, is treated, we must carefully distinguish, between *Liberty* and *Licentiousness*. I have perused many virulent Declamations against the *Liberty of the Press*, that have proceeded on Maxims evidently false: Not so much for want of Skill in the Compilers, as want of *Shame* and even common *Honesty*. They have supposed things which no good Man acquainted with the Nature of civil Government, would have supposed, and from those Principles weak and base, they have deduced Consequences equally weak and destructive of the Happiness of Societies. For, 'tis undoubtedly true, that there is a certain *Legerdemain* in Argument, by which, if you may suppose what you please; you may conclude what you will.

The Caprice and Fury of a Mobb undisciplined and under no Restraints from Law, may be as pernicious as the uncontroulable Edicts of an absolute Tyrant—The Extreams that seperate Liberty from License, are closer than most Men imagine; they ought therefore to be carefully distinguish'd.

By the *Liberty of the Press* then, I am far from understanding, (as I hope every *Englishman* is) a treasonable *Licence*, of calling into Question his most Sacred Majesty's undoubted Title, to the Realm of *Great-Britain*, or any his Dominions thereunto belonging. Nor do I think that his Conduct in private or public Life ought to be arraign'd. That *the King can do no wrong*, is a Maxim (a just Maxim too) in the *English* Law. His Ministers indeed are accountable to the Public for their Male Administration, and have frequently felt the Resentment of a good natured but an injur'd People.

Nor, by the *Liberty of the Press*, do I mean that unwarrantable License, which some People of much Fire, but little Judgment have taken of endeavouring to subvert the Fundamental Points of *Religion* or *Morality*. Religion ought to be treated with Veneration, and without Morality whose Doctrines true Religion always recommends and strengthens, Societies could not subsist. I have been astonish'd to hear some Men, who make high Pretences to Wit and Learning advance these and the like *Stupidities*; that Virtue and Vice are meer Words: That in the Nature of things there is no Distinction between the one and the other, that all Mankind are Villains; That what we call beautiful and generous in Life proceeds only from the sordid Motives of Pride or Self Interest; that Patriotism is a Word without a Meaning, and Public Virtue a thing to be laughed at—I must confess I don't know any Business such unnatural Wretches have in Society, to whom by their own avowed Principles, they publickly disclaim all manner of Relation.

But on the other Hand, to expose the ridiculous Claims of certain Priests, to examine with Freedom and Impartiality the Conduct of some spiritual Councils and Convocations, is a Liberty, I think every free People, is entitled to. Nor was I ever acquainted with a sensible and honest Clergyman, who did not acknowledge this to be true. Since I have mentioned that *Reverend Order of Men*, for some of whom, I entertain the highest Regards, allow me to say further, that the Observations I have made, proceed from no Prejudice.... I can never reflect on the brave Stand, the *Bishops* made in Favour of *English* Liberty, without the utmost Degree of Veneration. I think they ought to have their Statues erected in Brass, and I doubt not in the least that their Names will be transmitted with Honour to Ages yet to come. The Petulance of Tongue and the vile Scurrility with which the Gentlemen of that Robe have sometimes been treated provokes my Indignation, that they have their Foibles, is as true, as that they are Men: But, why the whole Order should be condemned in Gross, for the Whims or Vices of a few, is what I could never comprehend.

Nor, by the *Liberty of the Press*, do I understand a *License*, of traducing the Conduct, of those Gentlemen who are appointed our Lawful Governors: When they behave themselves well, they ought to be treated with all the Respect and Gratitude, that's due from an obliged People; should they behave themselves ill, their Measures are to be remonstrated against in Terms of *Decency*, and Moderation not of Fury or Scurrility.

Thanks to the indulgent Stars, that shed their kindly influence on *Pennsylvania*, a Country where the Goddess *Liberty*, hath chosen her particular Abode, we have nothing from that Quarter to dread. We are blest with Proprietors, who we have just Reason to hope, will imitate the Virtues of their renowned Father; a *Name*, a *Character* never to be forgotten! And, we have a *Governour*, who hath deservedly gained the Hearts of the People under his Care; to whom he hath been always willing to Grant any Favours, proper for them to ask.

But, should it please God, as a Punishment for our Sins, to visit us with a *Governor*, so far intoxicated with *Pride and Ambition*, as to endeavour to set himself above the *Laws*, and affect an independent Sway: Should he remove from Places of the highest Trust, those Persons, who had discharged them, with unquestioned Abilities and Integrity, in Order to promote the immediate *Creatures* of his own Will; should he presume to erect *Arbitrary Courts*, unknown to an English Constitution, and to Stop or Poison the streams of *Justice*. In such a Case, I doubt not in the least, but there would be found Men of *Spirit*, and *Honesty* enough, to let that Governor know that ——— *Such a Conduct did not become him.*

Nor, under the Colour of this *Liberty*, ought such Doctrines to be publish'd, as tend to lessen or take away, that sacred Veneration, which is due to the upright Dispensers of the *Laws*. Nor, should the *Press* be made use of as an Engine, to insult *Personal Deformities, Frailties* or *Misfortunes* much less to expose the secrets of Families. This is mean, and unbecoming a Writer. And indeed all such irregular Sallies are sufficiently provided against by the Laws in being.

But, by the *Freedom of the Press*, I mean a Liberty, within the Bounds of Law, for any Man to communicate to the Public, his Sentiments on the Important Points of *Religion* and *Government*; of proposing any Laws, which he apprehends may be for the Good of his Countrey, and of applying for the Repeal of such, as he Judges pernicious. I mean a *Liberty* of detecting the wicked and destructive Measures of *certain Politicians*; of dragging Villany out of it's obscure lurking Holes, and exposing it in it's full Deformity to open Day; of attacking Wickedness in high Places, of disintangling the intricate Folds of a wicked and corrupt Administration, and pleading freely for a Redress of *Grievances*: I mean a *Liberty* of examining the great Articles of our Faith, by the Lights of *Scripture and Reason*, a Privilege derived to us in it's fullest Latitude, from our most excellent *Charter*.

This is the *Liberty of the Press*, the great *Palladium* of all our other *Liberties*, which I hope the good People of this Province, will forever enjoy; and that every *Pennsylvanian*, will resent with *Scorn and Indignation*, the least Attempt to weaken or subvert it. For, it may be demonstrated from numerous Instances in History, that whenever this inestimable Jewel was lost, Slavery, Desolation and Ruine ensued.

This Doctrine of the *Liberty of the Press* can never be too much inculcated, tho' it hath been almost exhausted by Authors of signal Renown. I shall conclude this Paper with a Quotation from an excellent Pamphlet publish'd in the Reign of the late King *William*.

"All Sorts of Men, whose Interest it is, not to have their Actions exposed to the Publick, (which I am afraid) are no small Number, will be for *restraining the Press*; but, this is not the worst that may happen; because the *Press* may be so managed as to become the powerful Engine to overturn and subvert the Constitution it self: For, should a *Magistrate* arise with arbitrary Designs in his Head, no Papers that plead the *Rights and Privileges* of the People, could be publish'd with Security. The *Press* would be employ'd only to extol the Promoters of *arbitrary Power*, as the chief *Patriots* of their Country; and to traduce those that were really so, which would not only be the greatest Discouragement, to all brave and virtuous Actions; but be apt to make the People mistake their *Friends*, when they had not the *Liberty* to publish a Vindication of their *Principles* or *Actions* of their *Enemies*, in a Word, if the *Pulpits* and *Westminster-Hall*, should chime in with an *arbitrary Court*, what can warn the People of their Danger, except the *Press*? But, if that too be wholy against them, they may easily be so blinded as not to see the Chains that are preparing for them, till they are fettered beyond all Power of Redemption."

As therefore you love your *Liberties*, (my dear Countreymen) support and defend the *Liberty of the Press*.

ANDREW HAMILTON DEFENDS JOHN PETER ZENGER

Andrew Hamilton

Zenger's *New York Weekly Journal* was perhaps the first model for what was to become standard in American journalism—the party newspaper. Zenger himself, a German immigrant, seems not to have been heavily involved in the politics behind his paper; for him, the *Journal* was a commercial proposition that provided a livelihood. But the paper's criticism of the colonial administration infuriated New York governor William Cosby, who in 1735 instituted a prosecution against Zenger for seditious libel. When his original lawyers attempted to prove that the governor's newly appointed chief justice was not entitled to his office, that official disbarred them both. At this point, Philadelphia lawyer Andrew Hamilton volunteered his services to defend Zenger. His defense was one of the first in which the defense admitted performing the acts charged but argued that the law under which the prosecution had been brought was itself unconstitutional. This argument, a staple of civil liberties litigation today, was shockingly novel at the time. Hamilton's skillful argument led to what lawyers call "jury nullification"—the New York jury to whom his arguments were addressed simply ignored the judge's instruction as to the law and returned a verdict of "not guilty." The Zenger case established freedom

New York Weekly Journal, 1736. Reprinted in *John Peter Zenger, His Press, His Trial, and a Bibliography of Zenger Imprints* (New York: Dodd, Mead & Company, 1904).

of the press as one of the watchwords of the movement for American independence and made Hamilton (no relation to Alexander Hamilton of the next
generation) one of the foremost lawyers in the British New World.

... *Mr. Hamilton.* I know, may it please Your Honour, the Jury may do so; but I
do likewise know, they may do otherwise. I know they have the Right beyond
all Dispute, to determine both the Law and the Fact, and where they do not
doubt of the Law, they ought to do so. This of leaving it to the Judgment of
the Court, *whether the Words are libellous or not*, in Effect renders Juries useless
(to say no worse) in many Cases; but this I shall have Occasion to speak to by
and by; and I will with the Court's Leave proceed to examine the Inconveniences that must inevitably arise from the Doctrines Mr. Attorney has laid
down; and I observe, in support of this Prosecution, he has frequently
repeated the Words taken from the Case of *Libel, famosus*, in 5 *Co.* This is
indeed the leading case, and to which almost all the other Cases upon the
Subject of Libels do refer; and I must insist upon saying, That according as
this Case seems to be understood by the [Court] and Mr. Attorney, it is not
Law at this Day: For thou' I own it to be base and unworthy to scandalize any
Man, yet I think it is even villanous to scandalize a Person of publick Character, and I will go so far into Mr. Attorney's Doctrine as to agree, that if the
faults, Mistakes, nay even the Vices of such a Person be private and personal,
and don't affect the Peace of the Publick, or the Liberty or Property of our
Neighbour, it is unmanly and unmannerly to expose them either by Word or
Writing. But when a Ruler of the People brings his personal Failings, but
much more his Vices, into his Administration, and the People find themselves
affected by them, either in their Liberties or Properties, that will alter the
Case mightily, and all the high Things that are said in Favour of Rulers, and
of Dignities, and upon the side of Power, will not be able to stop People's
Mouths when they feel themselves oppressed, I mean in a free Government.
It is true in Times past it was a crime to speak Truth, and in that terrible
Court of Star Chamber, many worthy and brave Men suffered for so doing;
and yet even in that Court, and in those bad Times, a great and good Man
durst say, what I hope will not be taken amiss of me to say in this Place, *to wit,*
The Practice of informations for Libels is a Sword in the Hands of a wicked King, and
an arrant Coward, to cut down and destroy the innocent; the one cannot, because of his
high Station, and the other dares not, because of his want of Courage, revenge himself in
another Manner.

Mr. Attorney. Pray Mr. *Hamilton*, have a Care what you say, don't go too far neither, I don't like those Liberties.

Mr. Hamilton. Sure, Mr. Attorney, you won't make any Applications; all Men agree that we are governed by the best of Kings, and I cannot see the Meaning of Mr. Attorney's Caution; my well known Principles, and the Sense I have of the Blessings we enjoy under His present Majesty, makes it impossible for me to err, and I hope, even to be suspected, in that Point of Duty to my King. May it please Your Honour, I was saying, That notwithstanding all the Duty and Reverence claimed by Mr. Attorney to Men in Authority, they are not exempt from observing the Rules of Common Justice, even in their private or public Capacities; the Laws of our Mother Country know no Exemption. It is true, Men in Power are harder to be come at for Wrongs they do, either to a private Person, or to the Publick; especially a Governor in the Plantations, where they insist upon an Exemption from answering Complaints of any Kind in their own Government. We are indeed told, and it is true they are obliged to answer a Suit in the King's Courts at *Westminster*, for a Wrong done to any Person here: But do we not know how impracticable this is to most Men among us, to leave their Families (who depend upon their Labour and Care for their Livelihood) and carry Evidences to *Britain*, and at a great, nay, a far greater Expense than almost any of us are able to bear, only to prosecute a Governour for an Injury done here. But when the Oppression is general, there is no Remedy even that Way, no, our Constitution has (blessed be God) given us an Opportunity, if not to have such Wrongs redressed, yet by our Prudence and Resolution we may in a great Measure prevent the committing of such Wrongs, by making a Governour sensible that it is to his interest to be just to those under his Care; for such is the Sense that Men in General (I mean Freemen) have of common Justice, that when they come to know, that a chief Magistrate abuses the Power with which he is trusted, for the good of the People, and is attempting to turn that very Power against the Innocent, whether of high or low degree, I say, Mankind in general seldom fail to interpose, and as far as they can, prevent the Destruction of their fellow Subjects. And has it not often been seen (and I hope it will always be seen) that when the Representatives of a free People are by just Representations or Remonstrances, made sensible of the Sufferings of their Fellow-Subjects, by the Abuse of Power in the Hands of a Governour, they have declared (and loudly too) that they were not obliged by any Law to support a Governour who goes about to destroy a Province or Colony, or their Priviledges, which by His Majesty he was appointed, and by the Law he is bound to protect and encourage. But I pray it may be considered of what Use is this mighty Priviledge, if every Man that suffers must be silent? And if a Man must be taken up as a Libeller, for telling his Sufferings to his Neighbour? I know it may be answer'd, *Have you not a Legislature? Have you not a House of Representatives, to whom you may complain?* And to this I answer, we have. But what then? Is an Assembly to be troubled with every Injury done by a Governour? Or are they to hear of nothing but what those in the Administration will please to tell them? Or what Sort of a Tryal must a Man have? And how is he to be remedied; especially if the Case were, as I have known it to happen in *America* in my Time; That a Governour who has Places (I will not [say] Pensions, for I believe they seldom give that to another which they can take to themselves) to bestow, and can or will keep the same Assembly (after he has modeled them so as to get a Majority of the House in his Interest) for near *twice Seven Years* together? I pray, what Redress is to be expected for an honest Man, who makes his Complaint against a Governour to an Assembly who may properly enough be said, to be made by the same Governour against whom the Complaint is made? The Thing answers it self. No, it is natural, it is a Priviledge, I will go farther, it is a Right which all Freemen claim, and are entitled to complain when they are hurt; they have a Right publickly to remonstrate the Abuses of Power, in the strongest Terms, to put their Neighbours upon their Guard, against the Craft or open Violence of Men in Authority, and to assert with Courage the Sense they have of the Blessings of Liberty, the Value they put upon it, and their Resolution at all Hazards to preserve it, as one of the greatest Blessings Heaven can bestow....

...I beg Leave to insist, That the Right of complaining or remonstrating is natural; And the Restraint upon this natural Right is the Law only, and that those Restraints can only extend to what is *false*; For as it is Truth alone which can excuse or justify any Man for complaining of a bad Administration, I as frankly agree, that nothing ought to excuse a Man who raises a false Charge or Accusation, even against a private Person, and that no manner of Allowance ought to be made to him who does so against a publick Magistrate. *Truth* ought to govern the whole Affair of Libels, and yet the Party accused runs Risque enough even then; for if he fails of proving every Tittle of what he has wrote, and to the Satisfaction of the Court and Jury too, he may find to his Cost, that when the Prosecution is set on Foot by Men in Power, it seldom wants Friends to Favour it. And from thence (it is said) has arisen the great Diversity of Opinions among Judges, about what words were or were not scandalous or libellous. I believe it will be granted, that there is not greater Uncertainty in any Part of the Law than about Words of Scandal; it would be mispending of the Court's Time to mention the Cases; they may be said to be numberless; and therefore the uttermost Care ought to be taken in following Precedents; and the Times when the Judgments were given, which are quoted for Authorities in the Case of Libels, are much to be regarded. I think it will be agreed, That ever since the Time of the Star Chamber, where the most arbitrary and destructive Judgments and Opinions were given, that ever an *Englishman* heard of, at least in his own Country: I say, Prosecutions for Libels since the Time of that arbitrary Court, and until the glorious Revolution, have generally been set on Foot at the Instance of the Crown or its Ministers; and it is no small Reproach to the Law, that these Prosecutions were too often and too much countenanced by the Judges, who held their Places at Pleasure, (a disagreeable Tenure to any Officer, but a dangerous one in the Case of a Judge.) To say more to this Point may not be proper....

...If Power has had so great an Influence on Judges; how cautious ought we to be in determining by their Judgments, especially in the Plantations, and in the Case of Libels? There is Heresy in Law, as well as in Religion, and both have changed very much; and we well know that it is not two Centuries ago that a Man would have been burnt as an Heretick, for owning such Opinions in Matters of Religion as are publickly wrote and printed at this Day. They were fallible Men, it seems, and we take the Liberty not only to differ from them in religious Opinion, but to condemn them and their Opinions too; and I must presume, that in taking these Freedoms in thinking and speaking about Matters of Faith and Religion, we are in the right: For, tho' it is said there are very great Liberties of this Kind taken in *Newe York*, yet I have heard of no Information prefered by Mr. Attorney for any Offences of this Sort. From which I think it is pretty clear, That in *New-York* a Man may make very free with his God, but he must take special Care what he says of his Governour. It is agreed upon by all Men that this is a Reign of Liberty, and while Men keep within the Bounds of Truth, I hope they may with Safety both speak and write their Sentiments of the Conduct of Men in Power, I me[a]n of that Part of their Conduct only, which affects the Liberty or Property of the People under their Administration; were this to be denied, then the next Step may make them Slaves. For what Notions can be entertained of Slavery, beyond that of suffering the greatest Injuries and Oppressions, without the Liberty of complaining; or if they do, to be destroyed, Body and Estate, for so doing?

It is said and insisted upon by Mr. Attorney, *That Government is a sacred Thing; That it is to be supported and reverenced; It is Government that protects our Persons and Estates; That prevents Treasons, Murders, Robberies, Riots, and all the Train of Evils that overturns Kingdoms and States, and ruins particular Persons; and if those in the Administration, especially the Supream Magistrate, must have all their Conduct censured by private Men, Government cannot subsist.* This is called *a Licentiousness not to be tollerated.* It is said, *That it brings the Rulers of the People into Contempt, and their Authority not to be regarded, and so in the End the Laws cannot be put in Execution.* These I say, and such as these, are the general Topicks insisted upon by Men in Power, and their Advocates. But I wish it might be considered at the same Time, How often it has happened, that the Abuse of Power has been the primary Cause of these Evils, and that it was the Injustice and Oppression of these great Men, which has commonly brought them into Contempt with the People. The Craft and Art of such Men is great, and who, that is the least acquainted with History or Law, can be ignorant of the specious Pretences, which have often been made use of by Men in Power, to introduce arbitrary Rule, and destroy the Liberties of a free People....

... This is the second Information for Libelling of a Governour that I have known in America, And the first, tho' it may look like a Romance, yet as it is true, I will beg Leave to mention it. Governor Nicholson, who happened to be offended with one [of] his Clergy, met him one Day upon the Road, and as was usual with him (under the Protection of his Commission) used the poor Parson with the worst of Language, threatened to cut off his Ears, slit his Nose, and at last to shoot him through the Head. The Parson being a reverend Man, continued all this Time uncovered in the Heat of the Sun, until he found an Opportunity to fly for it; and coming to a Neighbours House felt himself very ill of a Fever, and immediately writes for a doctor; and that his Physician might the better judge of his Distemper, he acquainted him with the Usage he had received; concluding, that the Governor was certainly mad, for that no Man in his Senses would have behaved in that manner. The Doctor unhappily shews the Parson's Letter; the Governour came to hear of it; and so an Information was preferred against the poor Man for saying he believed the Governour was mad; and it was laid in the Information to be false, scandalous, and wicked, and wrote with Intent to move Sedition among the People, and bring His Excellency into Contempt. But by an Order from the late Queen Anne, there was a Stop put to that Prosecution, with sundry others set on foot by the same Governour, against Gentlemen of the greatest Worth and Honour in that Government.

And may not I be allowed, after all this, to say, That by a little Countenance, almost any Thing which a Man writes, may, with the Help of that useful Term of Art, called an *Innuendo*, be construed to be a Libel, according to Mr. Attorney's Definition of it....

...If a Libel is understood in the large and unlimited Sense urged by Mr. Attorney, there is scarce a Writing I know that may not be called a Libel, or scarce any Person safe from being called to an Account as a Libeller....

...The Danger is great, in Proportion to the Mischief that may happen, through our too great Credulity. A proper Confidence in a Court is commendable; but as the Verdict (whatever it is) will be yours, you ought to refer no Part of your Duty to the Discretion of other Persons. If you should be of Opinion, that there is no Falsehood in Mr. *Zenger's* Papers, you will, nay (pardon me for the Expression) you ought to say so; because you don't know whether others (I mean the Court) may be of that Opinion. It is your Right to do so, and there is much depending upon your Resolution, as well as upon your Integrity....

...I hope to be pardon'd Sir for my Zeal upon this Occasion; it is an old and wise Caution, *That when our Neighbours House is on Fire, we ought to take Care of our own.* For tho' Blessed be God, I live in a Government where Liberty is well understood, and freely enjoy'd; yet Experience has shewn us all (I'm sure it has to me) that a bad Precedent in one Government, is soon set up for an Authority in another; and therefore I cannot but think it mine, and every Honest Man's Duty, that (while we pay all due Obedience to Men in Authority) we ought at the same Time to be upon our Guard against Power, wherever we apprehend that it may affect ourselves or our Fellow-Subjects.

I am truely very unequal to such an Undertaking on many Accounts. And you see I labour under the Weight of many Years, and am born down with great Infirmities of Body; yet Old and Weak as I am, I should think of it my Duty, if required, to go to the utmost Part of the Land, where my Service could be of any Use in assisting to quench the Flame of Prosecutions upon Informations, set on Foot by the Government, to deprive a People of the Right of Remonstrating (and complaining too) of the arbitrary Attempts of Men in Power. Men who injure and oppress the People under the Administration provoke them to cry out and complain; and then make that very Complaint the Foundation for new Oppressions and Prosecutions. I wish I could say there were no Instances of this Kind. But to conclude; the Question before the Court and you, Gentlemen of the Jury, is not of small nor private Concern, it is not the Cause of a poor Printer, nor of *New-York* alone, which you are now trying: No! It may in its Consequence, affect every Freeman that lives under a British Government on the main of *America.* It is the best Cause. It is the Cause of Liberty; and I make no Doubt but your upright Conduct, this Day, will not only entitle you to the Love and Esteem of your Fellow-Citizens; but every Man who prefers Freedom to a Life of Slavery will bless and honour You, as Men who have baffled the Attempt of Tyranny; and by an impartial and incorrupt Verdict, have laid a noble Foundation for securing to ourselves, our Posterity, and our Neighbours, That, to which Nature and the Laws of our Country have given us a Right The Liberty both of exposing and opposing arbitrary Power (in these Parts of the World, at least) by speaking and writing Truth.

"LIBELS;
LIBERTY OF THE PRESS"

William Blackstone

Born in 1723 in England, William Blackstone became a distinguished barrister and the first professor of law at Oxford University in the 1750s. His landmark work, *Commentaries on the Laws of England*, published in four volumes between 1765 and 1769, has never gone out of print and is frequently cited by scholars and courts today as an authoritative exposition of the English common law. American lawyers were schooled in the *Commentaries*, not only before the Revolution but well into the nineteenth century. The Blackstone view of the common law held that prior restraint (such as licensing) was forbidden, but that the state was free to punish writers and printers after publication, if their work defamed individuals or ministers of the Crown. The presumption against "prior restraint" in this selection from the *Commentaries* is an important building block in American press-freedom law, from the early opinions of Justice Holmes to the landmark case of *Near v. Minnesota*.

...Of a nature very similar to challenges [to fight] are *libels*, *libelli famosi*, which, taken in their largest and most extensive sense, signify any writings, pictures, or the like, of an immoral or illegal tendency; but, in the sense under which we are now to consider them, are malicious defamations of any person,

William Blackstone, *Commentaries* (Chicago: Callaghan and Company, 1899), pp. 150–53.

and especially a magistrate, made public by either printing, writing, signs, or pictures, in order to provoke him to wrath, or expose him to public hatred, contempt, and ridicule. The direct tendency of these libels is the breach of the public peace, by stirring up the objects of them to revenge, and perhaps to bloodshed. The communication of a libel to any one person is a publication in the eye of the law: and therefore the sending an abusive private letter to a man is as much a libel as if it were openly printed, for it equally tends to a breach of the peace. For the same reason it is immaterial with respect to the essence of a libel, whether the matter of it be true or false; since the provocation, and not the falsity, is the thing to be punished criminally: though, doubtless, the falsehood of it may aggravate its guilt, and enhance its punishment. In a civil action, we may remember, a libel must appear to be false, as well as scandalous; for, if the charge be true, the plaintiff has received no private injury, and has no ground to demand a compensation for himself, whatever offence it may be against the public peace: and therefore, upon a civil action, the truth of the accusation may be pleaded in bar of the suit. But, in a criminal prosecution, the tendency which all libels have to create animosities, and to disturb the public peace, is the whole that the law considers. And therefore, in such prosecutions, the only facts to be considered are, first, the making or publishing of the book or writing; and secondly, whether the matter be criminal: and, if both these points are against the defendant, the offence against the public is complete. The punishment of such libellers, for either making, repeating, printing, or publishing the libel, is fine, and such corporal punishment as the court in their discretion shall inflict; regarding the quantity of the offence, and the quality of the offender....

Liberty of the press.—In this, and the other instances which we have lately considered, where blasphemous, immoral, treasonable, schismatical, seditious, or scandalous libels are punished by the English law, some with a greater, others with a less degree of severity; the *liberty of the press*, properly understood, is by no means infringed or violated. The liberty of the press is indeed essential to the nature of a free state: but this consists in laying no *previous* restraints upon publications, and not in freedom from censure for criminal matter when published. Every freeman has an undoubted right to lay what sentiments he pleases before the public: to forbid this, is to destroy the freedom of the press: but if he publishes what is improper, mischievous, or illegal, he must take the consequence of his own temerity. To subject the press to the restrictive power of a licenser, as was formerly done, both before and since the revolution, is to subject all freedom of sentiment to the prejudices of one man, and make him the arbitrary and infallible judge of all controverted points in learning, religion, and government. But to punish (as the law does at present) any dangerous or offensive writings, which, when published, shall on a fair and impartial trial be adjudged of a pernicious tendency, is necessary for the preservation of peace and good order, of government and religion, the only solid foundations of civil liberty. Thus the will of individuals is still left free; the abuse only of that free will is the object of legal punishment. Neither is any restraint hereby laid upon freedom of thought or enquiry: liberty of private sentiment is still left; the disseminating, or making public, of bad sentiments, destructive of the ends of society, is the crime which society corrects. A man (says a fine writer on this subject) may be allowed to keep poisons in his closet, but not publicly to vend them as cordials. And to this we may add, that the only plausible argument heretofore used for restraining the just freedom of the press, "that it was necessary to prevent the daily abuse of it," will entirely lose its force, when it is shewn (by a seasonable exertion of the laws) that the press cannot be abused to any bad purpose, without incurring a suitable punishment: whereas it never can be used to any good one, when under the control of an inspector. So true will it be found, that to censure the licentiousness, is to maintain the liberty, of the press.

"THE FEDERALIST NO. 84"
Alexander Hamilton

Thomas Jefferson wrote the birth announcement of the new nation; James Madison was the leading author of its Constitution; but many historians argue that Alexander Hamilton was the founder whose labors did most to establish the United States as a functioning state.

Scorned by John Adams as "the bastard brat of a Scotch pedlar," Hamilton was born out of wedlock on Nevis in the West Indies. He came to the United States to attend King's College in New York City (the forerunner of today's Columbia University), and remained a New Yorker the rest of his life. Barely twenty-one at the dawn of the Revolution, he realized his dreams of martial glory at the Battle of Yorktown, but his most effective service was as a junior officer on Washington's staff. A member of the Philadelphia Convention of 1787, he campaigned for ratification of the new Constitution even though he secretly harbored doubts about its structure and about republican government generally. As Washington's secretary of the treasury, he laid the foundation for a unified economy with a strong system of banking and finance. He and Secretary of State Thomas Jefferson began a deep political feud that quickly grew into the American two-party system. As a leader of the nascent Federalist Party, he had the poignant role of deciding whether Jefferson or his running

Federalist, 1788.

mate, Aaron Burr, would succeed the defeated Federalist president John Adams. Hamilton hated Burr even worse than Jefferson and threw the vote in the House of Representatives to Jefferson. Three years later, Burr killed Hamilton in a duel.

Early in the ratification struggle, it became clear that the Framers had erred grievously in omitting a bill of rights from the draft document. Hamilton argued that no such bill of rights was needed: "Why, for instance, should it be said that the liberty of the press shall not be restrained, when no power is given by which restrictions may be imposed?"

Despite Hamilton's argument that the new government had no power over the press, the Federalists in 1798 passed the Sedition Act, threatening dissenting editors with prison. Behind the scenes, Hamilton supported the act.

TO THE PEOPLE OF THE STATE OF NEW YORK:

... The most considerable of the remaining objections is that the plan of the convention contains no bill of rights. Among other answers given to this, it has been upon different occasions remarked that the constitutions of several of the States are in a similar predicament. I add that New York is of the number. And yet the opposers of the new system, in this State, who profess an unlimited admiration for its constitution, are among the most intemperate partisans of a bill of rights. To justify their zeal in this matter, they allege two things: one is that, though the constitution of New York has no bill of rights prefixed to it, yet it contains, in the body of it, various provisions in favor of particular privileges and rights, which, in substance, amount to the same thing; the other is, that the Constitution adopts, in their full extent, the common and statute law of Great Britain, by which many other rights, not expressed in it, are equally secured.

To the first I answer, that the Constitution proposed by the convention contains, as well as the constitution of this State, a number of such provisions.

I go further, and affirm that bill of rights, in the sense and to the extent in which they are contended for, are not only unnecessary in the proposed Constitution, but would even be dangerous. They would contain various exceptions to powers not granted; and, on this very account, would afford a colorable pretext to claim more than were granted. For why declare that things shall not be done which there is no power to do? Why, for instance, should it be said that the liberty of the press shall not be restrained, when no power is given by which restrictions may be imposed? I will not contend that such a provision would confer a regulating power; but it is evident that it would furnish, to men disposed to usurp, a plausible pretence for claiming that power. They might urge with a semblance of reason, that the Constitution ought not to be charged with the absurdity of providing against the abuse of an authority which was not given, and that the provision against restraining the liberty of the press afforded a clear implication, that a power to prescribe proper regulations concerning it was intended to be vested in the national government. This may serve as a specimen of the numerous handles which would be given to the doctrine of constructive powers, by the indulgence of an injudicious zeal for bills of rights.

On the subject of the liberty of the press, as much as has been said, I cannot forbear adding a remark or two: in the first place, I observe, that there is not a syllable concerning it in the constitution of this State; in the next, I contend, that whatever has been said about it in that of any other State, amounts to nothing. What signifies a declaration, that "the liberty of the press shall be inviolably preserved"? What is the liberty of the press? Who can give it any definition which would not leave the utmost latitude for evasion? I hold it to be impracticable; and from this I infer, that its security, whatever fine declarations may be inserted in any constitution respecting it, must altogether depend on public opinion, and on the general spirit of the people and of the government. And here, after all, as is intimated upon another occasion, must we seek for the only solid basis of all our rights....

PUBLIUS

REPLY TO THE PENNSYLVANIA MINORITY

Noah Webster

Historians frequently remark that the enemies of the new Constitution were not bound by any one consistent set of arguments. The same, however, is true of the Constitution's supporters, as the following excerpt from an essay by Noah Webster demonstrates. Webster, a Connecticut-born grammarian, editor, and lawyer, was allied with Madison and Hamilton in the cause of ratification; indeed, it was he who first coined the terms *Federalist* (for supporters of the Constitution) and *Anti-Federalists* (for its opponents). The first ratification of the Constitution came from a Pennsylvania state convention in Philadelphia in 1787. After the convention adjourned, the dissenting delegates issued a lengthy polemic against the Constitution and the tactics used to win approval at the convention; among its most effective criticisms was the lack of a bill of rights in general and of a press-freedom clause in particular. Webster's "Reply to the Philadelphia Minority," published under the pen name "America," was a no-holds-barred assault on the minority's arguments and character. In the excerpt reprinted here, Webster acidly mocked their concern for freedom of the press, a concept he derides as meaningless at best and dangerous at worst—for, after all, complete press freedom would mean that

"America," December 31, 1787. Reprinted in Bernard Bailyn, ed., *The Debate on the Constitution: Federalist and Antifederalist Speeches, Articles, and Letters during the Struggle over Ratification, Part One: September 1787 to February 1788* (New York: Library of America, 1993).

the state could not punish even "a man who should publish a treatise to *prove his maker a knave!*...I shudder at the thought."

===

...You object, Gentlemen, to the powers vested in Congress. Permit me, to ask you, where will you limit their powers? What bounds will you prescribe? You will reply, *we will reserve certain rights, which we deem invaluable, and restrain our rulers from abridging them.* But, Gentlemen, let me ask you, how will you define these rights? would you say, *the liberty of the Press shall not be restrained?* Well, what is this liberty of the Press? Is it an unlimited licence to publish *any thing and every thing* with impunity? If so, the Author, and Printer of any treatise, however obscene and blasphemous, will be screened from punishment. You know, Gentlemen, that there are books extant, so shockingly and infamously obscene and so daringly blasphemous, that no society on earth, would be vindicable in suffering the publishers to pass unpunished. You certainly know that such cases *have* happened, and *may* happen again—nay, you know that they are *probable.* Would not that indefinite expression, *the liberty of the Press,* extend to the justification of every *possible publication?* Yes, Gentlemen, you know, that under such a general licence, a man who should publish a treatise to *prove his maker a knave,* must be screened from legal punishment. I shudder at the thought!—But the truth must not be concealed. The Constitutions of several States *guarantee that very licence.*

But if you attempt to define the *liberty of the Press,* and ascertain what cases shall fall within that privilege, during the course of centuries, where will you *begin?* Or rather, where will you *end?* Here, Gentlemen, you will be puzzled. Some publications certainly *may* be a breach of civil law: You will not have the effrontery to deny a truth so obvious and intuitively evident. Admit that principle; and unless you can define precisely the cases, which are, and are not a breach of law, you have no right to say, the liberty of the Press shall not be retained; for such a licence would warrant *any breach of law.* Rather than hazard such an abuse of privilege, is it not better to leave the right altogether with your rulers and your posterity? No attempts have ever been made by a Legislative body in America, to abridge that privilege; and in this free enlightened country, no attempts could succeed, unless the public should be convinced that an abuse of it would warrant the restriction. Should this ever be the case, you have no right to say, that a future Legislature, or that posterity shall not abridge the privilege, or punish its abuses. The very attempt to establish a permanent, unalterable Constitution, is an act of consummate arrogance. It is a presumption that we have all possible wisdom—that we can foresee all possible circumstances—and judge for future generations, better than they can for themselves.

"LETTER TO EDWARD CARRINGTON"

Thomas Jefferson

The Founders of the United States were an eloquent and prolific bunch; most left behind a wealth of letters, pamphlets, published essays, and books. Even among this literate group, Thomas Jefferson understood more than most the power of the printed word. A silken aristocrat, he envisioned an egalitarian republic of independent yeoman farmers; a large-scale slaveholder, he changed history by writing into the Declaration of Independence the words "all men are created equal." On his tombstone in Virginia is written his own self-selected epitaph; two of the four accomplishments he claimed at the end of his life were written works—the Declaration and the Virginia Statue of Religious Freedom.

The letter that follows, written in the year the Constitution was drafted, is the origin of a famous Jefferson aphorism that is almost always quoted as making a stark choice of newspapers without government over government without newspapers. But in fact, in the letter, Jefferson makes clear that his libertarian choice is only valid if the public is educated and informed— readers must be willing to read the papers and understand what they read.

Jefferson was in Paris as American Minister when the Constitution was

January 16, 1787. Reprinted from Saul K. Padover, ed., *A Jefferson Profile* (New York: John Day Company, 1956).

drafted in Philadelphia, and he privately remonstrated with his protégé James Madison at the lack of a Bill of Rights in the new charter. After the Constitution went into effect, Jefferson also played a crucial role in the rise of American journalism. As secretary of state, he secretly funded an anti-administration newspaper dedicated to vicious attacks on his Cabinet rival, Alexander Hamilton, and even to snide criticism of President George Washington. He and James Madison led the powerful movement to protest the Sedition Act of 1798, which was aimed directly at him and the nascent party press supporting his Republican Party. As president, Jefferson frequently found it necessary to depart from his "strict constructionist" principles in order to achieve such things as the purchase of Louisiana from France. Nor was he entirely above using the courts to punish his political enemies.

One of Jefferson's paid scribes, James Callender, later turned on him; his attacks on President Jefferson were a major force in spreading the rumors (only recently proved true) that the widower Jefferson maintained a long-running alliance with his slave, Sally Hemmings, and fathered her children. Perhaps it was Callender who inspired some of Jefferson's later wistful comments to the effect that the doctrine of seditious libel had been perhaps too hastily rejected.

To Edward Carrington
January 16, 1787   *Paris*

I am persuaded myself, that the good sense of the people will always be found to be the best army. They may be led astray for a moment, but will soon correct themselves. The people are the only censors of their governors; and even their errors will tend to keep these to the true principles of their institution. To punish these errors too severely, would be to suppress the only safeguard of the public liberty. The way to prevent these irregular interpositions of the people, is to give them full information of their affairs through the channel of the public papers, and to contrive that those papers should penetrate the whole mass of the people. The basis of our government being the opinion of the people, the very first object should be to keep that right; and were it left to me to decide whether we should have a government without newspapers, or newspapers without a government, I should not hesitate a moment to prefer the latter. But I should mean that every man should receive those papers, and be capable of reading them. I am convinced that those societies (as the

Indians) which live without government, enjoy in their general mass an infinitely greater degree of happiness, than those who live under the European governments. Among the former, public opinion is in the place of law, and restrains morals as powerfully as laws ever did anywhere. Among the latter, under pretense of governing, they have divided their nations into two classes, wolves and sheep. I do not exaggerate. This is a true picture of Europe. Cherish, therefore, the spirit of our people, and keep alive their attention. Do not be too severe upon their errors, but reclaim them by enlightening them. If once they become inattentive to the public affairs, you and I, and Congress and assemblies, judges and governors, shall all become wolves. It seems to be the law of our general nature, in spite of individual exceptions, and experience declares that man is the only animal which devours his own kind, for I can apply no milder term to the governments of Europe, and to the general prey of the rich on the poor.

"THE VIRGINIA REPORT OF 1799"

James Madison

James Madison was the father of the United States Constitution and the principal force behind the adoption of the Bill of Rights. He began his public life at twenty-five as a member of the Virginia Convention in 1776 and served as a member of the House of Representatives, secretary of state, and fourth president of the United States. He was the clear intellectual leader of the Federal Convention of 1787 that wrote the Constitution, and was coauthor (with Alexander Hamilton and John Jay) of *The Federalist*, in which he argued that the new Constitution needed no Bill of Rights because the federal government would never have enough power to threaten individual rights. Once the Constitution was adopted, however, Madison served as the conscience of the new Congress and insisted that it supply amendments to provide the Bill of Rights the Constitution's supporters had promised during the close struggle over ratification.

Less than ten years after the new national government was launched, Madison and his close ally, Thomas Jefferson, found themselves in a political death-struggle against attempts by President John Adams to suppress their nascent Republican Party. The Alien and Sedition Acts were passed during a time of war between Britain and France. Jeffersonians sided with revolu-

Leonard W. Levy, ed., *Freedom of the Press from Zenger to Jefferson: Early American Libertarian Theories* (Indianapolis, IN: Bobbs-Merrill, 1966), pp. 212–26.

tionary France and agitated for United States help to the French; Adams and his fellow Federalists supported Britain and wished above all for the United States to remain neutral. Under the Sedition Act, it was a crime to publish "false, scandalous, and malicious writing" against the government or the president. The administration used the new statute to silence Jeffersonian newspapers across the country.

Jefferson and Madison prevailed upon the Virginia and Kentucky legislatures to pass resolutions proclaiming the acts unconstitutional and "interposing" state authority against them. This doctrine was widely criticized as a quasi-revolutionary attempt to break the Union. Madison wrote *The Virginia Report* as a response to that criticism and as an attempt to show the unconstitutionality of the laws. The Sedition Act expired in 1801. More than one hundred and fifty years later however, Supreme Court Justice William Brennan was to cite this struggle to justify his landmark opinion in *New York Times v. Sullivan*.

...In the attempts to vindicate the "sedition-act," it has been contended, 1. That the "freedom of the press" is to be determined by the meaning of these terms in the common law. 2. That the article supposes the power over the press to be in Congress, and prohibits them only from abridging the freedom allowed to it by the common law.

Although it will be shown, in examining the second of these positions, that the amendment is a denial to Congress of all power over the press, it may not be useless to make the following observations on the first of them.

It is deemed to be a sound opinion, that the sedition-act, in its definition of some of the crimes created, is an abridgment of the freedom of publication, recognised by principles of the common law in England.

The freedom of the press under the common law, is, in the defences of the sedition-act, made to consist in an exemption from all *previous* restraint on printed publications, by persons authorized to inspect and prohibit them. It appears to the committee, that this idea of the freedom of the press, can never be admitted to be the American idea of it: since a law inflicting penalties on printed publications, would have a similar effect with a law authorizing a previous restraint on them. It would seem a mockery to say, that no law should be passed, preventing publications from being made, but that laws might be passed for punishing them in case they should be made.

The essential difference between the British government, and the American constitutions, will place this subject in the clearest light.

In the British government, the danger of encroachments on the rights of the people, is understood to be confined to the executive magistrate. The representatives of the people in the legislature, are not only exempt themselves, from distrust, but are considered as sufficient guardians of the rights of their constituents against the danger from the executive. Hence it is a principle, that the parliament is unlimited in its power; or, in their own language, is omnipotent. Hence, too, all the ramparts for protecting the rights of the people, such as their magna charta, their bill of rights, &c., are not reared against the parliament, but against the royal prerogative. They are merely legislative precautions against executive usurpations. Under such a government as this, an exemption of the press from previous restraint by licensers appointed by the king, is all the freedom that can be secured to it.

In the United States, the case is altogether different. The people, not the government, possess the absolute sovereignty. The legislature, no less than the executive, is under limitations of power. Encroachments are regarded as possible from the one, as well as from the other. Hence, in the United States, the great and essential rights of the people are secured against legislative, as well as against executive ambition. They are secured, not by laws paramount to prerogative, but by constitutions paramount to laws. This security of the freedom of the press requires, that it should be exempt, not only from previous restraint by the executive, as in Great Britain, but from legislative restraint also; and this exemption, to be effectual, must be an exemption not only from the previous inspection of licensers, but from the subsequent penalty of laws.

The state of the press, therefore, under the common law, cannot, in this point of view, be the standard of its freedom in the United States.

But there is another view, under which it may be necessary to consider this subject. It may be alleged, that although the security for the freedom of the press, be different in Great Britain and in this country; being a legal security only in the former, and a constitutional security in the latter; and although there may be a further difference, in an extension of the freedom of the press here, beyond an exemption from previous restraint, to an exemption from subsequent penalties also; yet that the actual legal freedom of the press, under the common law, must determine the degree of freedom which is meant by the terms, and which is constitutionally secured against both previous and subsequent restraints.

The committee are not unaware of the difficulty of all general questions, which may turn on the proper boundary between the liberty and licentiousness of the press. They will leave it therefore for consideration only, how far the difference between the nature of the British government, and the nature of the American governments, and the practice under the latter, may show the degree of rigour in the former to be inapplicable to, and not obligatory in the latter.

The nature of governments elective, limited, and responsible, in all their branches, may well be supposed to require a greater freedom of animadversion than might be tolerated by the genius of such a government as that of Great Britain. In the latter, it is a maxim, that the king, an hereditary, not a responsible magistrate, can do no wrong; and that the legislature, which in two-thirds of its composition, is also hereditary, not responsible, can do what it pleases. In the United States, the executive magistrates are not held to be infallible, nor the legislatures to be omnipotent; and both being elective, are both responsible. Is it not natural and necessary, under such different circumstances, that a different degree of freedom, in the use of the press, should be contemplated?

Is not such an inference favoured by what is observable in Great Britain itself? Notwithstanding the general doctrine of the common law, on the subject of the press, and the occasional punishment of those who use it with a freedom offensive to the government; it is well known, that with respect to the responsible members of the government, where the reasons operating here, become applicable there, the freedom exercised by the press, and protected by the public opinion, far exceeds the limits prescribed by the ordinary rules of law. The ministry, who are responsible to impeachment, are at all times animadverted on, by the press, with peculiar freedom; and during the elections for the House of Commons, the other responsible part of the government, the press is employed with as little reserve towards the candidates.

The practice in America must be entitled to much more respect. In every state, probably, in the Union, the press has exerted a freedom in canvassing the merits and measures of public men, of every description, which has not been confined to the strict limits of the common law. On this footing, the freedom of the press has stood; on this footing it yet stands. And it will not be a breach, either of truth or of candour, to say, that no persons or presses are in the habit of more unrestrained animadversions on the proceedings and functionaries of the state governments, than the persons and presses most zealous in vindicating the act of Congress for punishing similar animadversions on the government of the United States.

The last remark will not be understood as claiming for the state governments an immunity greater than they have heretofore enjoyed. Some degree of abuse is inseparable from the proper use of everything; and in no instance is this more true, than in that of the press. It has accordingly been decided by the practice of the states, that it is better to leave a few of its noxious branches to their luxuriant growth, than by pruning them away, to injure the vigour of those yielding the proper fruits. And can the wisdom of this policy be doubted by any who reflect, that to the press alone, chequered as it is with abuses, the world is indebted for all the triumphs which have been gained by reason and humanity, over error and oppression; who reflect, that to the same beneficent source, the United States owe much of the lights which conducted them to the rank of a free and independent nation; and which have improved their political system into a shape so auspicious to their happiness. Had "sedition-acts," forbidding every publication that might bring the constituted agents into contempt or disrepute, or that might excite the hatred of the people against the authors of unjust or pernicious measures, been uniformly enforced against the press, might not the United States have been languishing at this day, under the infirmities of a sickly confederation? Might they not possibly be miserable colonies, groaning under a foreign yoke?

To these observations, one fact will be added, which demonstrates that the common law cannot be admitted as the *universal* expositor of American terms, which may be the same with those contained in that law. The freedom of conscience, and of religion, are found in the same instruments which assert the freedom of the press. It will never be admitted, that the meaning of the former, in the common law of England, is to limit their meaning in the United States.

Whatever weight may be allowed to these considerations, the committee do not, however, by any means intend to rest the question on them. They contend that the article of amendment, instead of supposing in Congress a power that might be exercised over the press, provided its freedom was not abridged, was meant as a positive denial to Congress, of any power whatever on the subject.

To demonstrate that this was the true object of the article, it will be sufficient to recall the circumstances which led to it, and to refer to the explanation accompanying the article.

When the Constitution was under the discussions which preceded its ratification, it is well known, that great apprehensions were expressed by many, lest the omission of some positive exception from the powers delegated, of certain rights, and of the freedom of the press particularly, might expose them to danger of being drawn by construction within some of the powers vested in Congress; more especially of the power to make all laws necessary and proper for carrying their other powers into execution. In reply to this objection, it was invariably urged to be a fundamental and characteristic principle of the Constitution, that all powers not given by it, were reserved; that no powers were given beyond those enumerated in the Constitution, and such as were fairly incident to them; that the power over the rights in question, and particularly over the press, was neither among the enumerated powers, nor incident to any of them; and consequently that an exercise of any such power, would be a manifest usurpation. It is painful to remark, how much the arguments now employed in behalf of the sedition-act, are at variance with the reasoning which then justified the Constitution, and invited its ratification.

From this posture of the subject, resulted the interesting question in so many of the conventions, whether the doubts and dangers ascribed to the Constitution, should be removed by any amendments previous to the ratification, or be postponed, in confidence that as far as they might be proper, they would be introduced in the form provided by the Constitution. The latter course was adopted; and in most of the states, the ratifications were followed by propositions and instructions for rendering the Constitution more explicit, and more safe to the rights not meant to be delegated by it. Among those rights, the freedom of the press, in most instances, is particularly and emphatically mentioned. The firm and very pointed manner, in which it is asserted in the proceedings of the convention of this state, will be hereafter seen.

In pursuance of the wishes thus expressed, the first Congress that assembled under the Constitution, proposed certain amendments which have since, by the necessary ratifications, been made a part of it; among which amendments, is the article containing, among other prohibitions on the Congress, an express declaration that they should make no law abridging the freedom of the press.

Without tracing farther the evidence on this subject, it would seem scarcely possible to doubt, that no power whatever over the press was supposed to be delegated by the Constitution, as it originally stood; and that the amendment was intended as a positive and absolute reservation of it.

But the evidence is still stronger. The proposition of amendment is made by Congress, is introduced in the following terms: "*The conventions of a number of the states having at the time of their adopting the Constitution expressed a desire, in order to prevent misconstructions or abuse of its powers, that further declaratory and restrictive clauses should be added; and as extending the ground of public confidence in the government, will best ensure the beneficent ends of its institutions.*"

Here is the most satisfactory and authentic proof, that the several amendments proposed, were to be considered as either declaratory or restrictive; and whether the one or the other, as corresponding with the desire expressed by a number of the states, and as extending the ground of public confidence in the government.

Under any other construction of the amendment relating to the press, than that it declared the press to be wholly exempt from the power of Congress, the amendment could neither be said to correspond with the desire expressed by a number of the states, nor be calculated to extend the ground of public confidence in the government.

Nay more; the construction employed to justify the "sedition-act," would exhibit a phenomenon, without a parallel in the political world. It would exhibit a number of respectable states, as denying first that any power over the press was delegated by the Constitution; as proposing next, that an amendment to it, should explicitly declare that no such power was delegated; and finally, as concurring in an amendment actually recognising or delegating such a power.

Is then the federal government, it will be asked, destitute of every authority for restraining the licentiousness of the press, and for shielding itself against the libellous attacks which may be made on those who administer it?

The Constitution alone can answer this question. If no such power be expressly delegated, and it be not both necessary and proper to carry into execution an express power; above all, if it be expressly forbidden by a declaratory amendment to the Constitution, the answer must be, that the federal government is destitute of all such authority.

And might it not be asked in turn, whether it is not more probable, under all the circumstances which have been reviewed, that the authority should be withheld by the Constitution, than that it should be left to a vague and violent construction; whilst so much pains were bestowed in enumerating other powers, and so many less important powers are included in the enumeration?

Might it not be likewise asked, whether the anxious circumspection which dictated so many *peculiar* limitations on the general authority, would be unlikely to exempt the press altogether from that authority? The peculiar magnitude of some of the powers necessarily committed to the federal government; the peculiar duration required for the functions of some of its departments; the peculiar distance of the seat of its proceedings from the great body of its constituents; and the peculiar difficulty of circulating an adequate knowledge of them through any other channel; will not these considerations, some or other of which produced other exceptions from the powers of ordinary governments, all together, account for the policy of binding the hand of the federal government, from touching the channel which alone can give efficacy to its responsibility to its constituents; and of leaving those who administer it, to a remedy for their their injured reputations, under the same laws, and in the same tribunals, which protect their lives, their liberties, and their properties?

But the question does not turn either on the wisdom of the Constitution, or on the policy which gave rise to its particular organization. It turns on the actual meaning of the instrument; by which it has appeared, that a power over the press is clearly excluded, from the number of powers delegated to the federal government.

...And in the opinion of the committee, well may it be said, as the resolution concludes with saying, that the unconstitutional power exercised over the press by the "sedition-act," ought "more than any other, to produce universal alarm; because it is levelled against that right of freely examining public characters and measures, and of free communication among the people thereon, which has ever been justly deemed the only effectual guardian of every other right."

Without scrutinizing minutely into all the provisions of the "sedition-act," it will be sufficient to cite so much of section 2, as follows: "And be it further enacted, that if any person shall write, print, utter, or publish, or shall cause or procure to be written, printed, uttered or published, or shall knowingly and willingly assist or aid in writing, printing, uttering or publishing any false, scandalous and malicious writing or writings against the government of the United States, or either house of the Congress of the United States, or the President of the United States, *with an intent to defame the said government, or either house of the said Congress, or the President, or to bring them, or either of them, into contempt or disrepute; or to excite against them, or either, or any of them, the hatred of the good people of the United States, &c. Then such person being thereof convicted before any court of the United States, having jurisdiction thereof, shall be punished by a fine not exceeding two thousand dollars, and by imprisonment not exceeding two years."*

On this part of the act, the following observations present themselves:

1. The Constitution supposes that the President, the Congress, and each of its houses may not discharge their trusts, either from defect of judgment or other causes. Hence, they are all made responsible to their constituents, at the returning periods of election; and the President, who is singly entrusted with very great powers, is, as a further guard, subjected to an intermediate impeachment.

2. Should it happen, as the Constitution supposes it may happen, that

either of these branches of the government may not have duly discharged its trust, it is natural and proper that, according to the cause and degree of their faults, they should be brought into contempt or disrepute, and incur the hatred of the people.

3. Whether it has, in any case, happened that the proceedings of either, or all of those branches, evince such a violation of duty as to justify a contempt, a disrepute or hatred among the people, can only be determined by a free examination thereof, and a free communication among the people thereon.

4. Whenever it may have actually happened, that proceedings of this sort are chargeable on all or either of the branches of the government, it is the duty as well as right of intelligent and faithful citizens, to discuss and promulge them freely, as well to control them by the censorship of the public opinion, as to promote a remedy according to the rules of the Constitution. And it cannot be avoided, that those who are to apply the remedy must feel, in some degree, a contempt or hatred against the transgressing party.

5. As the act was passed on July 14, 1798, and is to be in force until March 3, 1801, it was of course, that during its continuance, two elections of the entire House of Representatives, an election of a part of the Senate, and an election of a President, were to take place.

6. That consequently, during all these elections, intended by the Constitution to preserve the purity, or to purge the faults of the administration, the great remedial rights of the people were to be exercised, and the responsibility of their public agents to be screened, under the penalties of this act.

May it not be asked of every intelligent friend to the liberties of his country, whether the power exercised in such an act as this, ought not to produce great and universal alarm? Whether a rigid execution of such an act, in time past, would not have repressed that information and communication among the people, which is indispensable to the just exercise of their electoral rights? And whether such an act, if made perpetual, and enforced with rigour, would not, in time to come, either destroy our free system of government, or prepare a convulsion that might prove equally fatal to it?

In answer to such questions, it has been pleaded that the writings and publications forbidden by the act, are those only which are false and malicious, and intended to defame; and merit is claimed for the privilege allowed to authors to justify, by proving the truth of their publications, and for the limitations to which the sentence of fine and imprisonment is subjected.

To those who concurred in the act, under the extraordinary belief that the option lay between the passing of such an act, and leaving in force the common law of libels, which punishes truth equally with falsehood, and submits the fine and imprisonment to the indefinite discretion of the court, the merit of good intentions ought surely not to be refused. A like merit may perhaps be due for the discontinuance of the *corporal punishment*, which the common law also leaves to the discretion of the court. This merit of *intention*, however, would have been greater, if the several mitigations had not been limited to so short a period; and the apparent inconsistency would have been avoided, between justifying the act at one time, by contrasting it with the rigors of the common law, otherwise in force, and at another time by appealing to the nature of the crisis, as requiring the temporary rigour exerted by the act.

But, whatever may have been the meritorious intentions of all or any who contributed to the sedition-act, a very few reflections will prove, that its baneful tendency is little diminished by the privilege of giving in evidence the truth of the matter contained in political writings.

In the first place, where simple and naked facts alone are in question, there is sufficient difficulty in some cases, and sufficient trouble and vexation in all, of meeting a prosecution from the government, with the full and formal proof necessary in a court of law.

But in the next place, it must be obvious to the plainest minds, that opinions, and inferences, and conjectural observations, are not only in many cases inseparable from the facts, but may often be more the objects of the prosecution than the facts themselves; or may even be altogether abstracted from particular facts; and that opinions and inferences, and conjectural observations, cannot be subjects of that kind of proof which appertains to facts, before a court of law.

Again: It is no less obvious, that the *intent* to defame or bring into contempt or disrepute, or hatred, which is made a condition of the offence created by the act, cannot prevent its pernicious influence on the freedom of the press. For, omitting the inquiry, how far the malice of the intent is an inference of the law from the mere publication, it is manifestly impossible to punish the intent to bring those who administer the government into disrepute or contempt, without striking at the right of freely discussing public characters and measures: because those who engage in such discussions, must expect and *intend* to excite these unfavourable sentiments, so far as they may be thought to be deserved. To prohibit, therefore, the intent to excite those unfavourable sentiments against those who administer the government, is equivalent to a prohibition of the actual excitement of them; and to prohibit the actual excitement of them, is equivalent to a prohibition of discussions having that tendency and effect; which, again, is equivalent to a protection of those who administer the government, if they should at any time deserve the contempt or hatred of the people, against being exposed to it, by free animadversions on their characters and conduct. Nor can there be a doubt, if those in public trust be shielded by penal laws from such strictures of the press, as may expose them to contempt or disrepute, or hatred, where they may deserve it, in exact proportion as they may deserve to be exposed, will be the certainty and criminality of the intent to expose them, and the vigilance of prosecuting and punishing it; nor a doubt, that a government thus intrenched in penal statutes, against the just and natural effects of a culpable administration, will easily evade the responsibility, which is essential to a faithful discharge of its duty.

Let it be recollected, lastly, that the right of electing the members of the government, constitutes more particularly the essence of a free and responsible government. The value and efficacy of this right, depends on the knowledge of the comparative merits and demerits of the candidates for public trust; and on the equal freedom, consequently, of examining and discussing these merits and demerits of the candidates respectively. It has been seen, that a number of important elections will take place whilst the act is in force, although it should not be continued beyond the term to which it is limited. Should there happen, then, as is extremely probable in relation to some or other of the branches of the government, to be competitions between those who are, and those who are not, members of the government, what will be the situations of the competitors? Not equal; because the characters of the former will be covered by the "sedition-act" from animadversions exposing them to disrepute among the people; whilst the latter may be exposed to the contempt and hatred of the people, without a violation of the act. What will be the situation of the people? Not free; because they will be compelled to make their election between competitors, whose pretensions they are not permitted, by the act, equally to examine, to discuss, and to ascertain. And from both these situations, will not those in power derive an undue advantage for continuing themselves in it; which by impairing the right of election, endangers the blessings of the government founded on it?

It is with justice, therefore, that the General Assembly have affirmed in the resolution, as well that the right of freely examining public characters and measures, and free communication thereon, is the only effectual guardian of every other right, as that this particular right is levelled at, by the power exercised in the "sedition-act."

FROM
DEMOCRACY IN AMERICA
Alexis de Tocqueville

Perhaps the most famous and influential book analyzing American political culture was written by a Frenchman on the basis of a visit of a little over nine months during 1831 and 1832. Alexis de Tocqueville was born in Paris in 1805. His writings pioneered the discipline now known as sociology. His first book, *The U.S. Penitentiary System and Its Application in France*, compares the American prison system during the early 1800s to European systems. His second book, *Democracy in America*, is a close examination of America and the political institutions it produces.

Before coming to America, he had studied law and worked as a minor official of the government. Since its publication in English in 1840, Tocqueville's *Democracy in America* has been a perennial best seller, and analysis and elaboration of his insights have been a major sport of journalists, sociologists, political scientists, and lawyers. Tocqueville's emphasis on localism in government and voluntarism in society has appealed to the American imagination. His discussion of these concepts is so expansive that some writers have suggested one can find one's own position mirrored somehow in Tocqueville, no matter what it may be. But this universal quality may simply result from the profound affection Tocqueville shows for the new nation and its people.

Henry Reeve, trans., *Democracy in America* (Boston: John Allyn, 1882), pp. 230–41.

CHAPTER XI
LIBERTY OF THE PRESS IN THE UNITED STATES

...I confess that I do not entertain that firm and complete attachment to the liberty of the press which is wont to be excited by things that are supremely good in their very nature. I approve of it from a consideration more of the evils it prevents, than of the advantages it insures.

If any one could point out an intermediate and yet a tenable position between the complete independence and the entire servitude of opinion, I should, perhaps, be inclined to adopt it; but the difficulty is, to discover this intermediate position. Intending to correct the licentiousness of the press, and to restore the use of orderly language, you first try the offender by a jury; but if the jury acquits him, the opinion which was that of a single individual becomes the opinion of the whole country. Too much and too little has therefore been done; go farther, then. You bring the delinquent before permanent magistrates; but even here, the cause must be heard before it can be decided; and the very principles which no book would have ventured to avow are blazoned forth in the pleadings, and what was obscurely hinted at in a single composition is thus repeated in a multitude of other publications. The language is only the expression, and (if I may so speak) the body, of the thought, but it is not the thought itself. Tribunals may condemn the body, but the sense, the spirit, of the work is too subtile for their authority. Too much has still been done to recede, too little to attain your end; you must go still farther. Establish a censorship of the press. But the tongue of the public speaker will still make itself heard, and your purpose is not yet accomplished; you have only increased the mischief. Thought is not, like physical strength, dependent upon the number of its agents; nor can authors be counted like the troops which compose an army. On the contrary, the authority of a principle is often increased by the small number of men by whom it is expressed. The words of one strong-minded man, addressed to the passions of a listening assembly, have more power than the vociferations of a thousand orators; and if it be allowed to speak freely in any one public place, the consequence is the same as if free speaking was allowed in every village. The liberty of speech must therefore be destroyed, as well as the liberty of the press. And now you have succeeded, everybody is reduced to silence. But your object was to repress the abuses of liberty, and you are brought to the feet of a despot. You have been led from the extreme of independence to the extreme of servitude, without finding a single tenable position on the way at which you could stop.

There are certain nations which have peculiar reasons for cherishing the liberty of the press, independently of the general motives which I have just pointed out. For in certain countries which profess to be free, every individual agent of the government may violate the laws with impunity, since the constitution does not give to those who are injured a right of complaint before the courts of justice. In this case, the liberty of the press is not merely one of the guaranties, but it is the only guaranty, of their liberty and security which the citizens possess. If the rulers of these nations proposed to abolish the independence of the press, the whole people might answer, Give us the right of prosecuting your offences before the ordinary tribunals, and perhaps we may then waive our right of appeal to the tribunal of public opinion.

In countries where the doctrine of the sovereignty of the people ostensibly prevails, the censorship of the press is not only dangerous, but absurd. When the right of every citizen to a share in the government of society is acknowledged, every one must be presumed to be able to choose between the various opinions of his contemporaries, and to appreciate the different facts from which inferences may be drawn. The sovereignty of the people and the liberty of the press may therefore be regarded as correlative; just as the censorship of the press and universal suffrage are two things which are irreconcilably opposed, and which cannot long be retained among the institutions of the same people. Not a single individual of the [thirty] millions who inhabit the United States has, as yet, dared to propose any restrictions on the liberty of the press. The first newspaper over which I cast my eyes, upon my arrival in America, contained the following article:—

"In all this affair, the language of Jackson [the President] has been that of a heartless despot, solely occupied with the preservation of his own authority. Ambition is his crime, and it will be his punishment, too; intrigue is his native element, and intrigue will confound his tricks, and deprive him of his power. He governs by means of corruption, and his immoral practices will redound to his shame and confusion. His conduct in the political arena has been that of a shameless and lawless gamester. He succeeded at the time; but the hour of retribution approaches, and he will be obliged to disgorge his winnings, to throw aside his false dice, and to end his days in some retirement, where he may curse his madness at his leisure; for repentance is a virtue with which his heart is likely to remain forever unacquainted."

Many persons in France think, that the violence of the press originates in the instability of the social state, in our political passions, and the general feeling of uneasiness which consequently prevails; and it is therefore supposed that, as soon as society has resumed a certain degree of composure, the press will abandon its present vehemence. For my own part, I would willingly attribute to these causes the extraordinary ascendancy which the press has acquired over the nation; but I do not think that they do exercise much influence upon its language. The periodical press appears to me to have passions and instincts of its own, independent of the circumstances in which it is placed; and the present condition of America corroborates this opinion.

America is perhaps, at this moment, the country of the whole world which contains the fewest germs of revolution; but the press is not less destructive in its principles there than in France, and it displays the same violence without the same reasons for indignation. In America, as in France, it constitutes a singular power, so strangely composed of mingled good and evil, that liberty could not live without it, and public order can hardly be maintained against it. Its power is certainly much greater in France than in the United States; though nothing is more rare in the latter country than to hear of a prosecution being instituted against it. The reason of this is perfectly simple: The Americans, having once admitted the doctrine of the sovereignty of the people, apply it with perfect sincerity. It was never their intention out of elements which are changing every day to create institutions which should last forever; and there is consequently nothing criminal in an attack upon the existing laws, provided a violent infraction of them is not intended. They are also of opinion that courts of justice are powerless to check the abuses of the press; and that, as the subtilty of human language perpetually eludes judicial analysis, offences of this nature somehow escape the hand which attempts to seize them. They hold that, to act with efficacy upon the press, it would be necessary to find a tribunal, not only devoted to the existing order of things, but capable of surmounting the influence of public opinion; a tribunal which should conduct its proceedings without publicity, which should pronounce its decrees without assigning its motives, and punish the intentions, even more than the language, or a writer. Whoever should be able to create and maintain a tribunal of this kind, would waste his time in prosecuting the liberty of the press; for he would be as free to rid himself of the authors as of their writings. In this question, therefore, there is no medium between servitude and license; in order to enjoy the inestimable benefits which the liberty of the press insures, it is necessary to submit to the inevitable evils which it creates. To expect to acquire the former, and to escape the latter, is to cherish one of those illusions which commonly mislead nations in their times of sickness, when, tired with faction and exhausted by effort, they attempt to make hostile opinions and contrary principles coexist upon the same soil.

The small influence of the American journals is attributable to several reasons, amongst which are the following.

The liberty of writing, like all other liberty, is most formidable when it is a novelty; for a people who have never been accustomed to hear state affairs discussed before them, place implicit confidence in the first tribune who presents himself. The Anglo-Americans have enjoyed this liberty ever since the foundation of the Colonies; moreover, the press cannot create human passions, however skillfully it may kindle them where they exist. In America, political life is active, varied, even agitated, but is rarely affected by those deep passions which are excited only when material interests are impaired: and in the United States, these interests are prosperous. A glance at a French and an American newspaper is sufficient to show the difference which exists in this respect between the two nations. In France, the space allotted to commercial advertisements is very limited, and the news-intelligence is not considerable; but the essential part of the journal is the discussion of the politics of the day. In America, three quarters of the enormous sheet are filled with advertisements, and the remainder is frequently occupied by political intelligence or trivial anecdotes: it is only from time to time, that one finds a corner devoted to passionate discussions, like those which the journalists of France every day give to their readers.

It has been demonstrated by observation, and discovered by the sure instinct even of the pettiest despots, that the influence of a power is increased in proportion as its direction is centralized. In France, the press combines a two-fold centralization; almost all its power is centred in the same spot, and, so to speak, in the same hands; for its organs are far from numerous. The influence of a public press thus constituted, upon a skeptical nation, must be almost unbounded. It is an enemy with whom a government may sign an occasional truce, but which it is difficult to resist for any length of time.

Neither of these kinds of centralization exists in America. The United States have no metropolis; the intelligence and the power of the people are disseminated through all the parts of this vast country, and instead of radiating from a common point, they cross each other in every direction; the Americans have nowhere established any central direction of opinion, any more than of the conduct of affairs. This difference arises from local circumstances, and not from human power; but it is owing to the laws of the Union that there are no licenses to be granted to printers, no securities demanded from editors, as in France, and no stamp duty, as in France and England. The consequence is, that nothing is easier than to set up a newspaper, as a small number of subscribers suffices to defray the expenses.

Hence the number of periodical and semi-periodical publications in the United States is almost incredibly large. The most enlightened Americans attribute the little influence of the press to this excessive dissemination of its power; and it is an axiom of political science in that country, that the only way to neutralize the effect of the public journals is to multiply their number. I cannot see how a truth which is so self-evident should not already have been more generally admitted in Europe. I can see why the persons who hope to bring about revolutions by means of the press, should be desirous of confining it to a few powerful organs; but it is inconceivable that the official partisans of the existing state of things, and the natural supporters of the laws, should attempt to diminish the influence of the press by concentrating its power. The governments of Europe seem to treat the press with the courtesy which the knights of old showed to their opponents; having found from their own experience that centralization is a powerful weapon, they have furnished their enemies with it, in order doubtless to have more glory for overcoming them.

In America, there is scarcely a hamlet which has not its newspaper. It may readily be imagined, that neither discipline nor unity of action can be established among so many combatants; and each one consequently fights under his own standard. All the political journals of the United States are, indeed, arrayed on the side of the administration or against it; but they attack and defend it in a thousand different ways. They cannot form those great currents of opinion which sweep away the strongest dikes. This division of the influence of the press produces other consequences scarcely less remarkable. The facility with which newspapers can be established produces a multitude of them; but as the competition prevents any considerable profit, persons of much capacity are rarely led to engage in these undertakings. Such is the number of the public prints, that, even if they were a source of wealth, writers of ability could not be found to direct them all. The journalists of the United States are generally in a very humble position, with a scanty education and a vulgar turn of mind. The will of the majority is the most general of laws, and it establishes certain habits to which every one must then conform; the aggregate of these common habits is what is called the class-spirit (*esprit de corps*) of each profession; thus there is the class-spirit of the bar, of the court, &c. The class-spirit of the French journalists consists in a violent, but frequently an eloquent and lofty, manner of discussing the great interests of the state; and the exceptions to this mode of writing are only occasional. The characteristics of the American journalist consist in an open and coarse appeal to the passions of his readers; he abandons principles to assail the characters of individuals, to track them into private life, and disclose all their weaknesses and vices.

Nothing can be more deplorable than this abuse of the powers of thought; I shall have occasion to point out hereafter the influence of the newspapers upon the taste and the morality of the American people; but my present subject exclusively concerns the political world. It cannot be denied, that the political effects of this extreme license of the press tend indirectly to the maintenance of public order. The individuals who already stand high in the esteem of their fellow-citizens are afraid to write in the newspapers, and they are thus deprived of the most powerful instrument which they can use to excite the passions of the multitude to their own advantage.*

The personal opinion of the editors have no weight in the eyes of the public: what they seek in a newspaper is a knowledge of facts, and it is only by altering or distorting those facts, that a journalist can contribute to the support of his own views.

But although the press is limited to these resources, its influence in America is immense. It causes political life to circulate through all the parts of that vast territory. Its eye is constantly open to detect the secret springs of political designs, and to summon the leaders of all parties in turn to the bar of public opinion. It rallies the interests of the community round certain principles, and draws up the creed of every party; for it affords a means of intercourse between those who hear and address each other, without ever coming into immediate contact. When many organs of the press adopt the same line of conduct, their influence in the long run becomes irresistible; and public opinion, perpetually assailed from the same side, eventually yields to the attack. In the United States, each separate journal exercises but little authority; but the power of the periodical press is second only to that of the people.

---

*They only write in the papers when they choose to address the people in their own name; as, for instance, when they are called upon to repel calumnious imputations, or to correct a misstatement of facts.

The Opinions established in the United States, under the Influence of the Liberty of the Press, are frequently more firmly rooted than those which are formed elsewhere under the Sanction of a Censor.

In the United States, the democracy perpetually brings new men to the conduct of public affairs; and the administration consequently seldom preserves consistency or order in its measures. But the general principles of the government are more stable, and the chief opinions which regulate society are more durable, there than in many other countries. When once the Americans have taken up an idea, whether it be well or ill founded, nothing is more difficult than to eradicate it from their minds. The same tenacity of opinion has been observed in England, where, for the last century, greater freedom of thought and more invincible prejudices have existed than in any other country of Europe. I attribute this to a cause which may, at first sight, appear to have an opposite tendency, namely, to the liberty of the press. The nations amongst whom this liberty exists cling to their opinions as much from pride as from conviction. They cherish them because they hold them to be just, and because they chose them of their own free will; and they adhere to them, not only because they are true, but because they are their own. Several other reasons conduce to the same end.

It was remarked by a man of genius, that "ignorance lies at the two ends of knowledge." Perhaps it would have been more correct to say, that strong convictions are found only at the two ends, and that doubt lies in the middle. The human intellect, in truth, may be considered in three distinct states, which frequently succeed one another.

A man believes firmly, because he adopts a proposition without inquiry. He doubts as soon as objections present themselves. But he frequently succeeds in satisfying these doubts, and then he begins again to believe. This time, he has not a dim and casual glimpse of the truth, but sees it clearly before him, and advances by the light it gives.*

Then the liberty of the press acts upon men who are in the first of these three states, it does not immediately disturb their habit of believing implicitly without investigation, but it changes every day the objects of their unreflecting convictions. The human mind continues to discern but one point at a

---

*It may, however, be doubted whether this rational and self-guiding conviction arouses as much fervor or enthusiastic devotedness in men, as their first dogmatical belief.

time upon the whole intellectual horizon, and that point is constantly changing. This is the period of sudden revolutions. Woe to the generations which first abruptly adopt the freedom of the press.

The circle of novel ideas, however, is soon traveled over. Experience comes to undeceive men, and plunges them into doubt and general mistrust. We may rest assured that the majority of mankind will always stop in one of these two states, will either believe they know not wherefore, or will not know what to believe. Few are those who can ever attain to that other state of rational and independent conviction, which true knowledge can produce out of the midst of doubt.

It has been remarked that, in times of great religious fervor, men sometimes change their religious opinions; whereas, in times of general skepticism, every one clings to his old persuasion. The same thing takes place in politics under the liberty of the press. In countries where all the theories of social science have been contested in their turn, men who have adopted one of them stick to it, not so much because they are sure of its truth, as because they are not sure that there is any better to be had. In the present age, men are not very ready to die for their opinions, but they are rarely inclined to change them; there are few martyrs, as well as few apostates.

Another still more valid reason may be adduced: when no opinions are looked upon as certain, men cling to the mere instincts and material interests of their position, which are naturally more tangible, definite, and permanent than any opinions in the world.

It is a very difficult question to decide, whether an aristocracy or a democracy governs the best. But it is certain that democracy annoys one part of the community, and that aristocracy oppresses another. It is a truth which is self-established, and one which it is needless to discuss, that "you are rich and I am poor."

Part II

EXPANSION THROUGH CASE LAW

CONTEMPT OF COURT
Patterson v. Colorado

One of the earliest free-press cases arose not out of a restrictive statute but out of a state court's anger at being criticized in the press. *Patterson v. Colorado* raised the question of whether a court's contempt power could reach to punishing newspapers who held its decisions up to criticism and even ridicule.

In the early 1900s, Thomas M. Patterson, a US senator from Colorado, published articles and a cartoon concerning the conduct of Colorado Supreme Court justices. Patterson, the owner of the *Rocky Mountain News* since 1890 and later the *Denver Times*, was an attorney involved in a case pending before the Colorado Supreme Court. The Colorado Supreme Court held him in contempt for his published comments. Patterson appealed the case to the United States Supreme Court, arguing that the criminal contempt charge was invalid because the article he published was true and was a legitimate exercise of his First Amendment rights.

Justice Oliver Wendell Holmes, recently appointed to the United States Supreme Court, delivered the opinion of the Court. Holmes, who would later come to have a broader view of the First Amendment, in this early case wrote that the main purpose of the First Amendment was to prevent prior restraints on speech and press. He continued by reaffirming the Blackstonian view that subsequent punishment of public speech is constitutional.

205 U.S. 454 (1907).

99

The dissent by Justice John Marshall Harlan foreshadows the future application of the First Amendment, arguing that its protections go far beyond a rule against prior restraint, and that every American citizen had the write right to speak and publish freely without subsequent punishment. *Patterson* was later overruled by *Stromberg v. California* (1931).

Mr. Justice HOLMES delivered the opinion of the court:

This is a writ of error to review a judgment upon an information for contempt. The contempt alleged was the publication of certain articles and a cartoon, which, it was charged, reflected upon the motives and conduct of the Supreme Court of Colorado in cases still pending and were intended to embarrass the court in the impartial administration of justice.... The answer went on to narrate the transactions commented on, at length, intimating that the conduct of the court was unconstitutional and usurping, and alleging that it was in aid of a scheme, fully explained, to seat various Republican candidates, including the governor of the state, in place of Democrats who had been elected, and that two of the judges of the court got their seats as a part of the scheme. Finally the answer alleged that the respondent published the articles in pursuance of what he regarded as a public duty, repeated the previous objections to the information, averred the truth of the articles, and set up and claimed the right to prove the truth under the Constitution of the United States. Upon this answer the court, on motion, ordered judgment fining the plaintiff in error for contempt.

... The defense upon which the plaintiff in error most relies is raised by the allegation that the articles complained of are true, and the claim of the right to prove the truth. He claimed this right under the Constitutions both of the state and of the United States, but the latter ground alone comes into consideration here.... We leave undecided the question whether there is to be found in the Fourteenth Amendment a prohibition similar to that in the First. But even if we were to assume that freedom of speech and freedom of the press were protected from abridgment on the part not only of the United States but also of the states, still we should be far from the conclusion that the plaintiff in error would have us reach. In the first place, the main purpose of such constitutional provisions is "to prevent all such *previous restraints* upon publications as had been practised by other governments," and they do not prevent the subsequent punishment of such as may be deemed contrary to the public welfare. The preliminary freedom extends as well to the false as to the true; the subsequent punishment may extend as well to the true as to the false. This was the law of criminal libel apart from statute in most cases, if not in all.

In the next place, the rule applied to criminal libels applies yet more clearly to contempts. A publication likely to reach the eyes of a jury, declaring a witness in a pending cause a perjurer, would be none the less a contempt that it was true. It would tend to obstruct the administration of justice, because even a correct conclusion is not to be reached or helped in that way, if our system of trials is to be maintained. The theory of our system is that the conclusions to be reached in a case will be induced only by evidence and argument in open court, and not by any outside influence, whether of private talk or public print.

What is true with reference to a jury is true also with reference to a court. Cases like the present are more likely to arise, no doubt, when there is a jury and the publication may affect their judgment. Judges generally, perhaps, are less apprehensive that publications impugning their own reasoning or motives will interfere with their administration of the law. But if a court regards, as it may, a publication concerning a matter of law pending before it, as tending toward such an interference, it may punish it as in the instance put. When a case is finished, courts are subject to the same criticism as other people, but the propriety and necessity of preventing interference with the course of justice by premature statement, argument or intimidation hardly can be denied....

Mr. Justice HARLAN, dissenting:

I cannot agree that this writ of error should be dismissed.

...In *United States v. Cruikshank*, we held that the right of the people peaceably to assemble and to petition the government for a redress of grievances—one of the rights recognized in and protected by the First Amendment against hostile legislation by Congress—was an attribute of 'national citizenship.' So the First Amendment, although in form prohibitory, is to be regarded as having a reflex character, and as affirmatively recognizing freedom of speech and freedom of the press as rights belonging to citizens of the United States; that is, those rights are to be deemed attributes of national citizenship or citizenship of the United States....

Now, the Fourteenth Amendment declares, in express words, that "no state shall make or enforce any law which shall abridge the privileges or immunities of citizens of the United States." As the First Amendment guaranteed the rights of free speech and of a free press against hostile action by the United States, it would seem clear that when the Fourteenth Amendment prohibited the states from impairing or abridging the privileges of citizens of the United States it necessarily prohibited the states from impairing or abridging the constitutional rights of such citizens to free speech and a free press. But the court announces that it leaves undecided the specific question whether there is to be found in the Fourteenth Amendment a prohibition as to the rights of free speech and a free press similar to that in the First. It yet proceeds to say that the main purpose of such constitutional provisions was to prevent all such *previous restraints* upon publications as had been practised by other governments, but not to prevent the subsequent punishment of such as may be deemed contrary to the public welfare. I cannot assent to that view, if it be meant that the legislature may impair or abridge the rights of a free press and of free speech whenever it thinks that the public welfare requires that to be done. The public welfare cannot override constitutional privileges, and if the rights of free speech and of a free press are, in their essence, attributes of national citizenship, as I think they are, then neither Congress nor any state since the adoption of the Fourteenth Amendment, can, by legislative enactments or by judicial action, impair or abridge them. In my judgment the action of the court below was in violation of the rights of free speech and a free press as guaranteed by the Constitution.

I go further and hold that the privileges of free speech and of a free press, belonging to every citizen of the United States, constitute essential parts of every man's liberty, and are protected against violation by that clause of the Fourteenth Amendment forbidding a state to deprive any person of his liberty without due process of law. It is, I think, impossible to conceive of liberty, as secured by the Constitution against hostile action, whether by the nation or by the states, which does not embrace the right to enjoy free speech and the right to have a free press.

PUBLISHING DISSENTING VIEWS IN WARTIME

Frohwerk v. United States

A few weeks after the terrorist attacks on September 11, 2001, White House spokesman Ari Fleischer responded to a comment by comedian Bill Maher that the Al Qaeda hijackers were not, as they had been called, cowards. Maher had added that Americans were the cowards, because our military killed people from afar. Fleischer warned that "Americans...need to watch what they say, watch what they do. This is not a time for remarks like that; there never is." The next year, ABC decided not to renew Maher's talk show, *Politically Incorrect.*

When *is* the time for radical dissent? Should the government have more leeway to regulate and punish the media during times of war and national crisis? These issues first arose during the war that marked the emergence of the United States as a major world power, World War I. A substantial minority of the nation opposed our entry into the war, and the US government prosecuted many critics, including a former presidential candidate, for sedition. One seminal case concerned the rights of newspapers to question government policy. From June to December of 1917, two residents of the United States, Jacob Frohwerk and Carl Gleeser, published a series of articles in a Missouri-based German-language newspaper. The articles claimed that American public opinion was being manipulated by the British, that the Germans were

---

249 U.S. 204 (1919).

peace-loving people who were being misrepresented by the press, and that American draftee soldiers were unwitting dupes of wealthy Wall Street businessmen. At least one of the articles quoted in the decision urged American soldiers to "cease firing."

Frohwerk was arrested and charged with a conspiracy to violate the Espionage Act of 1917. He was convicted on twelve counts of obstructing the war effort and sentenced to ten years in prison, despite his claims that the First Amendment prevented Congress from restricting his ability to publish opinions, however unpopular they might be at the time.

In November of 1918, the Allies forced Germany to sign an armistice. In January of 1919, the Supreme Court heard Frohwerk's appeal. In May of 1919, the Court affirmed his conviction on the grounds that the "First Amendment...cannot have been, and obviously was not intended to give immunity for every possible use of language."

Mr. Justice HOLMES delivered the opinion of the Court.

This is an indictment in thirteen counts. The first alleges a conspiracy between the plaintiff in error and one Carl Gleeser, they then being engaged in the preparation and publication of a newspaper, the *Missouri Staats Zeitung*, to violate the Espionage Act of June 15, 1917.... It alleges as overt acts the preparation and circulation of twelve articles &c. in the said newspaper at different dates from July 6, 1917, to December 7 of the same year. The other counts allege attempts to cause disloyalty, mutiny and refusal of duty in the military and naval forces of the United States, by the same publications.... Motion to dismiss and a demurrer on constitutional and other grounds, especially that of the First Amendment as to free speech, were overruled, subject to exception, and the defendant refusing to plead the Court ordered a plea of not guilty to be filed. There was a trial and Frohwerk was found guilty on all the counts except the seventh, which needs no further mention. He was sentenced to a fine and to ten years imprisonment on each count, the imprisonment on the later counts to run concurrently with that on the first.

...With regard to [the constitutional question] we think it necessary to add to what has been said in *Schenck v. United States* only that the First Amendment while prohibiting legislation against free speech as such cannot have been, and obviously was not, intended to give immunity for every possible use of language.... We venture to believe that neither Hamilton nor Madison, nor any other competent person then or later, ever supposed that to make criminal the counselling of a murder within the jurisdiction of Congress would be an unconstitutional interference with free speech.

Whatever might be thought of the other counts on the evidence,...we have decided in *Schenck v. United States* that a person may be convicted of a conspiracy to obstruct recruiting by words of persuasion. The government argues that on the record the question is narrowed simply to the power of Congress to punish such a conspiracy to obstruct, but we shall take it in favor of the defendant that the publications [were] the only evidence of the conspiracy alleged. Taking it that way, however, so far as the language of the article goes there is not much to choose between expressions to be found in them and those before us in *Schenck v. United States.*

The first [article] begins by declaring it a monumental and inexcusable mistake to send our soldiers to France,...and later that it appears to be outright murder without serving anything practical; speaks of the unconquerable spirit and undiminished strength of the German nation, and characterizes its own discourse as words of warning to the American people....Later, on August 3, came discussion of the causes of the war, laying it to the administration and saying "that a few men and corporations might amass unprecedented fortunes we sold our honor, our very soul" with the usual repetition that we went to war to protect the loans of Wall Street. Later, after more similar discourse, comes "We say therefore, cease firing."

Next, on August 10,...the paper goes on to give a picture, made as moving as the writer was able to make it, of the sufferings of a drafted man, of his then recognizing that his country is not in danger and that he is being sent to a foreign land to fight in a cause that neither he nor any one else knows anything of, and reaching the conviction that this is but a war to protect some rich men's money....On August 17 there is quoted and applied to our own situation a remark to the effect that when rulers scheme to use it for their own aggrandizement loyalty serves to perpetuate wrong. On August 31 with more of the usual discourse, it is said that the sooner the public wakes up to the fact that we are led and ruled by England, the better; that our sons, our taxes and our sacrifices are only in the interest of England....There is much more to the general effect that we are in the wrong and are giving false and hypocritical reasons for our course, but the foregoing is enough to indicate the kind of matter with which we have to deal.

It may be that all this might be said or written even in time of war in circumstances that would not make it a crime. We do not lose our right to condemn either measures or men because the country is at war. It does not appear that there was any special effort to reach men who were subject to the draft; and if the evidence should show that the defendant was a poor man, turning out copy for Gleeser, his employer, at less than a day laborer's pay, for Gleeser to use or reject as he saw fit, in a newspaper of small circulation, there would be a natural inclination to test every question of law to be found in the record very thoroughly before upholding the very severe penalty imposed. But we must take the case on the record as it is, and on that record it is impossible to say that it might not have been found that the circulation of the paper was in quarters where a little breath would be enough to kindle a flame and that the fact was known and relied upon by those who sent the paper out. Small compensation would not exonerate the defendant if it were found that he expected the result, even if pay were his chief desire. When we consider that we do not know how strong the government's evidence may have been we find ourselves unable to say that the articles could not furnish a basis for a conviction upon the first count at least.... There is nothing before us that makes it possible to say that the judge's discretion was wrongly exercised. Upon the whole case we are driven to the conclusion that the record shows no ground upon which the judgment can be reversed.

   Judgment affirmed.

"PRIOR RESTRAINT"

Near v. Minnesota

Even the earliest Supreme Court cases recognized that the First Amendment barred government from enacting "prior restraints" on publication—systems of licensing or censorship that intervened before material was published. The doctrine originated in the eighteenth century, when William Blackstone used the term in a commentary reacting to the licensing system in England. Under the licensing system, the church or state had to approve all publications. In 1789, the Framers of the Bill of Rights created the First Amendment, at least in part to bar the new federal government from emulating the Crown in this regard.

In *Near v. Minnesota*, the US Supreme Court incorporated the doctrine of prior restraint into precedent. Currently, the best definition of prior restraint is an administrative or judicial order "forbidding certain communications when issued in advance of the time that such communications are to occur," *Alexandria v. United States.*

The publication at issue in *Near* was a scurrilous, anti-Semitic "scandal sheet," which author Fred W. Friendly, in his famous book about the case, dubbed a "Minnesota Rag." Its attacks on prominent officials and "Jewish gangsters" were raw even by the standards of the 1930s. The Court in *Near* was not concerned with whether the articles were truthful or malicious; if the

___

283 U.S. 697 (1931).

material was false and defamatory, subsequent litigation could establish liability. Instead, its concern was over the powerful tool created by a system of prior restraint. With such power, government could stifle any exposure of official corruption.

Since *Near*, the Supreme Court has extended the idea of forbidden prior restraint to cover injunctions barring publication of "national security" secrets (*New York v. United States*), licensing requirements for parades and demonstrations (*Nationalist Movement v. Forsyth*), and even a permit system allowing news racks on public property (*Lakewood v. Plain Dealer Publishing Co.*).

Mr. Chief Justice HUGHES delivered the opinion of the Court.

Chapter 285 of the Session Laws of Minnesota for the year 1925 provides for the abatement, as a public nuisance, of a "malicious, scandalous and defamatory newspaper, magazine or other periodical."

...Under this statute...the county attorney of Hennepin County brought this action to enjoin the publication of what was described as a "malicious, scandalous and defamatory newspaper, magazine or other periodical," known as *The Saturday Press*, published by the defendants in the city of Minneapolis. The complaint alleged that the defendants, on September 24, 1927, and on eight subsequent dates in October and November, 1927, published and circulated editions of that periodical which were 'largely devoted to malicious, scandalous and defamatory articles.'

...Without attempting to summarize the contents of the voluminous exhibits attached to the complaint, we deem it sufficient to say that the articles charged in substance that a Jewish gangster was in control of gambling, bootlegging, and racketeering in Minneapolis, and that law enforcing officers and agencies were not energetically performing their duties. Most of the charges were directed against the chief of police; he was charged with gross neglect of duty, illicit relations with gangsters, and with participation in graft. The county attorney was charged with knowing the existing conditions and with failure to take adequate measures to remedy them. The mayor was accused of inefficiency and dereliction. One member of the grand jury was stated to be in sympathy with the gangsters. A special grand jury and a special prosecutor were demanded to deal with the situation in general, and, in particular, to investigate an attempt to assassinate one Guilford, one of the original defendants, who, it appears from the articles, was shot by gangsters after the first issue of the periodical had been published. There is no question but that the articles made serious accusations against the public officers named and others in connection with the prevalence of crimes and the failure to expose and punish them....

The district court made findings of fact, which followed the allegations of the complaint and found in general terms that the editions in question were "chiefly devoted to malicious, scandalous and defamatory articles" concerning the individuals named. The court further found that the defendants through these publications "did engage in the business of regularly and customarily producing, publishing and circulating a malicious, scandalous and defamatory newspaper," and that "the said publication" "under said name of *The Saturday Press*, or any other name, constitutes a public nuisance under the laws of the State." Judgment was thereupon entered adjudging that "the newspaper, magazine and periodical known as *The Saturday Press*," as a public nuisance, "be and is hereby abated." The judgment perpetually enjoined the defendants "from producing, editing, publishing, circulating, having in their possession, selling or giving away any publication whatsoever which is a malicious, scandalous or defamatory newspaper, as defined by law," and also "from further conducting said nuisance under the name and title of said *The Saturday Press* or any other name or title."

... From the judgment as thus affirmed, the defendant Near appeals to this Court.

... It is no longer open to doubt that the liberty of the press and of speech is within the liberty safeguarded by the due process clause of the Fourteenth Amendment from invasion by state action. It was found impossible to conclude that this essential personal liberty of the citizen was left unprotected by the general guaranty of fundamental rights of person and property.... Liberty, in each of its phases, has its history and connotation, and, in the present instance, the inquiry is as to the historic conception of the liberty of the press and whether the statute under review violates the essential attributes of that liberty....

If we cut through mere details of procedure, the operation and effect of the statute in substance is that public authorities may bring the owner or publisher of a newspaper or periodical before a judge upon a charge of conducting a business of publishing scandalous and defamatory matter—in particular that the matter consists of charges against public officers of official dereliction—and, unless the owner or publisher is able and disposed to bring competent evidence to satisfy the judge that the charges are true and are published with good motives and for justifiable ends, his newspaper or periodical is suppressed and further publication is made punishable as a contempt. This is of the essence of censorship.

The question is whether a statute authorizing such proceedings in restraint of publication is consistent with the conception of the liberty of the press as historically conceived and guaranteed. In determining the extent of the constitutional protection, it has been generally, if not universally, considered that it is the chief purpose of the guaranty to prevent previous restraints upon publication. The struggle in England, directed against the legislative power of the licenser, resulted in renunciation of the censorship of the press. The liberty deemed to be established was thus described by Blackstone:

> The liberty of the press is indeed essential to the nature of a free state; but this consists in laying no *previous* restraints upon publications, and not in freedom from censure for criminal matter when published. Every freeman has an undoubted right to lay what sentiments he pleases before the public; to forbid this, is to destroy the freedom of the press; but if he publishes what is improper, mischievous or illegal, he must take the consequence of his own temerity.

The distinction was early pointed out between the extent of the freedom with respect to censorship under our constitutional system and that enjoyed in England. Here, as Madison said,

> the great and essential rights of the people are secured against legislative as well as against executive ambition. They are secured, not by laws paramount to prerogative, but by constitutions paramount to laws. This security of the freedom of the press requires that it should be exempt not only from previous restraint by the Executive, as in Great Britain, but from legislative restraint also.

This Court said, in *Patterson v. Colorado*: "In the first place, the main purpose of such constitutional provisions is 'to prevent all such *previous restraints* upon publications as had been practiced by other governments,' and they do not prevent the subsequent punishment of such as may be deemed contrary to the public welfare. The preliminary freedom extends as well to the false as to the true; the subsequent punishment may extend as well to the true as to the false...."

The objection has also been made that the principle as to immunity from previous restraint is stated too broadly, if every such restraint is deemed to be prohibited. That is undoubtedly true; the protection even as to previous restraint is not absolutely unlimited. But the limitation has been recognized only in exceptional cases: "When a nation is at war many things that might be said in time of peace are such a hindrance to its effort that their utterance will not be endured so long as men fight and that no Court could regard them as protected by any constitutional right." *Schenck v. United States.* No one would question but that a government might prevent actual obstruction to its recruiting service or the publication of the sailing dates of transports or the number and location of troops. On similar grounds, the primary requirements of decency may be enforced against obscene publications. The security of the community life may be protected against incitements to acts of violence and the overthrow by force of orderly government. The constitutional guaranty of free speech does not "protect a man from an injunction against uttering words that may have all the effect of force." *Schenck v. United States.* These limitations are not applicable here. Nor are we now concerned with questions as to the extent of authority to prevent publications in order to protect private rights according to the principles governing the exercise of the jurisdiction of courts of equity.

The exceptional nature of its limitations places in a strong light the general conception that liberty of the press, historically considered and taken up by the Federal Constitution, has meant, principally although not exclusively, immunity from previous restraints or censorship. The conception of the liberty of the press in this country had broadened with the exigencies of the colonial period and with the efforts to secure freedom from oppressive administration. That liberty was especially cherished for the immunity it afforded from previous restraint of the publication of censure of public officers and charges of official misconduct.... In the letter sent by the Continental Congress (October 26, 1774) to the Inhabitants of Quebec, referring to the "five great rights" it was said: "The last right we shall mention, regards the freedom of the press. The importance of this consists, besides the advancement of truth, science, morality, and arts in general, in its diffusion of liberal sentiments on the administration of Government, its ready communication of thoughts between subjects, and its consequential promotion of union among them, whereby oppressive officers are shamed or intimidated, into more honourable and just modes of conducting affairs." ...

The fact that for approximately 150 there has been almost an entire absence of attempts to impose previous restraints upon publications relating to the malfeasance of public officers is significant of the deep-seated conviction that such restraints would violate constitutional right. Public officers, whose character and conduct remain open to debate and free discussion in the press, find their remedies for false accusations in actions under libel laws providing for redress and punishment, and not in proceedings to restrain the publication of newspapers and periodicals. The general principle that the constitutional guaranty of the liberty of the press gives immunity from previous restraints has been approved in many decisions under the provisions of state constitutions.

The importance of this immunity has not lessened. While reckless assaults upon public men, and efforts to bring obloquy upon those who are endeavoring faithfully to discharge official duties, exert a baleful influence and deserve the severest condemnation in public opinion, it cannot be said that this abuse is greater, and it is believed to be less, than that which characterized the period in which our institutions took shape. Meanwhile, the administration of government has become more complex, the opportunities for malfeasance and corruption have multiplied, crime has grown to most serious proportions, and the danger of its protection by unfaithful officials and of the impairment of the fundamental security of life and property by criminal alliances and official neglect, emphasizes the primary need of a vigilant and courageous press, especially in great cities. The fact that the liberty of the press may be abused by miscreant purveyors of scandal does not make any the less necessary the immunity of the press from previous restraint in dealing with official misconduct. Subsequent punishment for such abuses as may exist is the appropriate remedy, consistent with constitutional privilege....

The statute in question cannot be justified by reason of the fact that the publisher is permitted to show, before injunction issues, that the matter published is true and is published with good motives and for justifiable ends. If such a statute, authorizing suppression and injunction on such a basis, is constitutionally valid, it would be equally permissible for the Legislature to provide that at any time the publisher of any newspaper could be brought before a court, or even an administrative officer (as the constitutional protection may not be regarded as resting on mere procedural details), and required to produce proof of the truth of his publication, or of what he intended to publish, and of his motives, or stand enjoined. If this can be done, the Legislature may provide machinery for determining in the complete exercise of its discretion what are justifiable ends and restrain publication accordingly. And it would be but a step to a complete system of censorship....

Equally unavailing is the insistence that the statute is designed to prevent the circulation of scandal which tends to disturb the public peace and to provoke assaults and the commission of crime. Charges of reprehensible conduct, and in particular of official malfeasance, unquestionably create a public scandal, but the theory of the constitutional guaranty is that even a more serious public evil would be caused by authority to prevent publication.... There is nothing new in the fact that charges of reprehensible conduct may create resentment and the disposition to resort to violent means of redress, but this well-understood tendency did not alter the determination to protect the press against censorship and restrain upon publication. As was said in *New Yorker Staats-Zeitung v. Nolan*: "If the township may prevent the circulation of a newspaper for no reason other than that some of its inhabitants may violently disagree with it, and resent its circulation by resorting to physical violence, there is no limit to what may be prohibited." The danger of violent reactions becomes greater with effective organization of defiant groups resenting exposure, and, if this consideration warranted legislative interference with the initial freedom of publication, the constitutional protection would be reduced to a mere form of words.

For these reasons we hold the statute, so far as it authorized the proceedings in this action...to be an infringement of the liberty of the press guaranteed by the Fourteenth Amendment.

Judgment reversed....

Mr. Justice BUTLER (dissenting).

...The Minnesota statute does not operate as a previous restraint on publication within the proper meaning of that phrase. It does not authorize administrative control in advance such as was formerly exercised by the licensers and censors, but prescribes a remedy to be enforced by a suit in equity. In this case there was previous publication made in the course of the business of regularly producing malicious, scandalous, and defamatory periodicals. The business and publications unquestionably constitute an abuse of the right of free press. The statute denounces the things done as a nuisance on the ground, as stated by the state Supreme Court, that they threaten morals, peace, and good order. There is no question of the power of the state to denounce such transgressions. The restraint authorized is only in respect of continuing to do what has been duly adjudged to constitute a nuisance....

It is well known, as found by the state Supreme Court, that existing libel laws are inadequate effectively to suppress evils resulting from the kind of business and publications that are shown in this case....

The judgment should be affirmed.

Mr. Justice VAN DEVANTER, Mr. Justice McREYNOLDS, and Mr. Justice SUTHERLAND concur in this opinion.

THE PRESS AND THE "TAXES ON KNOWLEDGE"

Grosjean v. American Press Company

The news media must pay their taxes, just like any other business. But what if government decides to tax the media *because* they are the media, or because of what they print? Louisiana governor and then senator Huey Long rose to prominence by attacking the oil and railroad industries. The state's daily newspapers, owned by prominent and wealthy families, opposed Long's populist agenda both during his years as governor and afterward, as he used his Senate seat to prepare for a possible presidential campaign in 1936. In response, Long and his allies in 1934 passed a state statute that imposed a new tax on large-circulation newspapers and then started their own paper that would escape taxation to compete with them.

In 1936 Justice George Sutherland wrote for a unanimous Court that Long's tax was an intrusion on the freedom of the press that violated the First Amendment. Sutherland reached back into eighteenth-century English political thought, which criticized "taxes of knowledge," that is, taxes targeted at the expression of ideas. Because the tax was implemented to attack large Louisiana newspapers while ignoring those with a smaller circulation, the court held that it was an unconstitutional prior restraint on publication. Sutherland wrote, "A free press stands as one of the great interpreters between the government and the people. To allow it to be fettered is to fetter ourselves."

297 U.S. 233 (1936).

115

In 1983 the Supreme Court reaffirmed the *Grosjean* doctrine and the ban on "taxes on knowledge" in an opinion striking down a special state tax on ink and paper (*Minneapolis Star & Tribune Co. v. Minn. Comm'r of Revenue* [1983]). At the same time, the Court has consistently followed Sutherland's dictum that "[i]t is not intended by anything we have said to suggest that the owners of newspapers are immune from any of the ordinary forms of taxation for support of the government." Newspapers must pay general taxes, and state laws that provide tax exemptions for religious newspapers but not others, for example, are also unconstitutional.

As for Senator Long, his spectacular career ended in his assassination in 1935. His last words reportedly were, "God, don't let me die. I have so much to do."

Mr. Justice SUTHERLAND delivered the opinion of the Court.

This suit was brought by appellees, nine publishers of newspapers in the state of Louisiana, to enjoin the enforcement against them of the provisions of § 1 of the act of the Legislature of Louisiana known as Act No. 23, passed and approved July 12, 1934, as follows: "That every person, firm, association or corporation, domestic or foreign, engaged in the business of selling, or making any charge for, advertising or for advertisements... in any newspaper, magazine, periodical or publication whatever having a circulation of more than 20,000 copies per week, or displayed and exhibited, or to be displayed and exhibited, by means of moving pictures, in the State of Louisiana, shall, in addition to all other taxes and licenses levied and assessed in this State, pay a license tax for the privilege of engaging in such business in this State of two percent (2%) of the gross receipts of such business."

The nine publishers who brought the suit publish thirteen newspapers; and these thirteen publications are the only ones within the state of Louisiana having each a circulation of more than 20,000 copies per week... [T]he lower court finds there are four other daily newspapers each having a circulation of "slightly less than 20,000 copies per week" which are in competition with those published by appellees both as to circulation and as to advertising. In addition, there are 120 weekly newspapers published in the state, also in competition, to a greater or less degree, with the newspapers of appellees. The revenue derived from appellees' newspapers comes almost entirely from regular subscribers or purchasers thereof and from payments received for the insertion of advertisements therein....

The validity of the act is assailed as violating the Federal Constitution in two particulars: (1) That it abridges the freedom of the press in contravention of the Due Process clause contained in § 1 of the Fourteenth Amendment; (2) that it denies appellees the equal protection of the laws in contravention of the same amendment.

1. The first point presents a question of the utmost gravity and importance; for, if well made, it goes to the heart of the natural right of the members of an organized society, united for their common good, to impart and acquire information about their common interests. The First Amendment to the Federal Constitution provides that "Congress shall make no law... abridging the freedom of speech, or of the press." While this provision is not a restraint upon the powers of the states, the states are precluded from abridging the freedom of speech or of the press by force of the due process clause of the Fourteenth Amendment....

That freedom of speech and of the press are rights of the same fundamental character, safeguarded by the due process of law clause of the Fourteenth Amendment against abridgement by state legislation, has likewise been settled by a series of decisions of this court....

The tax imposed is designated a "license tax for the privilege of engaging in such business," that is to say, the business of selling, or making any charge for, advertising. As applied to appellees, it is a tax of 2 percent on the gross receipts derived from advertisements carried in their newspapers when, and only when, the newspapers of each enjoy a circulation of more than 20,000 copies per week. It thus operates as a restraint in a double sense. First, its effect is to curtail the amount of revenue realized from advertising; and, second, its direct tendency is to restrict circulation. This is plain enough when we consider that, if it were increased to a high degree... it well might result in destroying both advertising and circulation.

A determination... whether the tax is valid in respect of the point now under review requires an examination of the history and circumstances which antedated and attended the adoption of the abridgement clause of the First Amendment....

For more than a century prior to the adoption of the amendment—and, indeed, for many years thereafter—history discloses a persistent effort on the part of the British government to prevent or abridge the free expression of any opinion which seemed to criticize... the agencies and operations of the government. The struggle between the proponents of measures to that end and those who asserted the right of free expression was continuous and unceasing. As early as 1644, John Milton, in an "Appeal for the Liberty of Unlicensed Printing," assailed an act of Parliament which had just been passed providing for censorship of the press previous to publication. He vigorously defended the right of every man to make public his honest views "without previous censure"; and declared the impossibility of finding any man base enough to accept the office of censor and at the same time good enough to be allowed to perform its duties. The act expired by its own terms in 1695. It was never renewed.... But mere exemption from previous censorship was soon recognized as too narrow a view of the liberty of the press.

In 1712, in response to a message from Queen Anne, Parliament imposed a tax upon all newspapers and upon advertisements. That the main purpose of these taxes was to suppress the publication of comments and criticisms objectionable to the Crown does not admit of doubt.... [T]hese taxes constituted one of the factors that aroused the American colonists to protest against taxation for the purposes of the home government; and...the revolution really began when, in 1765, that government sent stamps for newspaper duties to the American colonies.

These duties were quite commonly characterized as "taxes on knowledge," a phrase used for the purpose of describing the effect of the exactions and at the same time condemning them. That the taxes had, and were intended to have, the effect of curtailing the circulation of newspapers, and particularly the cheaper ones whose readers were generally found among the masses of the people, went almost without question, even on the part of those who defended the act....

... [T]he foregoing is enough to demonstrate...that in the adoption of the English newspaper stamp tax and the tax on advertisements, revenue was of subordinate concern; and that the dominant and controlling aim was to prevent, or curtail the opportunity for, the acquisition of knowledge by the people in respect of their governmental affairs. It is idle to suppose that so many of the best men of England would for a century of time have waged, as they did, stubborn and often precarious warfare against these taxes if a mere matter of taxation had been involved. The aim of the struggle was not to relieve taxpayers from a burden, but to establish and preserve the right of the English people to full information in respect of the doings or misdoings of their government. Upon the correctness of this conclusion the very characterization of the exactions as "taxes on knowledge" sheds a flood of corroborative light. In the ultimate, an informed and enlightened public opinion was the thing at stake....

In 1785, only four years before Congress had proposed the First Amendment, the Massachusetts Legislature, following the English example, imposed a stamp tax on all newspapers and magazines. The following year an advertisement tax was imposed. Both taxes met with such violent opposition that the former was repealed in 1786, and the latter in 1788....

The framers of the First Amendment were familiar with the English struggle, which then had continued for nearly eighty years.... The framers were likewise familiar with the then recent Massachusetts episode; and while that occurrence did much to bring about the adoption of the amendment... the predominant influence must have come from the English experience. It is impossible to concede that by the words "freedom of the press" the framers of the amendment intended to adopt merely the narrow view then reflected by the law of England that such freedom consisted only in immunity from previous censorship; for this abuse had then permanently disappeared from English practice. It is equally impossible to believe that it was not intended to bring within the reach of these words such modes of restraint as were embodied in the two forms of taxation already described....

In the light of all that has now been said, it is evident that the restricted rules of the English law in respect of the freedom of the press in force when the Constitution was adopted were never accepted by the American colonists, and that by the First Amendment it was meant to preclude the national government, and by the Fourteenth Amendment to preclude the states, from adopting any form of previous restraint upon printed publications, or their circulation, including that which had theretofore been effected by these two well known and odious methods.

This court had occasion in *Near v. Minnesota*... to discuss at some length the subject in its general aspect. The conclusion there stated is that the object of the constitutional provisions was to prevent previous restraints on publication; and the court was careful not to limit the protection of the right to any particular way of abridging it. Liberty of the press within the meaning of the constitutional provision, it was broadly said, meant "principally although not exclusively, immunity from previous restraints or (from) censorship."...

It is not intended by anything we have said to suggest that the owners of newspapers are immune from any of the ordinary forms of taxation for support of the government. But this is not an ordinary form of tax, but one single in kind, with a long history of hostile misuse against the freedom of the press.

The predominant purpose of the grant of immunity here invoked was to preserve an untrammeled press as a vital source of public information. The newspapers, magazines, and other journals of the country, it is safe to say, have shed and continue to shed, more light on the public and business affairs of the nation than any other instrumentality of publicity; and since informed public opinion is the most potent of all restraints upon misgovernment, the suppression or abridgement of the publicity afforded by a free press cannot be regarded otherwise than with grave concern. The tax here involved is bad not because it takes money from the pockets of the appellees. If that were all, a wholly different question would be presented. It is bad because, in the light of its history and of its present setting, it is seen to be a deliberate and calculated device in the guise of a tax to limit the circulation of information to which the public is entitled in virtue of the constitutional guaranties. A free press stands as one of the great interpreters between the government and the people. To allow it to be fettered is to fetter ourselves....

Decree affirmed.

THE END OF
SEDITIOUS LIBEL

New York Times v. Sullivan

In what is widely regarded as the single most important free-press decision ever made, the Supreme Court in 1964 held that public officials could not sue a news organization for defamation unless they could prove that the statements were made with "actual malice"—meaning that the news medium either knew it was telling an untruth or entertained subjective doubt that the statement was true.

The case thwarted a concerted attempt by southern state governments to intimidate national media, whose coverage of the attacks on civil rights demonstrators had electrified public opinion. In 1960 the *New York Times* published an editorial advertisement called "Heed Their Rising Voices." The advertisement solicited funds to defend the Rev. Martin Luther King Jr. against tax evasion charges and criticized repressive actions by Alabama officials against civil rights protesters. The commissioner in charge of police in Birmingham, Alabama, claimed that, though he was not mentioned by name, small factual errors in the criticism of the police meant that the article defamed him. A state-court jury granted substantial damages against the *Times*; many other officials across the South began filing suits, openly boasting that they would use this mechanism to silence the hated national media.

---

376 U.S. 254 (1964).

In a sweeping opinion, Justice Brennan wrote that any rule requiring a guarantee of the truth on all factual assertions would "dampen the vigor and limit the variety of public debate." The Court harked back to the struggle against the Sedition Acts under President John Adams to hold that the First Amendment barred officials from using defamation law to punish critics for their official performance. Subsequent cases have extended the "actual malice" rule to news coverage of "public figures," even those who don't hold public office.

Even at the time, the case was seen as crucial for the development of a free mass media in the United States. When it was decided, philosopher Alexander Meikeljohn famously reacted by saying, "It is an occasion for dancing in the streets."

Mr. Justice BRENNAN delivered the opinion of the Court.

We are required in this case to determine for the first time the extent to which the constitutional protections for speech and press limit a State's power to award damages in a libel action brought by a public official against critics of his official conduct.

Respondent L. B. Sullivan is one of the three elected Commissioners of the City of Montgomery, Alabama. He testified that he was "Commissioner of Public Affairs and the duties are supervision of the Police Department, Fire Department, Department of Cemetery and Department of Scales." He brought this civil libel action against the four individual petitioners, who are Negroes and Alabama clergymen, and against petitioner the New York Times Company, a New York corporation which publishes the *New York Times*, a daily newspaper. A jury in the Circuit Court of Montgomery County awarded him damages of $ 500,000, the full amount claimed, against all the petitioners, and the Supreme Court of Alabama affirmed.

Respondent's complaint alleged that he had been libeled by statements in a full-page advertisement that was carried in the *New York Times* on March 29, 1960....

The text appeared over the names of 64 persons, many widely known for their activities in public affairs, religion, trade unions, and the performing arts. Below these names, and under a line reading "We in the south who are struggling daily for dignity and freedom warmly endorse this appeal," appeared the names of the four individual petitioners and of 16 other persons, all but two of whom were identified as clergymen in various Southern cities. The advertisement was signed at the bottom of the page by the "Committee to Defend Martin Luther King and the Struggle for Freedom in the South," and the officers of the Committee were listed.

Of the 10 paragraphs of text in the advertisement, the third and a portion of the sixth were the basis of respondent's claim of libel. They read as follows:

Third paragraph:

"In Montgomery, Alabama, after students sang 'My Country, 'Tis of Thee' on the State Capitol steps, their leaders were expelled from school, and truckloads of police armed with shotguns and tear-gas ringed the Alabama State College Campus. When the entire student body protested to state authorities by refusing to re-register, their dining hall was padlocked in an attempt to starve them into submission."

Sixth paragraph:

"Again and again the Southern violators have answered Dr. King's peaceful protests with intimidation and violence. They have bombed his home almost killing his wife and child. They have assaulted his person. They have arrested him seven times—for 'speeding,' 'loitering' and similar 'offenses.' And now they have charged him with 'perjury'—a *felony* under which they could imprison him for *ten years....*"

Although neither of these statements mentions respondent by name, he contended that the word "police" in the third paragraph referred to him as the Montgomery Commissioner who supervised the Police Department, so that he was being accused of "ringing" the campus with police. He further claimed that the paragraph would be read as imputing to the police, and hence to him, the padlocking of the dining hall in order to starve the students into submission. As to the sixth paragraph, he contended that since arrests are ordinarily made by the police, the statement "They have arrested [Dr. King] seven times" would be read as referring to him; he further contended that the "They" who did the arresting would be equated with the "They" who committed the other described acts and with the "Southern violators." Thus, he argued, the paragraph would be read as accusing the Montgomery police, and hence him, of answering Dr. King's protests with "intimidation and violence," bombing his home, assaulting his person, and charging him with perjury. Respondent and six other Montgomery residents testified that they read some or all of the statements as referring to him in his capacity as Commissioner.

It is uncontroverted that some of the statements contained in the two paragraphs were not accurate descriptions of events which occurred in Montgomery. Although Negro students staged a demonstration on the State Capitol steps, they sang the National Anthem and not "My Country, 'Tis of Thee." Although nine students were expelled by the State Board of Education, this was not for leading the demonstration at the Capitol, but for demanding service at a lunch counter in the Montgomery County Courthouse on another day. Not the entire student body, but most of it, had protested the expulsion, not by refusing to register, but by boycotting classes on a single day; virtually all the students did register for the ensuing semester. The campus dining hall was not padlocked on any occasion, and the only students who may have been barred from eating there were the few who had neither signed a preregistration application nor requested temporary meal tickets. Although the police were deployed near the campus in large numbers on three occasions, they did not at any time "ring" the campus, and they were not called to the campus in connection with the demonstration on the State Capitol steps, as the third paragraph implied. Dr. King had not been arrested seven times, but only four; and although he claimed to have been assaulted some years earlier in connection with his arrest for loitering outside a courtroom, one of the officers who made the arrest denied that there was such an assault.

On the premise that the charges in the sixth paragraph could be read as referring to him, respondent was allowed to prove that he had not participated in the events described. Although Dr. King's home had in fact been bombed twice when his wife and child were there, both of these occasions antedated respondent's tenure as Commissioner, and the police were not only not implicated in the bombings, but had made every effort to apprehend those who were. Three of Dr. King's four arrests took place before respondent became Commissioner. Although Dr. King had in fact been indicted (he was subsequently acquitted) on two counts of perjury, each of which carried a possible five-year sentence, respondent had nothing to do with procuring the indictment.

Respondent made no effort to prove that he suffered actual pecuniary loss as a result of the alleged libel. One of his witnesses, a former employer, testified that if he had believed the statements, he doubted whether he "would want to be associated with anybody who would be a party to such things that are stated in that ad," and that he would not re-employ respondent if he believed "that he allowed the Police Department to do the things that the paper say he did." But neither this witness nor any of the others testified that he had actually believed the statements in their supposed reference to respondent. . . .

The trial judge submitted the case to the jury under instructions that the statements in the advertisement were "libelous *per se*" and were not privileged, so that petitioners might be held liable if the jury found that they had published the advertisement and that the statements were made "of and concerning" respondent. The jury was instructed that, because the statements were libelous *per se*, "the law … implies legal injury from the bare fact of publication itself," "falsity and malice are presumed," "general damages need not be alleged or proved but are presumed," and "punitive damages may be awarded by the jury even though the amount of actual damages is neither found nor shown." … The judge rejected petitioners' contention that his rulings abridged the freedoms of speech and of the press that are guaranteed by the First and Fourteenth Amendments.

In affirming the judgment, the Supreme Court of Alabama sustained the trial judge's rulings and instructions in all respects. …

We reverse the judgment. We hold that the rule of law applied by the Alabama courts is constitutionally deficient for failure to provide the safeguards for freedom of speech and of the press that are required by the First and Fourteenth Amendments in a libel action brought by a public official against critics of his official conduct. We further hold that under the proper safeguards the evidence presented in this case is constitutionally insufficient to support the judgment for respondent.

I.

We may dispose at the outset of two grounds asserted to insulate the judgment of the Alabama courts from constitutional scrutiny. The first is the proposition relied on by the State Supreme Court—that "The Fourteenth Amendment is directed against State action and not private action." That proposition has no application to this case. Although this is a civil lawsuit between private parties, the Alabama courts have applied a state rule of law which petitioners claim to impose invalid restrictions on their constitutional freedoms of speech and press. …

The second contention is that the constitutional guarantees of freedom of speech and of the press are inapplicable here, at least so far as the *Times* is concerned, because the allegedly libelous statements were published as part of a paid, "commercial" advertisement. The argument relies on *Valentine v. Chrestensen*, where the Court held that a city ordinance forbidding street distribution of commercial and business advertising matter did not abridge the First Amendment freedoms, even as applied to a handbill having a commercial message on one side but a protest against certain official action on the other. The reliance is wholly misplaced. The Court in *Chrestensen* reaffirmed the constitutional protection for "the freedom of communicating information and disseminating opinion"; its holding was based upon the factual conclusions that the handbill was "purely commercial advertising" and that the protest against official action had been added only to evade the ordinance.

The publication here was not a "commercial" advertisement in the sense in which the word was used in *Chrestensen*. It communicated information, expressed opinion, recited grievances, protested claimed abuses, and sought financial support on behalf of a movement whose existence and objectives are matters of the highest public interest and concern. That the *Times* was paid for publishing the advertisement is as immaterial in this connection as is the fact that newspapers and books are sold. Any other conclusion would discourage newspapers from carrying "editorial advertisements" of this type, and so might shut off an important outlet for the promulgation of information and ideas by persons who do not themselves have access to publishing facilities— who wish to exercise their freedom of speech even though they are not members of the press. The effect would be to shackle the First Amendment in its attempt to secure "the widest possible dissemination of information from diverse and antagonistic sources." *Associated Press v. United States*. To avoid placing such a handicap upon the freedoms of expression, we hold that if the allegedly libelous statements would otherwise be constitutionally protected from the present judgment, they do not forfeit that protection because they were published in the form of a paid advertisement.

II.

...Respondent relies heavily, as did the Alabama courts, on statements of this Court to the effect that the Constitution does not protect libelous publications. Those statements do not foreclose our inquiry here. None of the cases sustained the use of libel laws to impose sanctions upon expression critical of the official conduct of public officials.... In deciding the question now, we are compelled by neither precedent nor policy to give any more weight to the epithet "libel" than we have to other "mere labels" of state law. Like insurrection, contempt, advocacy of unlawful acts, breach of the peace, obscenity, solicitation of legal business, and the various other formulae for the repression of expression that have been challenged in this Court, libel can claim no talismanic immunity from constitutional limitations. It must be measured by standards that satisfy the First Amendment.

The general proposition that freedom of expression upon public questions is secured by the First Amendment has long been settled by our decisions. The constitutional safeguard, we have said, "was fashioned to assure unfettered interchange of ideas for the bringing about of political and social changes desired by the people." *Roth v. United States.* "The maintenance of the opportunity for free political discussion to the end that government may be responsive to the will of the people and that changes may be obtained by lawful means, an opportunity essential to the security of the Republic, is a fundamental principle of our constitutional system." *Stromberg v. California.* "It is a prized American privilege to speak one's mind, although not always with perfect good taste, on all public institutions," *Bridges v. California,* and this opportunity is to be afforded for "vigorous advocacy" no less than "abstract discussion." *N.A.A.C.P. v. Button.* The First Amendment, said Judge Learned Hand, "presupposes that right conclusions are more likely to be gathered out of a multitude of tongues, than through any kind of authoritative selection. To many this is, and always will be, folly; but we have staked upon it our all." *United States v. Associated Press.* Mr. Justice Brandeis, in his concurring opinion in *Whitney v. California,* gave the principle its classic formulation:

> Those who won our independence believed...that public discussion is a political duty; and that this should be a fundamental principle of the American government. They recognized the risks to which all human institutions are subject. But they knew that order cannot be secured merely through fear of punishment for its infraction; that it is hazardous to discourage thought, hope and imagination; that fear breeds repression; that repression breeds hate; that hate menaces stable government; that the path of safety lies in the opportunity to discuss freely supposed grievances and proposed remedies; and that the fitting remedy for evil counsels is good ones. Believing in the power of reason as applied through public discussion, they eschewed silence coerced by law—the argument of force in its worst form. Recognizing the occasional tyrannies of governing majorities, they amended the Constitution so that free speech and assembly should be guaranteed.

Thus we consider this case against the background of a profound national commitment to the principle that debate on public issues should be uninhibited, robust, and wide-open, and that it may well include vehement, caustic, and sometimes unpleasantly sharp attacks on government and public officials. The present advertisement, as an expression of grievance and protest on one of the major public issues of our time, would seem clearly to qualify for the constitutional protection. The question is whether it forfeits that protection by the falsity of some of its factual statements and by its alleged defamation of respondent.

Authoritative interpretations of the First Amendment guarantees have consistently refused to recognize an exception for any test of truth—whether administered by judges, juries or administrative officials—and especially one that puts the burden of proving truth on the speaker. The constitutional protection does not turn upon "the truth, popularity, or social utility of the ideas and beliefs which are offered." *N.A.A.C.P. v. Button.* As Madison said, "Some degree of abuse is inseparable from the proper use of every thing; and in no instance is this more true than in that of the press." ...

Injury to official reputation affords no more warrant for repressing speech that would otherwise be free than does factual error. Where judicial officers are involved, this Court has held that concern for the dignity and reputation of the courts does not justify the punishment as criminal contempt of criticism of the judge or his decision. This is true even though the utterance contains "half-truths" and "misinformation." Such repression can be justified, if at all, only by a clear and present danger of the obstruction of justice. If judges are to be treated as "men of fortitude, able to thrive in a hardy climate," surely the same must be true of other government officials, such as elected city commissioners. Criticism of their official conduct does not lose its constitutional protection merely because it is effective criticism and hence diminishes their official reputations.

If neither factual error nor defamatory content suffices to remove the constitutional shield from criticism of official conduct, the combination of the two elements is no less inadequate. This is the lesson to be drawn from the great controversy over the Sedition Act of 1798 ... which first crystallized a national awareness of the central meaning of the First Amendment. That statute made it a crime, punishable by a $5,000 fine and five years in prison, "if any person shall write, print, utter or publish ... any false, scandalous and malicious writing or writings against the government of the United States, or

either house of the Congress..., or the President..., with intent to defame...
or to bring them, or either of them, into contempt or disrepute; or to excite
against them, or either or any of them, the hatred of the good people of the
United States." The Act allowed the defendant the defense of truth, and provided that the jury were to be judges both of the law and the facts. Despite
these qualifications, the Act was vigorously condemned as unconstitutional in
an attack joined in by Jefferson and Madison....

Earlier, in a debate in the House of Representatives, Madison had said: "If
we advert to the nature of Republican Government, we shall find that the censorial power is in the people over the Government, and not in the Government over the people." Of the exercise of that power by the press, his *Report*
said: "In every state, probably, in the Union, the press has exerted a freedom
in canvassing the merits and measures of public men, of every description,
which has not been confined to the strict limits of the common law. On this
footing the freedom of the press has stood; on this foundation it yet stands...."
The right of free public discussion of the stewardship of public officials was
thus, in Madison's view, a fundamental principle of the American form of
government.

Although the Sedition Act was never tested in this Court, the attack upon
its validity has carried the day in the court of history.... The invalidity of the
Act has also been assumed by Justices of this Court. These views reflect a
broad consensus that the Act, because of the restraint it imposed upon criticism of government and public officials, was inconsistent with the First
Amendment.

There is no force in respondent's argument that the constitutional limitations implicit in the history of the Sedition Act apply only to Congress and
not to the States. It is true that the First Amendment was originally addressed
only to action by the Federal Government...[b]ut this distinction was eliminated with the adoption of the Fourteenth Amendment and the application to
the States of the First Amendment's restrictions.

What a State may not constitutionally bring about by means of a criminal
statute is likewise beyond the reach of its civil law of libel. The fear of damage
awards under a rule such as that invoked by the Alabama courts here may be
markedly more inhibiting than the fear of prosecution under a criminal statute.
...The judgment awarded in this case—without the need for any proof of
actual pecuniary loss—was one thousand times greater than the maximum fine
provided by the Alabama criminal statute, and one hundred times greater than

that provided by the Sedition Act. And since there is no double-jeopardy limitation applicable to civil lawsuits, this is not the only judgment that may be awarded against petitioners for the same publication. Whether or not a newspaper can survive a succession of such judgments, the pall of fear and timidity imposed upon those who would give voice to public criticism is an atmosphere in which the First Amendment freedoms cannot survive....

The constitutional guarantees require, we think, a federal rule that prohibits a public official from recovering damages for a defamatory falsehood relating to his official conduct unless he proves that the statement was made with "actual malice"—that is, with knowledge that it was false or with reckless disregard of whether it was false or not....

Such a privilege for criticism of official conduct is appropriately analogous to the protection accorded a public official when *he* is sued for libel by a private citizen. In *Barr v. Matteo*, this Court held the utterance of a federal official to be absolutely privileged if made "within the outer perimeter" of his duties. The States accord the same immunity to statements of their highest officers, although some differentiate their lesser officials and qualify the privilege they enjoy. But all hold that all officials are protected unless actual malice can be proved. The reason for the official privilege is said to be that the threat of damage suits would otherwise "inhibit the fearless, vigorous, and effective administration of policies of government" and "dampen the ardor of all but the most resolute, or the most irresponsible, in the unflinching discharge of their duties." Analogous considerations support the privilege for the citizen-critic of government. It is as much his duty to criticize as it is the official's duty to administer. As Madison said, "the censorial power is in the people over the Government, and not in the Government over the people." It would give public servants an unjustified preference over the public they serve, if critics of official conduct did not have a fair equivalent of the immunity granted to the officials themselves.

We conclude that such a privilege is required by the First and Fourteenth Amendments.

III.

We hold today that the Constitution delimits a State's power to award damages for libel in actions brought by public officials against critics of their official conduct. Since this is such an action, the rule requiring proof of actual malice is applicable....

Since respondent may seek a new trial, we deem that considerations of effective judicial administration require us to review the evidence in the present record to determine whether it could constitutionally support a judgment for respondent. This Court's duty is not limited to the elaboration of constitutional principles; we must also in proper cases review the evidence to make certain that those principles have been constitutionally applied....

Applying these standards, we consider that the proof presented to show actual malice lacks the convincing clarity which the constitutional standard demands, and hence that it would not constitutionally sustain the judgment for respondent under the proper rule of law....

We think the evidence against the Times supports at most a finding of negligence in failing to discover the misstatements, and is constitutionally insufficient to show the recklessness that is required for a finding of actual malice.

We also think the evidence was constitutionally defective in another respect: it was incapable of supporting the jury's finding that the allegedly libelous statements were made "of and concerning" respondent.... There was no reference to respondent in the advertisement, either by name or official position.... The statements upon which respondent principally relies as referring to him are the two allegations that did concern the police or police functions: that "truckloads of police...ringed the Alabama State College Campus" after the demonstration on the State Capitol steps, and that Dr. King had been "arrested...seven times." These statements were false only in that the police had been "deployed near" the campus but had not actually "ringed" it and had not gone there in connection with the State Capitol demonstration, and in that Dr. King had been arrested only four times.... Although the statements may be taken as referring to the police, they did not on their face make even an oblique reference to respondent as an individual.

...We hold that such a proposition may not constitutionally be utilized to establish that an otherwise impersonal attack on governmental operations was a libel of an official responsible for those operations. Since it was relied on exclusively here, and there was no other evidence to connect the statements with respondent, the evidence was constitutionally insufficient to support a finding that the statements referred to respondent.

The judgment of the Supreme Court of Alabama is reversed and the case is remanded to that court for further proceedings not inconsistent with this opinion.

Reversed and remanded.

Mr. Justice BLACK, with whom Mr. Justice DOUGLAS joins, concurring.

I base my vote to reverse on the belief that the First and Fourteenth Amendments not merely "delimit" a State's power to award damages to "public officials against critics of their official conduct" but completely prohibit a State from exercising such a power.... Unlike the Court, therefore, I vote to reverse exclusively on the ground that the *Times* and the individual defendants had an absolute, unconditional constitutional right to publish in the *Times* advertisement their criticisms of the Montgomery agencies and officials....

BROADCAST LICENSEES AND "FAIRNESS"

Red Lion Broadcasting Company v. FCC

The First Amendment clearly suggests that government cannot tell news-papers what they *must* print. But what about broadcast media? Unlike news-papers, radio and television frequencies are limited, and broadcasters must have a license to use airwaves that, in theory at least, belong to the public. Congress, by setting up a licensing system, decreed that license holders must at least in part serve "the public interest."

In 1934 Congress regulated broadcasting and created the Federal Com-munications Commission to implement its rules. Congress acted because the broadcast spectrum is a limited resource; it is impossible for two stations to broadcast on one frequency at the same time. To prevent interference on the receiving end, the FCC issues licenses for individual radio stations, to regu-late how close together geographically and in the spectrum two stations can be situated and how much power each station may use to broadcast its signal.

Along with the power to license, the FCC was instructed to ensure that the new communication medium functioned properly for listeners. To guar-antee that the listener's interest was protected, the FCC enforced the Fairness Doctrine, which required any radio (and later, television) station that endorsed a political candidate or attacked any person to provide equal time to the opposing point of view.

395 U.S. 367 (1969).

In *Red Lion Broadcasting Company v. FCC*, the Supreme Court held that the First Amendment did not bar the FCC from enforcing the Fairness Doctrine. Requiring a station owner to broadcast political opinions is a restriction of the owner's rights of free speech and press, but that right had to be balanced against those of listeners, considering that the broadcast spectrum was limited.

In 1987 the FCC repealed the Fairness Doctrine. Almost immediately afterward, right-wing talk radio became a major political force.

Mr. Justice WHITE delivered the opinion of the Court.

The Federal Communications Commission has for many years imposed on radio and television broadcasters the requirement that discussion of public issues be presented on broadcast stations, and that each side of those issues must be given fair coverage. This is known as the fairness doctrine.... Two aspects of the fairness doctrine, relating to personal attacks in the context of controversial public issues and to political editorializing, were codified more precisely in the form of FCC regulations in 1967. The two cases before us now, which were decided separately below, challenge the constitutional and statutory bases of the doctrine and component rules. *Red Lion* involves the application of the fairness doctrine to a particular broadcast, and [the companion case] arises as an action to review the FCC's 1967 promulgation of the personal attack and political editorializing regulations, which were laid down after the Red Lion litigation had begun.

I.

A.

The Red Lion Broadcasting Company is licensed to operate a Pennsylvania radio station, WGCB. On November 27, 1964, WGCB carried a 15-minute broadcast by the Reverend Billy James Hargis as part of a "Christian Crusade" series. A book by Fred J. Cook entitled *Goldwater—Extremist on the Right* was discussed by Hargis, who said that Cook had been fired by a newspaper for making false charges against city officials; that Cook had then worked for a Communist-affiliated publication; that he had defended Alger Hiss and attacked J. Edgar Hoover and the Central Intelligence Agency; and that he had now written a "book to smear and destroy Barry Goldwater." When Cook heard of the broadcast he concluded that he had been personally attacked and demanded free reply time, which the station refused. After an exchange of letters among Cook, Red Lion, and the FCC, the FCC declared that the Hargis broadcast constituted a personal attack on Cook; that Red Lion had failed to meet its obligation under the fairness doctrine ..., to send a tape, transcript, or summary of the broadcast to Cook and offer him reply time; and that the station must provide reply time whether or not Cook would pay for it....

Not long after the Red Lion litigation was begun, the FCC issued a Notice of Proposed Rule Making, with an eye to making the personal attack aspect of the fairness doctrine more precise and more readily enforceable, and to specifying its rules relating to political editorials. After considering written comments supporting and opposing the rules, the FCC adopted them substantially as proposed. Twice amended, the rules were held unconstitutional ... by the Court of Appeals for the Seventh Circuit, on review of the rule-making proceeding, as abridging the freedoms of speech and press.

As they now stand amended, the regulations [require that when an identifiable American person or group is attacked in a television or radio broadcast, the broadcaster must notify the person or group who was attacked and provide an opportunity for them to respond on the original broadcaster's station, within a week of the original broadcast. This rule applies except when the attacker and the victim are both candidates for political office, or when the attack is made in the context of an interview or while covering an event that is newsworthy in its own right. The regulations also require any broadcaster who endorses or opposes a candidate for elected office to notify that candidate's opponents, and to provide those opponents with an opportunity to respond, using the broadcaster's facilities and airtime, free of charge, and with enough advance notice that the opponent has a reasonable opportunity to respond before the election takes place.] ...

... We cannot say that the FCC's declaratory ruling in *Red Lion*, or the regulations ... are beyond the scope of the congressionally conferred power to assure that stations are operated by those whose possession of a license serves "the public interest."

III.

The broadcasters challenge the fairness doctrine and its specific manifestations in the personal attack and political editorial rules on conventional First

Amendment grounds, alleging that the rules abridge their freedom of speech and press. Their contention is that the First Amendment protects their desire to use their allotted frequencies continuously to broadcast whatever they choose, and to exclude whomever they choose from ever using that frequency. No man may be prevented from saying or publishing what he thinks, or from refusing in his speech or other utterances to give equal weight to the views of his opponents. This right, they say, applies equally to broadcasters.

A.

Although broadcasting is clearly a medium affected by a First Amendment interest, differences in the characteristics of new media justify differences in the First Amendment standards applied to them. For example, the ability of new technology to produce sounds more raucous than those of the human voice justifies restrictions on the sound level, and on the hours and places of use, of sound trucks so long as the restrictions are reasonable and applied without discrimination.

Just as the Government may limit the use of sound-amplifying equipment potentially so noisy that it drowns out civilized private speech, so may the Government limit the use of broadcast equipment. The right of free speech of a broadcaster, the user of a sound truck, or any other individual does not embrace a right to snuff out the free speech of others. *Associated Press v. United States.*

When two people converse face to face, both should not speak at once if either is to be clearly understood. But the range of the human voice is so limited that there could be meaningful communications if half the people in the United States were talking and the other half listening. Just as clearly, half the people might publish and the other half read. But the reach of radio signals is incomparably greater than the range of the human voice and the problem of interference is a massive reality. The lack of know-how and equipment may keep many from the air, but only a tiny fraction of those with resources and intelligence can hope to communicate by radio at the same time if intelligible communication is to be had, even if the entire radio spectrum is utilized in the present state of commercially acceptable technology.

It was this fact, and the chaos which ensued from permitting anyone to use any frequency at whatever power level he wished, which made necessary the enactment of the Radio Act of 1927 and the Communications Act of 1934, as the Court has noted at length before. It was this reality which at the very least necessitated first the division of the radio spectrum into portions reserved respectively for public broadcasting and for other important radio uses such as amateur operation, aircraft, police, defense, and navigation; and then the subdivision of each portion, and assignment of specific frequencies to individual users or groups of users. Beyond this, however, because the frequencies reserved for public broadcasting were limited in number, it was essential for the Government to tell some applicants that they could not broadcast at all because there was room for only a few.

Where there are substantially more individuals who want to broadcast than there are frequencies to allocate, it is idle to posit an unabridgeable First Amendment right to broadcast comparable to the right of every individual to speak, write, or publish. If one hundred persons want broadcast licenses but there are only ten frequencies to allocate, all of them may have the same "right" to a license; but if there is to be any effective communication by radio, only a few can be licensed and the rest must be barred from the airwaves. It would be strange if the First Amendment, aimed at protecting and furthering communications, prevented the Government from making radio communication possible by requiring licenses to broadcast and by limiting the number of licenses so as not to overcrowd the spectrum.

This has been the consistent view of the Court. Congress unquestionably has the power to grant and deny licenses and to eliminate existing stations. No one has a First Amendment right to a license or to monopolize a radio frequency; to deny a station license because "the public interest" requires it "is not a denial of free speech." *National Broadcasting Co. v. United States.*

By the same token, as far as the First Amendment is concerned those who are licensed stand no better than those to whom licenses are refused. A license permits broadcasting, but the licensee has no constitutional right to be the one who holds the license or to monopolize a radio frequency to the exclusion of his fellow citizens. There is nothing in the First Amendment which prevents the Government from requiring a licensee to share his frequency with others and to conduct himself as a proxy or fiduciary with obligations to present those views and voices which are representative of his community and which would otherwise, by necessity, be barred from the airwaves.

This is not to say that the First Amendment is irrelevant to public broadcasting. On the contrary, it has a major role to play as the Congress itself recognized in §326, which forbids FCC interference with "the right of free speech by means of radio communication." Because of the scarcity of radio frequencies, the Government is permitted to put restraints on licensees in favor of others whose views should be expressed on this unique medium. But the people as a whole retain their interest in free speech by radio and their collective right to have the medium function consistently with the ends and purposes of the First Amendment. It is the right of the viewers and listeners, not the right of the broadcasters, which is paramount. It is the purpose of the First Amendment to preserve an uninhibited marketplace of ideas in which truth will ultimately prevail, rather than to countenance monopolization of that market, whether it be by the Government itself or a private licensee.... It is the right of the public to receive suitable access to social, political, esthetic, moral, and other ideas and experiences which is crucial here. That right may not constitutionally be abridged either by Congress or by the FCC.

B.

Rather than confer frequency monopolies on a relatively small number of licensees, in a nation of 200,000,000, the Government could surely have decreed that each frequency should be shared among all or some of those who wish to use it, each being assigned a portion of the broadcast day or the broadcast week. The ruling and regulations at issue here do not go quite so far. They assert that under specified circumstances, a licensee must offer to make available a reasonable amount of broadcast time to those who have a view different from that which has already been expressed on his station. The expression of a political endorsement, or of a personal attack while dealing with a controversial public issue, simply triggers this time sharing. As we have said, the First Amendment confers no right on licensees to prevent others from broadcasting on "their" frequencies and no right to an unconditional monopoly of a scarce resource which the Government has denied others the right to use.

    In terms of constitutional principle, and as enforced sharing of a scarce resource, the personal attack and political editorial rules are indistinguishable from the equal-time provision of §315, a specific enactment of Congress requiring stations to set aside reply time under specified circumstances and to which the fairness doctrine and these constituent regulations are important complements. That provision, which has been part of the law since 1927, has been held valid by this Court as an obligation of the licensee relieving him of any power in any way to prevent or censor the broadcast, and thus insulating him from liability for defamation. The constitutionality of the statute under the First Amendment was unquestioned.

Nor can we say that it is inconsistent with the First Amendment goal of producing an informed public capable of conducting its own affairs to require a broadcaster to permit answers to personal attacks occurring in the course of discussing controversial issues, or to require that the political opponents of those endorsed by the station be given a chance to communicate with the public. Otherwise, station owners and a few networks would have unfettered power to make time available only to the highest bidders, to communicate only their own views on public issues, people and candidates, and to permit on the air only those with whom they agreed. There is no sanctuary in the First Amendment for unlimited private censorship operating in a medium not open to all. "Freedom of the press from governmental interference under the First Amendment does not sanction repression of that freedom by private interests." *Associated Press v. United States.*

C.

It is strenuously argued, however, that if political editorials or personal attacks will trigger an obligation in broadcasters to afford the opportunity for expression to speakers who need not pay for time and whose views are unpalatable to the licensees, then broadcasters will be irresistibly forced to self-censorship and their coverage of controversial public issues will be eliminated or at least rendered wholly ineffective. Such a result would indeed be a serious matter, for should licensees actually eliminate their coverage of controversial issues, the purposes of the doctrine would be stifled.

At this point, however, as the Federal Communications Commission has indicated, that possibility is at best speculative. The communications industry, and in particular the networks, have taken pains to present controversial issues in the past, and even now they do not assert that they intend to abandon their efforts in this regard. It would be better if the FCC's encouragement were never necessary to induce the broadcasters to meet their responsibility. And if experience with the administration of those doctrines indicates that they have the net effect of reducing rather than enhancing the volume and quality of coverage, there will be time enough to reconsider the constitutional implications. The fairness doctrine in the past has had no such overall effect.

...It does not violate the First Amendment to treat licensees given the privilege of using scarce radio frequencies as proxies for the entire community, obligated to give suitable time and attention to matters of great public concern. To condition the granting or renewal of licenses on a willingness to present representative community views on controversial issues is consistent with the ends and purposes of those constitutional provisions forbidding the abridgment of freedom of speech and freedom of the press. Congress need not stand idly by and permit those with licenses to ignore the problems which beset the people or to exclude from the airways anything but their own views of fundamental questions....

E.

It is argued that even if at one time the lack of available frequencies for all who wished to use them justified the Government's choice of those who would best serve the public interest by acting as proxy for those who would present differing views, or by giving the latter access directly to broadcast facilities, this condition no longer prevails so that continuing control is not justified. To this there are several answers.

Scarcity is not entirely a thing of the past....

The rapidity with which technological advances succeed one another to create more efficient use of spectrum space on the one hand, and to create new uses for that space by ever growing numbers of people on the other, makes it unwise to speculate on the future allocation of that space. It is enough to say that the resource is one of considerable and growing importance whose scarcity impelled its regulation by an agency authorized by Congress. Nothing in this record, or in our own researches, convinces us that the resource is no longer one for which there are more immediate and potential uses than can be accommodated, and for which wise planning is essential.

In view of the scarcity of broadcast frequencies, the Government's role in allocating those frequencies, and the legitimate claims of those unable without governmental assistance to gain access to those frequencies for expression of their views, we hold the regulations and ruling at issue here are both authorized by statute and constitutional....

CENSORSHIP AND "NATIONAL SECURITY"
New York Times v. United States

New York Times v. United States was, in its way, as dramatic as *Bush v. Gore* thirty years later. The Court reached its decision in only days, while the eyes of the world were fixed on Washington to discover whether the guarantee of free press even included the right to publish information in wartime that the government insisted was crucial to "national security." The Pentagon Papers were a secret study ordered by the Department of Defense of US involvement in Vietnam since the 1950s. When former National Security staffer Daniel Ellsberg gave the papers to several major newspapers, American troops were still fighting in Indochina. The papers revealed, among other things, illegal acts committed by the United States, such as bombing in Cambodia and Laos. They clearly showed that officials had repeatedly lied to Congress and to the public about the extent and nature of the war.

No statute forbade the newspapers from publishing summaries of the Pentagon Papers. Nonetheless, the government persuaded a district court in New York to issue an injunction against the *New York Times*, the first paper to reveal the contents of the papers. After that, Ellsberg gave a copy to the *Washington Post*, which began its own series of articles. The government then sought an injunction against the *Post*, but this time the district court refused. Only a few days later, the Supreme Court resolved the case.

---

403 U.S. 713 (1971).

The sharp divide in public opinion was reflected in the Court's decision, which struck down the injunction against publication as an unconstitutional prior restraint but then split into separate opinions by each of the nine justices. Justices Black and Douglas suggested that the executive branch might be acting in bad faith to prevent political embarrassment. Justice Marshall based his decision on separation of powers concerns. Chief Justice Burger protested the Court's haste. And Justice Blackmun laid the responsibility for future deaths of American soldiers in Vietnam at the feet of the *New York Times*.

The decision left open the question of whether Congress could pass a statute prohibiting the publication of classified information in wartime.

PER CURIAM

... The United States seeks to enjoin the *New York Times* and the *Washington Post* from publishing the contents of a classified study entitled "History of U.S. Decision-Making Process on Viet Nam Policy."

"Any system of prior restraints of expression comes to this Court bearing a heavy presumption against its constitutional validity." *Bantam Books, Inc. v. Sullivan*. The government "thus carries a heavy burden of showing justification for the imposition of such a restraint." *Organization for a Better Austin v. Keefe*. The District Court for the Southern District of New York in the *New York Times* case and the District Court for the District of Columbia and the Court of Appeals for the District of Columbia Circuit in the *Washington Post* case held that the government had not met that burden. We agree....

Mr. Justice BLACK, with whom Mr. Justice DOUGLAS joins, concurring.

I adhere to the view that the government's case against the *Washington Post* should have been dismissed and that the injunction against the *New York Times* should have been vacated without oral argument when the cases were first presented to this Court. I believe that every moment's continuance of the injunctions against these newspapers amounts to a flagrant, indefensible, and continuing violation of the First Amendment.... In my view it is unfortunate that some of my Brethren are apparently willing to hold that the publication of news may sometimes be enjoined. Such a holding would make a shambles of the First Amendment.

... Now, for the first time in the 182 years since the founding of the

Republic, the federal courts are asked to hold that the First Amendment does not mean what it says, but rather means that the government can halt the publication of current news of vital importance to the people of this country.

In seeking injunctions against these newspapers and in its presentation to the Court, the Executive Branch seems to have forgotten the essential purpose and history of the First Amendment.... In response to an overwhelming public clamor, James Madison...proposed what later became the First Amendment..., which proclaimed: "The people shall not be deprived or abridged of their right to speak, to write, or to publish their sentiments; and the freedom of the press, as one of the great bulwarks of liberty, shall be inviolable." The amendments were offered to curtail and restrict the general powers granted to the Executive, Legislative, and Judicial Branches two years before in the original Constitution. The Bill of Rights changed the original Constitution into a new charter under which no branch of government could abridge the people's freedoms of press, speech, religion, and assembly. Yet the Solicitor General argues and some members of the Court appear to agree that the general powers of the government adopted in the original Constitution should be interpreted to limit and restrict the specific and emphatic guarantees of the Bill of Rights adopted later. I can imagine no greater perversion of history. Madison and the other Framers of the First Amendment, able men that they were, wrote in language they earnestly believed could never be misunderstood: "Congress shall make no law...abridging the freedom...of the press...." Both the history and language of the First Amendment support the view that the press must be left free to publish news, whatever the source, without censorship, injunctions, or prior restraints.

In the First Amendment the Founding Fathers gave the free press the protection it must have to fulfill its essential role in our democracy. The press was to serve the governed, not the governors. The government's power to censor the press was abolished so that the press would remain forever free to censure the government. The press was protected so that it could bare the secrets of government and inform the people. Only a free and unrestrained press can effectively expose deception in government. And paramount among the responsibilities of a free press is the duty to prevent any part of the government from deceiving the people and sending them off to distant lands to die of foreign fevers and foreign shot and shell. In my view, far from deserving condemnation for their courageous reporting, the *New York Times*, the *Washington Post*, and other newspapers should be commended for serving the purpose that the Founding Fathers saw so clearly. In revealing the workings of government that led to the Vietnam War, the newspapers nobly did precisely that which the Founders hoped and trusted they would do.

... To find that the President has "inherent power" to halt the publication of news by resort to the courts would wipe out the First Amendment and destroy the fundamental liberty and security of the very people the government hopes to make "secure." No one can read the history of the adoption of the First Amendment without being convinced beyond any doubt that it was injunctions like those sought here that Madison and his collaborators intended to outlaw in this nation for all time.

The word "security" is a broad, vague generality whose contours should not be invoked to abrogate the fundamental law embodied in the First Amendment. The guarding of military and diplomatic secrets at the expense of informed representative government provides no real security for our republic. The Framers of the First Amendment, fully aware of both the need to defend a new nation and the abuses of the English and Colonial governments, sought to give this new society strength and security by providing that freedom of speech, press, religion, and assembly should not be abridged....

Mr. Justice DOUGLAS, with whom Mr. Justice BLACK joins, concurring.

... It should be noted at the outset that the First Amendment provides that "Congress shall make no law... abridging the freedom of speech, or of the press." That leaves, in my view, no room for governmental restraint on the press.

There is, moreover, no statute barring the publication by the press of the material which the *Times* and the *Post* seek to use....

Thus Congress has been faithful to the command of the First Amendment in this area.

... [A]ny power [to restrain publication] that the government possesses must come from its "inherent power."

The power to wage war is "the power to wage war successfully." But the war power stems from a declaration of war. The Constitution by Art. I, § 8, gives Congress, not the President, power "[to] declare war." Nowhere are presidential wars authorized. We need not decide therefore what leveling effect the war power of Congress might have.

These disclosures may have a serious impact. But that is no basis for sanctioning a previous restraint on the press....

The government says that it has inherent powers to go into court and obtain an injunction to protect the national interest, which in this case is alleged to be national security. *Near v. Minnesota* repudiated that expansive doctrine in no uncertain terms.

The dominant purpose of the First Amendment was to prohibit the widespread practice of governmental suppression of embarrassing information. It is common knowledge that the First Amendment was adopted against the widespread use of the common law of seditious libel to punish the dissemination of material that is embarrassing to the powers-that-be.... The present cases will, I think, go down in history as the most dramatic illustration of that principle. A debate of large proportions goes on in the Nation over our posture in Vietnam....

...On public questions there should be "uninhibited, robust, and wide-open" debate. *New York Times Co. v. Sullivan*....

Mr. Justice BRENNAN, concurring.

I

I write separately in these cases only to emphasize what should be apparent: that our judgments in the present cases may not be taken to indicate the propriety, in the future, of issuing temporary stays and restraining orders to block the publication of material sought to be suppressed by the government. So far as I can determine, never before has the United States sought to enjoin a newspaper from publishing information in its possession.... [T]he First Amendment stands as an absolute bar to the imposition of judicial restraints in circumstances of the kind presented by these cases.

II

... The entire thrust of the government's claim throughout these cases has been that publication of the material sought to be enjoined "could," or "might," or "may" prejudice the national interest in various ways. But the First Amendment tolerates absolutely no prior judicial restraints of the press predicated upon surmise or conjecture that untoward consequences may result. Our cases, it is true, have indicated that there is a single, extremely narrow class of cases in which the First Amendment's ban on prior judicial restraint may be overridden. Our cases have thus far indicated that such cases may arise only when the Nation "is at war," *Schenk v. United States*, during which times "[n]o one would question but that a government might prevent actual obstruction to its recruiting service or the publication of the sailing dates of transports or the number and location of troops." *Near v. Minnesota.* Even if the present world situation were assumed to be tantamount to a time of war, or if the power of presently available armaments would justify even in peacetime the suppression of information that would set in motion a nuclear holocaust, in neither of these actions has the government presented or even alleged that publication of items from or based upon the material at issue would cause the happening of an event of that nature. "[T]he chief purpose of [the First Amendment's] guaranty [is] to prevent previous restraints upon publication." *Near v. Minnesota ex rel Olson.* Thus, only governmental allegation and proof that publication must inevitably, directly, and immediately cause the occurrence of an event kindred to imperiling the safety of a transport already at sea can support even the issuance of an interim restraining order. In no event may mere conclusions be sufficient: for if the Executive Branch seeks judicial aid in preventing publication, it must inevitably submit the basis upon which that aid is sought to scrutiny by the judiciary....

Mr. Justice STEWART, with whom Mr. Justice WHITE joins, concurring.
... [W]ithout an informed and free press there cannot be an enlightened people.
Yet it is elementary that the successful conduct of international diplomacy and the maintenance of an effective national defense require both confidentiality and secrecy....
I think there can be but one answer to this dilemma, if dilemma it be. The responsibility must be where the power is. If the Constitution gives the Executive a large degree of unshared power in the conduct of foreign affairs and the maintenance of our national defense, then under the Constitution the Executive must have the largely unshared duty to determine and preserve the degree of internal security necessary to exercise that power successfully. It is an awesome responsibility, requiring judgment and wisdom of a high order. I should suppose that moral, political, and practical considerations would dictate that a very first principle of that wisdom would be an insistence upon avoiding secrecy for its own sake. For when everything is classified, then nothing is classified.... [I]t is clear to me that it is the constitutional duty of the Executive—as a matter of sovereign prerogative and not as a matter of law

as the courts know law—through the promulgation and enforcement of executive regulations, to protect the confidentiality necessary to carry out its responsibilities in the fields of international relations and national defense.

This is not to say that Congress and the courts have no role to play. Undoubtedly Congress has the power to enact specific and appropriate criminal laws to protect government property and preserve government secrets. Congress has passed such laws, and several of them are of very colorable relevance to the apparent circumstances of these cases. And if a criminal prosecution is instituted, it will be the responsibility of the courts to decide the applicability of the criminal law under which the charge is brought. Moreover, if Congress should pass a specific law authorizing civil proceedings in this field, the courts would likewise have the duty to decide the constitutionality of such a law as well as its applicability to the facts proved.

But in the cases before us we are asked neither to construe specific regulations nor to apply specific laws. We are asked, instead, to perform a function that the Constitution gave to the Executive, not the Judiciary. We are asked, quite simply, to prevent the publication by two newspapers of material that the Executive Branch insists should not, in the national interest, be published. I am convinced that the Executive is correct with respect to some of the documents involved. But I cannot say that disclosure of any of them will surely result in direct, immediate, and irreparable damage to our Nation or its people. That being so, there can under the First Amendment be but one judicial resolution of the issues before us. I join the judgments of the Court.

Mr. Justice WHITE, with whom Mr. Justice STEWART joins, concurring.

I concur in today's judgments, but only because of the concededly extraordinary protection against prior restraints enjoyed by the press under our constitutional system. I do not say that in no circumstances would the First Amendment permit an injunction against publishing information about government plans or operations. Nor, after examining the materials the government characterizes as the most sensitive and destructive, can I deny that revelation of these documents will do substantial damage to public interests. Indeed, I am confident that their disclosure will have that result. But I nevertheless agree that the United States has not satisfied the very heavy burden that it must meet to warrant an injunction against publication in these cases, at least in the absence of express and appropriately limited congressional authorization for prior restraints in circumstances such as these....

It is not easy to reject the proposition urged by the United States and to deny relief on its good-faith claims in these cases that publication will work serious damage to the country. But that discomfiture is considerably dispelled by the infrequency of prior-restraint cases. Normally, publication will occur and the damage be done before the government has either opportunity or grounds for suppression. So here, publication has already begun and a substantial part of the threatened damage has already occurred. The fact of a massive breakdown in security is known, access to the documents by many unauthorized people is undeniable, and the efficacy of equitable relief against these or other newspapers to avert anticipated damage is doubtful at best.

What is more, terminating the ban on publication of the relatively few sensitive documents the government now seeks to suppress does not mean that the law either requires or invites newspapers or others to publish them or that they will be immune from criminal action if they do. Prior restraints require an unusually heavy justification under the First Amendment; but failure by the government to justify prior restraints does not measure its constitutional entitlement to a conviction for criminal publication. That the government mistakenly chose to proceed by injunction does not mean that it could not successfully proceed in another way....

... I am not, of course, saying that either of these newspapers has yet committed a crime or that either would commit a crime if it published all the material now in its possession. That matter must await resolution in the context of a criminal proceeding if one is instituted by the United States....

Mr. Justice MARSHALL, concurring.

.... It would ... be utterly inconsistent with the concept of separation of powers for this Court to use its power of contempt to prevent behavior that Congress has specifically declined to prohibit....

Even if it is determined that the government could not in good faith bring criminal prosecutions against the *New York Times* and the *Washington Post*, it is clear that Congress has specifically rejected passing legislation that would have clearly given the President the power he seeks here and made the current activity of the newspapers unlawful. When Congress specifically declines to make conduct unlawful it is not for this Court to re-decide those issues to overrule Congress....

Mr. Chief Justice BURGER, dissenting.

...In these cases, the imperative of a free and unfettered press comes into collision with another imperative, the effective functioning of a complex modern government and specifically the effective exercise of certain constitutional powers of the Executive. Only those who view the First Amendment as an absolute in all circumstances—a view I respect, but reject—can find such cases as these to be simple or easy.

These cases are not simple for another and more immediate reason. We do not know the facts of the cases. No District Judge knew all the facts. No Court of Appeals Judge knew all the facts. No member of this Court knows all the facts....

...An issue of this importance should be tried and heard in a judicial atmosphere conducive to thoughtful, reflective deliberation, especially when haste, in terms of hours, is unwarranted in light of the long period the *Times*, by its own choice, deferred publication.

It is not disputed that the *Times* has had unauthorized possession of the documents for three to four months, during which it has had its expert analysts studying them, presumably digesting them and preparing the material for publication. During all of this time, the *Times*, presumably in its capacity as trustee of the public's "right to know," has held up publication for purposes it considered proper and thus public knowledge was delayed. No doubt this was for a good reason; the analysis of 7,000 pages of complex material drawn from a vastly greater volume of material would inevitably take time and the writing of good news stories takes time. But why should the United States government, from whom this information was illegally acquired by someone, along with all the counsel, trial judges, and appellate judges be placed under needless pressure? After these months of deferral, the alleged "right to know" has somehow and suddenly become a right that must be vindicated instantly.

Would it have been unreasonable, since the newspaper could anticipate the government's objections to release of secret material, to give the government an opportunity to review the entire collection and determine whether agreement could be reached on publication?...

Mr. Justice HARLAN, with whom THE CHIEF JUSTICE and Mr. Justice BLACKMUN join, dissenting....

With all respect, I consider that the Court has been almost irresponsibly feverish in dealing with these cases....

...Due regard for the extraordinarily important and difficult questions involved in these litigations should have led the Court to shun such a precipitate timetable. . . .

. . . I cannot believe that the doctrine prohibiting prior restraints reaches to the point of preventing courts from maintaining the status quo long enough to act responsibly in matters of such national importance as those involved here.

Mr. Justice BLACKMUN, dissenting. . . .

The First Amendment, after all, is only one part of an entire Constitution. Article II of the great document vests in the Executive Branch primary power over the conduct of foreign affairs and places in that branch the responsibility for the Nation's safety. Each provision of the Constitution is important, and I cannot subscribe to a doctrine of unlimited absolutism for the First Amendment at the cost of downgrading other provisions. First Amendment absolutism has never commanded a majority of this Court. What is needed here is a weighing, upon properly developed standards, of the broad right of the press to print and of the very narrow right of the government to prevent. Such standards are not yet developed. The parties here are in disagreement as to what those standards should be. But even the newspapers concede that there are situations where restraint is in order and is constitutional. . . .

I strongly urge, and sincerely hope, that these two newspapers will be fully aware of their ultimate responsibilities to the United States of America. . . . I hope that damage has not already been done. If, however, damage has been done, and if, with the Court's action today, these newspapers proceed to publish the critical documents and there results therefrom "the death of soldiers, the destruction of alliances, the greatly increased difficulty of negotiation with our enemies, the inability of our diplomats to negotiate," to which list I might add the factors of prolongation of the war and of further delay in the freeing of United States prisoners, then the Nation's people will know where the responsibility for these sad consequences rests.

IS THERE A "JOURNALIST'S PRIVILEGE"?

Branzburg v. Hayes

Investigative journalists rely heavily on sources who wish to remain anonymous. Often these sources describe acts of malfeasance or lawbreaking. A frequent condition of an interview is a promise that the journalist will protect the source's identity even from law enforcement officials and grand juries. From time to time, journalists are jailed for contempt when they assert this "journalist's privilege." Whether the First Amendment protects journalistic confidentiality was the issue in *Branzburg v. Hayes*.

The case arose in 1972, during a period of intense and often violent protest against an unpopular war in Asia and racism and police practices at home. The case consolidated appeals by reporters from three different news organizations. Each reporter had agreed to keep the identity of his sources confidential. One reporter had witnessed his sources making raw marijuana into hashish, and the other two had interviewed members of the Black Panther Party about their activities. Each was subpoenaed by a federal grand jury to testify about the possible crimes that they had witnessed, and each reporter asserted the First Amendment as a "shield."

In an opinion by Justice Byron White, the Court held that reporters had no more right than any other citizen to refuse to testify before a grand jury, and that

408 U.S. 665 (1972).

151

society's interest in upholding the rule of law outweighed any theoretical concerns about the ability of the press to gather news from confidential sources. Justice Powell's concurrence was less categorical in its rejection of reporter's privilege, and suggested that a case may yet arise where the interest in preserving confidentiality of a particular source would outweigh the grand jury's need for testimony. Powell's concurrence was noted in briefs filed by *New York Times* reporter Judy Miller, *Time* correspondent Matthew Cooper, and Tim Russert of NBC News, who were unsuccessfully opposing subpoenas from special prosecutor Patrick Fitzgerald requiring their testimony about confidential sources alleged to have leaked the identity of CIA case officer Valerie Plame Wilson.

Efforts to pass a federal shield law have been unsuccessful, but a majority of states have passed statutes protecting journalists against compelled testimony in most cases.

Opinion of the Court by MR. JUSTICE WHITE, announced by THE CHIEF JUSTICE.

The issue in these cases is whether requiring newsmen to appear and testify before state or federal grand juries abridges the freedom of speech and press guaranteed by the First Amendment. We hold that it does not....

I

... On November 15, 1969, the *Courier-Journal* [of Louisville, Kentucky] carried a story under petitioner's by-line describing in detail his observations of two young residents of Jefferson County synthesizing hashish from marihuana, an activity which, they asserted, earned them about $5,000 in three weeks. The article included a photograph of a pair of hands working above a laboratory table on which was a substance identified by the caption as hashish. The article stated that petitioner had promised not to reveal the identity of the two hashish makers. Petitioner was shortly subpoenaed by the Jefferson County grand jury; he appeared, but refused to identify the individuals he had seen possessing marihuana or the persons he had seen making hashish from marihuana. A state trial court judge ordered petitioner to answer these questions and rejected his contention that the Kentucky reporters' privilege statute, the First Amendment of the United States Constitution, or ss 1, 2 and 8 of the Kentucky Constitution authorized his refusal to answer....

The second case involving petitioner Branzburg arose out of his later story published on January 10, 1971, which described in detail the use of drugs in Frankfort, Kentucky. The article reported that in order to provide a comprehensive survey of the "drug scene" in Frankfort, petitioner had "spent two weeks interviewing several dozen drug users in the capital city" and had seen some of them smoking marihuana. A number of conversations with and observations of several unnamed drug users were recounted. Subpoenaed to appear before a Franklin County grand jury "to testify in the matter of violation of statutes concerning use and sale of drugs," petitioner Branzburg moved to quash the summons; the motion was denied, although an order was issued protecting Branzburg from revealing "confidential associations, sources or information" but requiring that he "answer any questions which concern or pertain to any criminal act, the commission of which was actually observed by [him]." ...

In re Pappas originated when petitioner Pappas, a television newsman-photographer ... was called to New Bedford on July 30, 1970, to report on civil disorders there.... He intended to cover a Black Panther news conference at that group's headquarters in a boarded-up store. Petitioner found the streets around the store barricaded, but he ultimately gained entrance to the area and recorded and photographed a prepared statement read by one of the Black Panther leaders at about 3 p.m. He then asked for and received permission to re-enter the area. Returning at about 9 o'clock, he was allowed to enter and remain inside Panther headquarters. As a condition of entry, Pappas agreed not to disclose anything he saw or heard inside the store except an anticipated police raid, which Pappas, "on his own," was free to photograph and report as he wished. Pappas stayed inside the headquarters for about three hours, but there was no police raid, and petitioner wrote no story and did not otherwise reveal what had occurred in the store while he was there. Two months later, petitioner was summoned before the Bristol County Grand Jury and appeared, answered questions as to his name, address, employment, and what he had seen and heard outside Panther headquarters, but refused to answer any questions about what had taken place inside headquarters while he was there, claiming that the First Amendment afforded him a privilege to protect confidential informants and their information.... His motion to quash on First Amendment and other grounds was denied by the trial judge who, noting the absence of a statutory newsman's privilege in Massachusetts, ruled that petitioner had no constitutional privilege to refuse to divulge to the grand jury what he had seen and heard, including the identity of persons he had observed....

United States v. Caldwell arose from subpoenas issued by a federal grand jury in the Northern District of California to respondent Earl Caldwell, a reporter for the *New York Times* assigned to cover the Black Panther Party and other black militant groups. A subpoena *duces tecum* was served on respondent on February 2, 1970, ordering him to appear before the grand jury to testify and to bring with him notes and tape recordings of interviews given him for publication by officers and spokesmen of the Black Panther Party concerning the aims, purposes, and activities of that organization. Respondent objected to the scope of this subpoena, and an agreement between his counsel and the Government attorneys resulted in a continuance. A second subpoena, served on March 16, omitted the documentary requirement and simply ordered Caldwell "to appear...to testify before the Grand Jury." Respondent and his employer, the *New York Times*, moved to quash on the ground that the unlimited breadth of the subpoenas and the fact that Caldwell would have to appear in secret before the grand jury would destroy his working relationship with the Black Panther Party and "suppress vital First Amendment freedoms...by driving a wedge of distrust and silence between the news media and the militants." Respondent argued that "so drastic an incursion upon First Amendment freedoms" should not be permitted "in the absence of a compelling governmental interest—not shown here—in requiring Mr. Caldwell's appearance before the grand jury."...

[T]he [District] court accepted respondent's First Amendment arguments to the extent of issuing a protective order providing that although respondent had to divulge whatever information had been given to him for publication, he "shall not be required to reveal confidential associations, sources or information received, developed or maintained by him as a professional journalist in the course of his efforts to gather news for dissemination to the public through the press or other news media." The court held that the First Amendment afforded respondent a privilege to refuse disclosure of such confidential information until there had been "a showing by the Government of a compelling and overriding national interest in requiring Mr. Caldwell's testimony which cannot be served by any alternative means."...

II

Petitioners Branzburg and Pappas and respondent Caldwell press First Amendment claims that may be simply put: that to gather news it is often necessary to agree either not to identify the source of information published or to publish only part of the facts revealed, or both; that if the reporter is nevertheless forced to reveal these confidences to a grand jury, the source so identified and other confidential sources of other reporters will be measurably deterred from furnishing publishable information, all to the detriment of the free flow of information protected by the First Amendment. Although the newsmen in these cases do not claim an absolute privilege against official interrogation in all circumstances, they assert that the reporter should not be forced either to appear or to testify before a grand jury or at trial until and unless sufficient grounds are shown for believing that the reporter possesses information relevant to a crime the grand jury is investigating, that the information the reporter has is unavailable from other sources, and that the need for the information is sufficiently compelling to override the claimed invasion of First Amendment interests occasioned by the disclosure.... The heart of the claim is that the burden on news gathering resulting from compelling reporters to disclose confidential information outweighs any public interest in obtaining the information....

The sole issue before us is the obligation of reporters to respond to grand jury subpoenas as other citizens do and to answer questions relevant to an investigation into the commission of crime. Citizens generally are not constitutionally immune from grand jury subpoenas; and neither the First Amendment nor any other constitutional provision protects the average citizen from disclosing to a grand jury information that he has received in confidence. The claim is, however, that reporters are exempt from these obligations because if forced to respond to subpoenas and identify their sources or disclose other confidences, their informants will refuse or be reluctant to furnish newsworthy information in the future. This asserted burden on news gathering is said to make compelled testimony from newsmen constitutionally suspect and to require a privileged position for them....

Despite the fact that news gathering may be hampered, the press is regularly excluded from grand jury proceedings, our own conferences, the meetings of other official bodies gathered in executive session, and the meetings of private organizations. Newsmen have no constitutional right of access to the scenes of crime or disaster when the general public is excluded, and they may be prohibited from attending or publishing information about trials if such restrictions are necessary to assure a defendant a fair trial before an impartial tribunal....

It is thus not surprising that the great weight of authority is that newsmen are not exempt from the normal duty of appearing before a grand jury and answering questions relevant to a criminal investigation. At common law, courts consistently refused to recognize the existence of any privilege authorizing a newsman to refuse to reveal confidential information to a grand jury. In 1958, a news gatherer asserted for the first time that the First Amendment exempted confidential information from public disclosure pursuant to a subpoena issued in a civil suit, but the claim was denied, and this argument has been almost uniformly rejected since then, although there are occasional dicta that, in circumstances not presented here, a newsman might be excused. These courts have applied the presumption against the existence of an asserted testimonial privilege, and have concluded that the First Amendment interest asserted by the newsman was outweighed by the general obligation of a citizen to appear before a grand jury or at trial, pursuant to a subpoena, and give what information he possesses....

The prevailing constitutional view of the newsman's privilege is very much rooted in the ancient role of the grand jury that has the dual function of determining if there is probable cause to believe that a crime has been committed and of protecting citizens against unfounded criminal prosecutions....

A number of States have provided newsmen a statutory privilege of varying breadth, but the majority have not done so, and none has been provided by federal statute. Until now the only testimonial privilege for unofficial witnesses that is rooted in the Federal Constitution is the Fifth Amendment privilege against compelled self-incrimination. We are asked to create another by interpreting the First Amendment to grant newsmen a testimonial privilege that other citizens do not enjoy. This we decline to do. Fair and effective law enforcement aimed at providing security for the person and property of the individual is a fundamental function of government, and the grand jury plays an important, constitutionally mandated role in this process. On the records now before us, we perceive no basis for holding that the public interest in law enforcement and in ensuring effective grand jury proceedings is insufficient to override the consequential, but uncertain, burden on news gathering that is said to result from insisting that reporters, like other citizens, respond to relevant questions put to them in the course of a valid grand jury investigation or criminal trial.

This conclusion itself involves no restraint on what newspapers may publish or on the type or quality of information reporters may seek to acquire, nor does it threaten the vast bulk of confidential relationships between reporters and their sources. . . . Only where news sources themselves are implicated in crime or possess information relevant to the grand jury's task need they or the reporter be concerned about grand jury subpoenas. . . .

The preference for anonymity of those confidential informants involved in actual criminal conduct is presumably a product of their desire to escape criminal prosecution, and this preference, while understandable, is hardly deserving of constitutional protection. It would be frivolous to assert—and no one does in these cases—that the First Amendment, in the interest of securing news or otherwise, confers a license on either the reporter or his news sources to violate valid criminal laws. Although stealing documents or private wiretapping could provide newsworthy information, neither reporter nor source is immune from conviction for such conduct, whatever the impact on the flow of news. . . .

Thus, we cannot seriously entertain the notion that the First Amendment protects a newsman's agreement to conceal the criminal conduct of his source, or evidence thereof, on the theory that it is better to write about crime than to do something about it. . . .

There remain those situations where a source is not engaged in criminal conduct but has information suggesting illegal conduct by others. Newsmen frequently receive information from such sources pursuant to a tacit or express agreement to withhold the source's name and suppress any information that the source wishes not published. Such informants presumably desire anonymity in order to avoid being entangled as a witness in a criminal trial or grand jury investigation. They may fear that disclosure will threaten their job security or personal safety or that it will simply result in dishonor or embarrassment.

The argument that the flow of news will be diminished by compelling reporters to aid the grand jury in a criminal investigation is not irrational, nor are the records before us silent on the matter. But we remain unclear how often and to what extent informers are actually deterred from furnishing information when newsmen are forced to testify before a grand jury.

. . . [W]e cannot accept the argument that the public interest in possible future news about crime from undisclosed, unverified sources must take precedence over the public interest in pursuing and prosecuting those crimes reported to the press by informants and in thus deterring the commission of such crimes in the future. . . .

... [C]oncealment of crime and agreements to do so are not looked upon with favor. Such conduct deserves no encomium, and we decline now to afford it First Amendment protection by denigrating the duty of a citizen, whether reporter or informer, to respond to grand jury subpoena and answer relevant questions put to him.

Of course, the press has the right to abide by its agreement not to publish all the information it has, but the right to withhold news is not equivalent to a First Amendment exemption from the ordinary duty of all other citizens to furnish relevant information to a grand jury performing an important public function....

Neither are we now convinced that a virtually impenetrable constitutional shield, beyond legislative or judicial control, should be forged to protect a private system of informers operated by the press to report on criminal conduct, a system that would be unaccountable to the public, would pose a threat to the citizen's justifiable expectations of privacy, and would equally protect well-intentioned informants and those who for pay or otherwise betray their trust to their employer or associates....

We are admonished that refusal to provide a First Amendment reporter's privilege will undermine the freedom of the press to collect and disseminate news. But this is not the lesson history teaches us. As noted previously, the common law recognized no such privilege, and the constitutional argument was not even asserted until 1958. From the beginning of our country the press has operated without constitutional protection for press informants, and the press has flourished. The existing constitutional rules have not been a serious obstacle to either the development or retention of confidential news sources by the press.

It is said that currently press subpoenas have multiplied, that mutual distrust and tension between press and officialdom have increased, that reporting styles have changed, and that there is now more need for confidential sources, particularly where the press seeks news about minority cultural and political groups or dissident organizations suspicious of the law and public officials. These developments, even if true, are treacherous grounds for a far-reaching interpretation of the First Amendment fastening a nationwide rule on courts, grand juries, and prosecuting officials everywhere. The obligation to testify in response to grand jury subpoenas will not threaten these sources not involved with criminal conduct and without information relevant to grand jury investigations, and we cannot hold that the Constitution places the sources in these two categories either above the law or beyond its reach....

The requirements of those cases which hold that a State's interest must be "compelling" or "paramount" to justify even an indirect burden on First Amendment rights, are also met here. As we have indicated, the investigation of crime by the grand jury implements a fundamental governmental role of securing the safety of the person and property of the citizen....

Similar considerations dispose of the reporters' claims that preliminary to requiring their grand jury appearance, the State must show that a crime has been committed and that they possess relevant information not available from other sources, for only the grand jury itself can make this determination. The role of the grand jury as an important instrument of effective law enforcement necessarily includes an investigatory function with respect to determining whether a crime has been committed and who committed it. To this end it must call witnesses, in the manner best suited to perform its task.... We see no reason to hold that these reporters, any more than other citizens, should be excused from furnishing information that may help the grand jury in arriving at its initial determinations.

The privilege claimed here is conditional, not absolute; given the suggested preliminary showings and compelling need, the reporter would be required to testify. Presumably, such a rule would reduce the instances in which reporters could be required to appear, but predicting in advance when and in what circumstances they could be compelled to do so would be difficult.... If newsmen's confidential sources are as sensitive as they are claimed to be, the prospect of being unmasked whenever a judge determines the situation justifies it is hardly a satisfactory solution to the problem....

We are unwilling to embark the judiciary on a long and difficult journey to such an uncertain destination. The administration of a constitutional newsman's privilege would present practical and conceptual difficulties of a high order. Sooner or later, it would be necessary to define those categories of newsmen who qualified for the privilege, a questionable procedure in light of the traditional doctrine that liberty of the press is the right of the lonely pamphleteer who uses carbon paper or a mimeograph just as much as of the large metropolitan publisher.... The informative function asserted by representatives of the organized press in the present cases is also performed by lecturers, political pollsters, novelists, academic researchers, and dramatists. Almost any author may quite accurately assert that he is contributing to the flow of information to the public, that he relies on confidential sources of information, and that these sources will be silenced if he is forced to make disclosures before a grand jury.

At the federal level, Congress has freedom to determine whether a statutory newsman's privilege is necessary and desirable and to fashion standards and rules as narrow or broad as deemed necessary to deal with the evil discerned and, equally important, to refashion those rules as experience from time to time may dictate. There is also merit in leaving state legislatures free, within First Amendment limits, to fashion their own standards in light of the conditions and problems with respect to the relations between law enforcement officials and press in their own areas. It goes without saying, of course, that we are powerless to bar state courts from responding in their own way and construing their own constitutions so as to recognize a newsman's privilege, either qualified or absolute.

Finally, as we have earlier indicated, news gathering is not without its First Amendment protections, and grand jury investigations if instituted or conducted other than in good faith, would pose wholly different issues for resolution under the First Amendment. Official harassment of the press undertaken not for purposes of law enforcement but to disrupt a reporter's relationship with his news sources would have no justification....

Mr. Justice POWELL, concurring.

I add this brief statement to emphasize what seems to me to be the limited nature of the Court's holding. The Court does not hold that newsmen, subpoenaed to testify before a grand jury, are without constitutional rights with respect to the gathering of news or in safeguarding their sources. Certainly, we do not hold, as suggested in Mr. Justice STEWART's dissenting opinion, that state and federal authorities are free to "annex" the news media as "an investigative arm of government." The solicitude repeatedly shown by this Court for First Amendment freedoms should be sufficient assurance against any such effort, even if one seriously believed that the media—properly free and untrammeled in the fullest sense of these terms—were not able to protect themselves.

As indicated in the concluding portion of the opinion, the Court states that no harassment of newsmen will be tolerated. If a newsman believes that the grand jury investigation is not being conducted in good faith he is not without remedy. Indeed, if the newsman is called upon to give information bearing only a remote and tenuous relationship to the subject of the investigation, or if he has some other reason to believe that his testimony implicates confidential source relationship without a legitimate need of law enforcement, he will have access to the court on a motion to quash and an appropriate protective order may be entered. The asserted claim to privilege should be judged on its facts by the striking of a proper balance between freedom of the press and the obligation of all citizens to give relevant testimony with respect to criminal conduct. The balance of these vital constitutional and societal interests on a case-by-case basis accords with the tried and traditional way of adjudicating such questions.

In short, the courts will be available to newsmen under circumstances where legitimate First Amendment interests require protection.

Mr. Justice STEWART, with whom Mr. Justice BRENNAN and Mr. Justice MARSHALL join, dissenting.

The Court's crabbed view of the First Amendment reflects a disturbing insensitivity to the critical role of an independent press in our society.... While Mr. Justice POWELL's enigmatic concurring opinion gives some hope of a more flexible view in the future, the Court in these cases holds that a newsman has no First Amendment right to protect his sources when called before a grand jury. The Court thus invites state and federal authorities to undermine the historic independence of the press by attempting to annex the journalistic profession as an investigative arm of government. Not only will this decision impair performance of the press' constitutionally protected functions, but it will, I am convinced, in the long run, harm rather than help the administration of justice.

I respectfully dissent.

I

The reporter's constitutional right to a confidential relationship with his source stems from the broad societal interest in a full and free flow of information to the public....

Enlightened choice by an informed citizenry is the basic ideal upon which an open society is premised, and a free press is thus indispensable to a free society. Not only does the press enhance personal self-fulfillment by providing the people with the widest possible range of fact and opinion, but it also is an incontestable precondition of self-government. The press "has been a mighty catalyst in awakening public interest in governmental affairs, exposing corruption among public officers and employees and generally informing the citizenry of public events and occurrences."...As private and public aggregations of power burgeon in size and the pressures for conformity necessarily mount, there is obviously a continuing need for an independent press to disseminate a robust variety of information and opinion through reportage, investigation, and criticism, if we are to preserve our constitutional tradition of maximizing freedom of choice by encouraging diversity of expression.

A

...A corollary of the right to publish must be the right to gather news. The full flow of information to the public protected by the free-press guarantee would be severely curtailed if no protection whatever were afforded to the process by which news is assembled and disseminated. We have, therefore, recognized that there is a right to publish without prior governmental approval, a right to distribute information, and a right to receive printed matter.

No less important to the news dissemination process is the gathering of information. News must not be unnecessarily cut off at its source, for without freedom to acquire information the right to publish would be impermissibly compromised. Accordingly, a right to gather news, of some dimensions, must exist....

B

The right to gather news implies, in turn, a right to a confidential relationship between a reporter and his source. This proposition follows as a matter of simple logic once three factual predicates are recognized: (1) newsmen require informants to gather news; (2) confidentiality—the promise or understanding that names or certain aspects of communications will be kept off the record—is essential to the creation and maintenance of a news-gathering relationship with informants; and (3) an unbridled subpoena power—the absence of a constitutional right protecting, in *any* way, a confidential relationship from compulsory process—will either deter sources from divulging information or deter reporters from gathering and publishing information.

It is equally obvious that the promise of confidentiality may be a necessary prerequisite to a productive relationship between a newsman and his informants. An officeholder may fear his superior; a member of the bureaucracy, his associates; a dissident, the scorn of majority opinion. All may have information valuable to the public discourse, yet each may be willing to relate that information only in confidence to a reporter whom he trusts, either because of excessive caution or because of a reasonable fear of reprisals or censure for unorthodox views. The First Amendment concern must not be with the motives of any particular news source, but rather with the conditions in which informants of all shades of the spectrum may make information available through the press to the public....

Finally, and most important, when governmental officials possess an unchecked power to compel newsmen to disclose information received in confidence, sources will clearly be deterred from giving information, and reporters will clearly be deterred from publishing it, because uncertainty about exercise of the power will lead to "self-censorship." *Smith v. California.*...

F

Thus, we cannot escape the conclusion that when neither the reporter nor his source can rely on the shield of confidentiality against unrestrained use of the grand jury's subpoena power, valuable information will not be published and the public dialogue will inevitably be impoverished.

II

Accordingly, when a reporter is asked to appear before a grand jury and reveal confidences, I would hold that the government must (1) show that there is probable cause to believe that the newsman has information that is clearly relevant to a specific probable violation of law; (2) demonstrate that the information sought cannot be obtained by alternative means less destructive of First Amendment rights; and (3) demonstrate a compelling and overriding interest in the information.

... The sad paradox of the Court's position is that when a grand jury may exercise an unbridled subpoena power, and sources involved in sensitive matters become fearful of disclosing information, the newsman will not only cease to be a useful grand jury witness; he will cease to investigate and publish information about issues of public import. I cannot subscribe to such an anomalous result, for, in my view, the interests protected by the First Amendment are not antagonistic to the administration of justice....

NARROWING OBSCENITY
Miller v. California

In 1957 the Supreme Court held that obscenity, material appealing to "prurient interest" in sex, was unprotected by the First Amendment (*Roth v. United States* [1957]). But after *Roth*, the Court splintered in an attempt to define exactly what obscenity is. The question was of grave importance in a nation undergoing a sexual revolution, and in which, not long before, as great a work as *Ulysses* by James Joyce had been banned for alleged obscenity. No clear majority emerged, and in 1964, Justice Stewart seemed to speak for many justices when he figuratively threw up his hands, writing that he could not define obscenity, "[b]ut I know it when I see it." (*Jacobellis v. Ohio* [1964]). *Miller v. California*, a 5-4 decision, finally set a majority test for obscenity, requiring that it be narrowly defined by statute and that valid statutes only cover the most hard-core material. In addition, the work, taken as a whole, must lack "serious literary, artistic, political, or scientific value." This represented a subtle shift, since works with *some* merit could be criminalized if that merit did not redeem the work "taken as a whole."

Since *Miller*, the test for obscenity has not changed, although the court has explained it in subsequent cases. In *Jenkins v. Georgia* (1974), the Court held that nudity alone is not enough to make something obscene. Sexually explicit

413 U.S. 15 (1973).

material, unless legally obscene, enjoys the protection of the First Amendment. In *Pope v. Illinois* (1987), the Court held that the artistic, literary, political, or scientific value of a work must be judged by a national, not a state or local, standard. The Court has further held that the mere possession of obscene material in a home cannot be made criminal (*Stanley v. Georgia* [1969]), but that states may enact laws designed to protect minors from exposure to sexually explicit nonobscene material, *Ginsberg v. New York* (1968). Finally, in *New York v. Ferber* (1982), the Court made clear that sexually explicit material containing photographs of minors could be banned regardless of lack of obscenity. The government may even ban private possession of such material (*Osborne v. Ohio* [1990]).

Mr. Chief Justice BURGER delivered the opinion of the Court....

Appellant conducted a mass mailing campaign to advertise the sale of illustrated books, euphemistically called "adult" material. After a jury trial, he was convicted of violating, a misdemeanor, by knowingly distributing obscene matter,... Appellant's conviction was specifically based on his conduct in causing five unsolicited advertising brochures to be sent through the mail in an envelope addressed to a restaurant in Newport Beach, California. The envelope was opened by the manager of the restaurant and his mother. They had not requested the brochures; they complained to the police.

The brochures advertise four books entitled "Intercourse," "Man-Woman," "Sex Orgies Illustrated," and "An Illustrated History of Pornography," and a film entitled "Marital Intercourse." While the brochures contain some descriptive printed material, primarily they consist of pictures and drawings very explicitly depicting men and women in groups of two or more engaging in a variety of sexual activities, with genitals often prominently displayed.

I

This case involves the application of a State's criminal obscenity statute to a situation in which sexually explicit materials have been thrust by aggressive sales action upon unwilling recipients who had in no way indicated any desire to receive such materials. This Court has recognized that the States have a legitimate interest in prohibiting dissemination or exhibition of obscene material when the mode of dissemination carries with it a significant danger of offending the sensibilities of unwilling recipients or of exposure to juveniles. It is in this context that we are called on to define the standards which must be used to identify obscene material that a State may regulate without infringing on the First Amendment as applicable to the States through the Fourteenth Amendment....

Apart from the initial formulation in the *Roth* case, no majority of the Court has at any given time been able to agree on a standard to determine what constitutes obscene, pornographic material subject to regulation under the States' police power.... This is not remarkable, for in the area of freedom of speech and press the courts must always remain sensitive to any infringement on genuinely serious literary, artistic, political, or scientific expression. This is an area in which there are few eternal verities....

II

This much has been categorically settled by the Court, that obscene material is unprotected by the First Amendment. We acknowledge, however, the inherent dangers of undertaking to regulate any form of expression. State statutes designed to regulate obscene materials must be carefully limited. As a result, we now confine the permissible scope of such regulation to works which depict or describe sexual conduct....

The basic guidelines for the trier of fact must be: (a) whether "the average person, applying contemporary community standards" would find that the work, taken as a whole, appeals to the prurient interest; (b) whether the work depicts or describes, in a patently offensive way, sexual conduct specifically defined by the applicable state law; and (c) whether the work, taken as a whole, lacks serious literary, artistic, political, or scientific value. We do not adopt as a constitutional standard the "*utterly* without redeeming social value" test of *Memoirs v. Massachusetts*; that concept has never commanded the adherence of more than three Justices at one time....

Under the holdings announced today, no one will be subject to prosecution for the sale or exposure of obscene materials unless these materials depict or describe patently offensive "hard core" sexual conduct specifically defined by the regulating state law, as written or construed. We are satisfied that these specific prerequisites will provide fair notice to a dealer in such materials that his public and commercial activities may bring prosecution. If the inability to define regulated materials with ultimate, god-like precision altogether removes the power of the States or the Congress to regulate, then "hard core" pornography may be exposed without limit to the juvenile, the passerby, and the consenting adult alike....

III

Under a National Constitution, fundamental First Amendment limitations on the powers of the States do not vary from community to community, but this does not mean that there are, or should or can be, fixed, uniform national standards of precisely what appeals to the "prurient interest" or is "patently offensive."...

...It is neither realistic nor constitutionally sound to read the First Amendment as requiring that the people of Maine or Mississippi accept public depiction of conduct found tolerable in Las Vegas, or New York City. People in different States vary in their tastes and attitudes, and this diversity is not to be strangled by the absolutism of imposed uniformity....

IV

The dissenting Justices sound the alarm of repression. But, in our view, to equate the free and robust exchange of ideas and political debate with commercial exploitation of obscene material demeans the grand conception of the First Amendment and its high purposes in the historic struggle for freedom.... The First Amendment protects works which, taken as a whole, have serious literary, artistic, political, or scientific value, regardless of whether the government or a majority of the people approve of the ideas these works represent.... But the public portrayal of hard-core sexual conduct for its own sake, and for the ensuing commercial gain, is a different matter.

There is no evidence, empirical or historical, that the stern 19th century American censorship of public distribution and display of material relating to sex, in any way limited or affected expression of serious literary, artistic, political, or scientific ideas. On the contrary, it is beyond any question that the era following Thomas Jefferson to Theodore Roosevelt was an "extraordinarily vigorous period," not just in economics and politics, but in belles lettres and in "the outlying fields of social and political philosophies." We do not see the harsh hand of censorship of ideas—good or bad, sound or unsound—and "repression" of political liberty lurking in every state regulation of commercial exploitation of human interest in sex....

In sum, we (a) reaffirm the *Roth* holding that obscene material is not protected by the First Amendment; (b) hold that such material can be regulated by the States, subject to the specific safeguards enunciated above, without a showing that the material is "*utterly* without redeeming social value"; and (c) hold that obscenity is to be determined by applying "contemporary community standards." *Roth v. United States....*

Vacated and remanded.

Mr. Justice DOUGLAS, dissenting.

I

... Today the Court retreats from the earlier formulations of the constitutional test and undertakes to make new definitions. This effort, like the earlier ones, is earnest and well intentioned. The difficulty is that we do not deal with constitutional terms, since "obscenity" is not mentioned in the Constitution or Bill of Rights. And the First Amendment makes no such exception from "the press" which it undertakes to protect nor, as I have said on other occasions, is an exception necessarily implied, for there was no recognized exception to the free press at the time the Bill of Rights was adopted which treated "obscene" publications differently from other types of papers, magazines, and books. So there are no constitutional guidelines for deciding what is and what is not "obscene." The Court is at large because we deal with tastes and standards of literature. What shocks me may be sustenance for my neighbor. What causes one person to boil up in rage over one pamphlet or movie may reflect only his neurosis, not shared by others. We deal here with a regime of censorship which, if adopted, should be done by constitutional amendment after full debate by the people....

III

... The idea that the First Amendment permits punishment for ideas that are "offensive" to the particular judge or jury sitting in judgment is astounding. No greater leveler of speech or literature has ever been designed. To give the power to the censor, as we do today, is to make a sharp and radical break with the traditions of a free society. The First Amendment was not fashioned as a vehicle for dispensing tranquilizers to the people. Its prime function was to keep debate open to "offensive" as well as to "staid" people. The tendency throughout history has been to subdue the individual and to exalt the power of government. The use of the standard "offensive" gives authority to government that cuts the very vitals out of the First Amendment. As is intimated by the Court's opinion, the materials before us may be garbage. But so is much of what is said in political campaigns, in the daily press, on TV, or over the radio. By reason of the First Amendment—and solely because of it—speakers and publishers have not been threatened or subdued because their thoughts and ideas may be "offensive" to some....

We deal with highly emotional, not rational, questions. To many the Song of Solomon is obscene. I do not think we, the judges, were ever given the constitutional power to make definitions of obscenity. If it is to be defined, let the people debate and decide by a constitutional amendment what they want to ban as obscene and what standards they want the legislatures and the courts to apply....

NEWSPAPERS AND "THE RIGHT OF REPLY"

Miami Herald v. Tornillo

News media do more than report. Very often they express their owners' opinions, in sweeping and sometimes unfair terms. When should an individual have a "right of reply" against criticism from a newspaper? And can a government, consistent with the First Amendment, require a newspaper to observe what it considers the rules of fairness? *Miami Herald v. Tornillo* states in no uncertain terms that governments may not impose any general obligations on newspapers to publish information they do not choose to.

In 1972 Pat Tornillo was running for a seat in the Florida state legislature. The *Miami Herald* ran two editorials attacking him for his involvement with the local teachers' union. Tornillo sued the newspaper under a Florida state law that was intended to force newspapers to print opposing points of view. The Florida Supreme Court upheld his claim.

However, in 1974 the US Supreme Court held that forcing a newspaper to print material was as great an intrusion upon editorial freedom as was outright censorship, and, therefore, the Florida law could not stand. The principle of editorial freedom for print media in *Miami Herald v. Tornillo* largely survives to this day. Broadcast media, because they are licensed to use public airwaves, may, however, be required to follow more restrictive rules.

418 U.S. 241 (1974).

Mr. Chief Justice BURGER delivered the opinion of the Court.

The issue in this case is whether a state statute granting a political candidate a right to equal space to reply to criticism and attacks on his record by a newspaper violates the guarantees of a free press.

I

In the fall of 1972, appellee... was a candidate for the Florida House of Representatives. On September 20, 1972, and again on September 29, 1972, appellant printed editorials critical of appellee's candidacy. In response to these editorials appellee demanded that appellant print verbatim his replies.... Appellant declined to print the appellee's replies and appellee brought suit in Circuit Court, Dade County, seeking declaratory and injunctive relief and actual and punitive damages in excess of $5,000. The action was premised on Florida Statute §104.38 (1973), F.S.A., a "right of reply" statute which provides that if a candidate for nomination or election is assailed regarding his personal character or official record by any newspaper, the candidate has the right to demand that the newspaper print, free of cost to the candidate, any reply the candidate may make to the newspaper's charges. The reply must appear in as conspicuous a place and in the same kind of type as the charges which prompted the reply, provided it does not take up more space than the charges. Failure to comply with the statute constitutes a first-degree misdemeanor....

The challenged statute creates a right to reply to press criticism of a candidate for nomination or election. The statute was enacted in 1913, and this is only the second recorded case decided under its provisions.

Appellant contends the statute is void on its face because it purports to regulate the content of a newspaper in violation of the First Amendment.... It is also contended that the statute fails to distinguish between critical comment which is and which is not defamatory.

B

The appellee and supporting advocates of an enforceable right of access to the press vigorously argue that government has an obligation to ensure that a wide variety of views reach the public. The contentions of access proponents will be set out in some detail. It is urged that at the time the First Amendment to the Constitution was ratified in 1791 as part of our Bill of Rights the press was broadly representative of the people it was serving. While many of the newspapers were intensely partisan and narrow in their views, the press collectively presented a broad range of opinions to readers. Entry into publishing was inexpensive; pamphlets and books provided meaningful alternatives to the organized press for the expression of unpopular ideas and often treated events and expressed views not covered by conventional newspapers. A true marketplace of ideas existed in which there was relatively easy access to the channels of communication.

Access advocates submit that although newspapers of the present are superficially similar to those of 1791 the press of today is in reality very different from that known in the early years of our national existence. In the past half century a communications revolution has seen the introduction of radio and television into our lives, the promise of a global community through the use of communications satellites, and the spectre of a "wired" nation by means of an expanding cable television network with two-way capabilities. The printed press, it is said, has not escaped the effects of this revolution. Newspapers have become big business and there are far fewer of them to serve a larger literate population. Chains of newspapers, national newspapers, national wire and news services, and one-newspaper towns, are the dominant features of a press that has become noncompetitive and enormously powerful and influential in its capacity to manipulate popular opinion and change the course of events. Major metropolitan newspapers have collaborated to establish news services national in scope. Such national news organizations provide syndicated "interpretive reporting" as well as syndicated features and commentary, all of which can serve as part of the new school of "advocacy journalism."

The elimination of competing newspapers in most of our large cities, and the concentration of control of media that results from the only newspaper's being owned by the same interests which own a television station and a radio station, are important components of this trend toward concentration of control of outlets to inform the public.

The result of these vast changes has been to place in a few hands the power to inform the American people and shape public opinion. Much of the editorial opinion and commentary that is printed is that of syndicated columnists distributed nationwide and, as a result, we are told, on national and world issues there tends to be a homogeneity of editorial opinion, commentary, and interpretive analysis. The abuses of bias and manipulative reportage are, likewise, said to be the result of the vast accumulations of unreviewable power in the modern media empires. In effect, it is claimed, the public has lost any ability to respond or to contribute in a meaningful way to the debate on issues. The monopoly of the means of communication allows for little or no critical analysis of the media except in professional journals of very limited readership....

The obvious solution, which was available to dissidents at an earlier time when entry into publishing was relatively inexpensive, today would be to have additional newspapers. But the same economic factors which have caused the disappearance of vast numbers of metropolitan newspapers have made entry into the marketplace of ideas served by the print media almost impossible. It is urged that the claim of newspapers to be "surrogates for the public" carries with it a concomitant fiduciary obligation to account for that stewardship. From this premise it is reasoned that the only effective way to insure fairness and accuracy and to provide for some accountability is for government to take affirmative action. The First Amendment interest of the public in being informed is said to be in peril because the "marketplace of ideas" is today a monopoly controlled by the owners of the market.

Proponents of enforced access to the press take comfort from language in several of this Court's decisions which suggests that the First Amendment acts as a sword as well as a shield, that it imposes obligations on the owners of the press in addition to protecting the press from government regulation. In *Associated Press v. United States*, the Court, in rejecting the argument that the press is immune from the antitrust laws by virtue of the First Amendment, stated:

> The First Amendment, far from providing an argument against application of the Sherman Act, here provides powerful reasons to the contrary. That Amendment rests on the assumption that the widest possible dissemination of information from diverse and antagonistic sources is essential to the welfare of the public, that a free press is a condition of a free society. Surely a command that the government itself shall not impede the free flow of ideas does not afford non-governmental combinations a refuge if they impose restraints upon that constitutionally guaranteed freedom. Freedom to publish means freedom for all and not for some. Freedom to publish is guaranteed by the Constitution, but freedom to combine to keep others from publishing is not. Freedom of the press from governmental interference under the First Amendment does not sanction repression of that freedom by private interests.

In *New York Times Co. v. Sullivan*, the Court spoke of "a profound national commitment to the principle that debate on public issues should be uninhibited, robust, and wide-open." It is argued that the "uninhibited, robust" debate is not "wide-open" but open only to a monopoly in control of the press....

IV

However much validity may be found in these arguments, at each point the implementation of a remedy such as an enforceable right of access necessarily calls for some mechanism, either governmental or consensual. If it is governmental coercion, this at once brings about a confrontation with the express provisions of the First Amendment and the judicial gloss on that Amendment developed over the years....

Appellee's argument that the Florida statute does not amount to a restriction of appellant's right to speak because "the statute in question here has not prevented the *Miami Herald* from saying anything it wished" begs the core question. Compelling editors or publishers to publish that which "reason tells them should not be published" is what is at issue in this case. The Florida statute operates as a command in the same sense as a statue or regulation forbidding appellant to publish specified matter. Governmental restraint on publishing need not fall into familiar or traditional patterns to be subject to constitutional limitations on governmental powers. The Florida statute exacts a penalty on the basis of the content of a newspaper. The first phase of the penalty resulting from the compelled printing of a reply is exacted in terms of the cost in printing and composing time and materials and in taking up space that could be devoted to other material the newspaper may have preferred to print....

Faced with the penalties that would accrue to any newspaper that published news or commentary arguably within the reach of the right-of-access statute, editors might well conclude that the safe course is to avoid controversy. Therefore, under the operation of the Florida statute, political and electoral coverage would be blunted or reduced. Government-enforced right of access inescapably "dampens the vigor and limits the variety of public debate," *New York Times Co. v. Sullivan*....

Even if a newspaper would face no additional costs to comply with a compulsory access law and would not be forced to forgo publication of news or opinion by the inclusion of a reply, the Florida statute fails to clear the barriers of the First Amendment because of its intrusion into the function of editors. A newspaper is more than a passive receptacle or conduit for news, comment, and advertising. The choice of material to go into a newspaper, and the decisions made as to limitations on the size and content of the paper, and treatment of public issues and public officials—whether fair or unfair—constitute the exercise of editorial control and judgment. It has yet to be demonstrated how governmental regulation of this crucial process can be exercised consistent with First Amendment guarantees of a free press as they have evolved to this time. Accordingly, the judgment of the Supreme Court of Florida is reversed.

Mr. Justice BRENNAN, with whom Mr. Justice REHNQUIST joins, concurring.

I join the Court's opinion which, as I understand it, addresses only "right of reply" statutes and implies no view upon the constitutionality of "retraction" statutes affording plaintiffs able to prove defamatory falsehoods a statutory action to require publication of a retraction.

Mr. Justice WHITE, concurring.

The Court today holds that the First Amendment bars a State from requiring a newspaper to print the reply of a candidate for public office whose personal character has been criticized by that newspaper's editorials. According to our accepted jurisprudence, the First Amendment erects a virtually insurmountable barrier between government and the print media so far as government tampering, in advance of publication, with news and editorial content is concerned. A newspaper or magazine is not a public utility subject to "reasonable" governmental regulation in matters affecting the exercise of journalistic judgment as to what shall be printed....

To justify this statute, Florida advances a concededly important interest of ensuring free and fair elections by means of an electorate informed about the issues. But prior compulsion by government in matters going to the very nerve center of a newspaper—the decision as to what copy will or will not be included in any given edition—collides with the First Amendment.

...Quite the contrary, this law runs afoul of the elementary First Amendment proposition that government may not force a newspaper to print copy which, in its journalistic discretion, it chooses to leave on the newsroom floor....

FREE PRESS AND FAIR TRIAL

Nebraska Press Association v. Stuart

In sensational criminal cases, the First Amendment freedom of the press can conflict with the Sixth Amendment guarantee of a fair trial in front of an impartial jury. Jurors who have been exposed to the kind of publicity that attends cases like the trials of O. J. Simpson or Kobe Bryant may understandably have a difficult time reaching a verdict based only on the evidence presented in the courtroom.

Judges have several tools at their disposal to ensure a fair trial. The trial judge in *Nebraska Press Association v. Stuart* chose to use a tool that the Supreme Court has never recognized as valid: a prior restraint on publication. The case involved a multiple murder in a town of only eight hundred and fifty people; the crime itself received a great deal of local publicity not just in the newspaper but on radio and television as well. When a suspect apparently confessed to the crimes, the confession and the identity of the accused murderer received a great deal of exposure. Concerned that the suspect would not be able to receive a fair trial, the judge ordered a halt to the publication of any material discussing the case.

The Supreme Court concluded that such a classic prior restraint on publication amounts to censorship. Judges may order changes of venue (the place of trial), or venire (the community from which the jury pool is drawn); they may order law enforcement and parties to the case not to discuss some or all

427 U.S. 539 (1976).

176

of the facts; but they cannot assume jurisdiction over media and tell them not to print truthful accounts of what is happening in the criminal courts.

Mr. Chief Justice BURGER delivered the opinion of the Court.

I

On the evening of October 18, 1975, local police found the six members of the Henry Kellie family murdered in their home in Sutherland, Neb., a town of about 850 people. Police released the description of a suspect, Erwin Charles Simants, to the reporters who had hastened to the scene of the crime. Simants was arrested and arraigned in Lincoln County Court the following morning, ending a tense night for this small rural community.

The crime immediately attracted widespread news coverage, by local, regional, and national newspapers, radio and television stations. Three days after the crime, the County Attorney and Simants' attorney joined in asking the County Court to enter a restrictive order relating to "matters that may or may not be publicly reported or disclosed to the public," because of the "mass coverage by news media" and the "reasonable likelihood of prejudicial news which would make difficult, if not impossible, the impaneling of an impartial jury and tend to prevent a fair trial." The County Court heard oral argument but took no evidence; no attorney for members of the press appeared at this stage. The County Court granted the prosecutor's motion for a restrictive order and entered it the next day, October 22. The order prohibited everyone in attendance from "releas[ing] or authoriz[ing] the release for public dissemination in any form or manner whatsoever any testimony given or evidence adduced"; the order also required members of the press to observe the Nebraska Bar-Press Guidelines.

Simants' preliminary hearing was held the same day, open to the public but subject to the order.... The charges, as amended to reflect the autopsy findings, were that Simants had committed the murders in the course of a sexual assault.

Petitioners, several press and broadcast associations, publishers, and individual reporters moved on October 23 for leave to intervene in the District Court, asking that the restrictive order imposed by the County Court be vacated.... The District Judge granted petitioners' motion to intervene and, on October 27, entered his own restrictive order. The judge found "because of the nature of the crimes charged in the complaint that there is a clear and present danger that pre-trial publicity could impinge upon the defendant's right to a fair trial." The order applied only until the jury was impaneled, and specifically prohibited petitioners from reporting five subjects: (1) the existence or contents of a confession Simants had made to law enforcement officers, which had been introduced in open court at arraignment; (2) the fact or nature of statements Simants had made to other persons; (3) the contents of a note he had written the night of the crime; (4) certain aspects of the medical testimony at the preliminary hearing; and (5) the identity of the victims of the alleged sexual assault and the nature of the assault. It also prohibited reporting the exact nature of the restrictive order itself. Like the County Court's order, this order incorporated the Nebraska Bar-Press Guidelines.

...We are informed by the parties that since we granted certiorari, Simants has been convicted of murder and sentenced to death. His appeal is pending in the Nebraska Supreme Court.

III

...Neither in the Constitution nor in contemporaneous writings do we find that the conflict between these two important rights was anticipated, yet it is inconceivable that the authors of the Constitution were unaware of the potential conflicts between the right to an unbiased jury and the guarantee of freedom of the press....

The trial of Aaron Burr in 1807 presented Mr. Chief Justice Marshall, presiding as a trial judge, with acute problems in selecting an unbiased jury. Few people in the area of Virginia from which jurors were drawn had not formed some opinions concerning Mr. Burr or the case, from newspaper accounts and heightened discussion both private and public. The Chief Justice conducted a searching voir dire of the two panels eventually called.... Burr was acquitted, so there was no occasion for appellate review to examine the problem of prejudicial pretrial publicity. Mr. Chief Justice Marshall's careful voir dire inquiry into the matter of possible bias makes clear that the problem is not a new one.

The speed of communication and the pervasiveness of the modern news media have exacerbated these problems, however, as numerous appeals demonstrate. The trial of Bruno Hauptmann in a small New Jersey community for the abduction and murder of the Charles Lindberghs' infant child probably was the most widely covered trial up to that time, and the nature of the coverage produced widespread public reaction. Criticism was directed at the "carnival" atmosphere that pervaded the community and the courtroom itself. Responsible leaders of press and the legal profession including other judges pointed out that much of this sorry performance could have been controlled by a vigilant trial judge and by other public officers subject to the control of the court.

The excesses of press and radio and lack of responsibility of those in authority in the *Hauptmann* case and others of that era led to efforts to develop voluntary guidelines for courts, lawyers, press, and broadcasters. The effort was renewed in 1965 when the American Bar Association embarked on a project to develop standards for all aspects of criminal justice, including guidelines to accommodate the right to a fair trial and the rights of a free press.... In the wake of these efforts, the cooperation between bar associations and members of the press led to the adoption of voluntary guidelines like Nebraska's.

In practice, of course, even the most ideal guidelines are subjected to powerful strains when a case such as Simants' arises, with reporters from many parts of the country on the scene. Reporters from distant places are unlikely to consider themselves bound by local standards. They report to editors outside the area covered by the guidelines, and their editors are likely to be guided only by their own standards. To contemplate how a state court can control acts of a newspaper or broadcaster outside its jurisdiction, even though the newspapers and broadcasts reach the very community from which jurors are to be selected, suggests something of the practical difficulties of managing such guidelines....

IV

The Sixth Amendment in terms guarantees "trial, by an impartial jury..." in federal criminal prosecutions. Because "trial by jury in criminal cases is fundamental to the American scheme of justice," the Due Process Clause of the Fourteenth Amendment guarantees the same right in state criminal prosecutions....

In the overwhelming majority of criminal trials, pretrial publicity presents few unmanageable threats to this important right. But when the case is a "sensational" one tensions develop between the right of the accused to trial by an impartial jury and the rights guaranteed others by the First Amendment.

... The trial judge has a major responsibility. What the judge says about a case, in or out of the courtroom, is likely to appear in newspapers and broadcasts. More important, the measures a judge takes or fails to take to mitigate the effects of pretrial publicity ... may well determine whether the defendant receives a trial consistent with the requirements of due process....

The state trial judge in the case before us acted responsibly, out of a legitimate concern, in an effort to protect the defendant's right to a fair trial. What we must decide is not simply whether the Nebraska courts erred in seeing the possibility of real danger to the defendant's rights, but whether in the circumstances of this case the means employed were foreclosed by another provision of the Constitution.

V

The First Amendment provides that "Congress shall make no law ... abridging the freedom ... of the press...." The Court has interpreted these guarantees to afford special protection against orders that prohibit the publication or broadcast of particular information or commentary orders that impose a "previous" or "prior" restraint on speech. None of our decided cases on prior restraint involved restrictive orders entered to protect a defendant's right to a fair and impartial jury, but the opinions on prior restraint have a common thread relevant to this case.

In *Near v. Minnesota*, the Court held invalid a Minnesota statute providing for the abatement as a public nuisance of any "malicious, scandalous and defamatory newspaper, magazine or other periodical."...

The principles enunciated in *Near* were so universally accepted that the precise issue did not come before us again until *Organization for a Better Austin v. Keefe*. There the state courts had enjoined the petitioners from picketing or passing out literature of any kind in a specified area. Noting the similarity to *Near v. Minnesota*, a unanimous Court held:

> Here, as in that case, the injunction operates, not to redress alleged private wrongs, but to suppress, on the basis of previous publications, distribution of literature 'of any kind' in a city of 18,000.
>
> Any prior restraint on expression comes to this Court with a 'heavy pre-

sumption' against its constitutional validity. Respondent thus carries a heavy burden of showing justification for the imposition of such a restraint. He has not met that burden....

More recently in *New York Times Co. v. United States*, the Government sought to enjoin the publication of excerpts from a massive, classified study of this nation's involvement in the Vietnam conflict, going back to the end of the Second World War. The dispositive opinion of the Court simply concluded that the Government had not met its heavy burden of showing justification for the prior restraint.... "[E]very member of the Court, tacitly or explicitly, accepted the *Near* and *Keefe* condemnation of prior restraint as presumptively unconstitutional." *Pittsburgh Press Co. v. Human Rel. Commission* (Burger, C. J., dissenting). The Court's conclusion in *New York Times* suggests that the burden on the Government is not reduced by the temporary nature of a restraint....

The thread running through all these cases is that prior restraints on speech and publication are the most serious and the least tolerable infringement on First Amendment rights. A criminal penalty or a judgment in a defamation case is subject to the whole panoply of protections afforded by deferring the impact of the judgment until all avenues of appellate review have been exhausted. Only after judgment has become final, correct or otherwise, does the law's sanction become fully operative.

A prior restraint, by contrast and by definition, has an immediate and irreversible sanction. If it can be said that a threat of criminal or civil sanctions after publication "chills" speech, prior restraint "freezes" it at least for the time.

The damage can be particularly great when the prior restraint falls upon the communication of news and commentary on current events. Truthful reports of public judicial proceedings have been afforded special protection against subsequent punishment. For the same reasons the protection against prior restraint should have particular force as applied to reporting of criminal proceedings, whether the crime in question is a single isolated act or a pattern of criminal conduct.

... The extraordinary protections afforded by the First Amendment carry with them something in the nature of a fiduciary duty to exercise the protected rights responsibly—a duty widely acknowledged but not always observed by editors and publishers. It is not asking too much to suggest that those who exercise First Amendment rights in newspapers or broadcasting enterprises direct some effort to protect the rights of an accused to a fair trial by unbiased jurors.

Of course, the order at issue like the order requested in *New York Times* does not prohibit but only postpones publication. Some news can be delayed and most commentary can even more readily be delayed without serious injury, and there often is a self-imposed delay when responsible editors call for verification of information. But such delays are normally slight and they are self-imposed. Delays imposed by governmental authority are a different matter....

The authors of the Bill of Rights did not undertake to assign priorities as between First Amendment and Sixth Amendment rights, ranking one as superior to the other. In this case, the petitioners would have us declare the right of an accused subordinate to their right to publish in all circumstances. But if the authors of these guarantees, fully aware of the potential conflicts between them, were unwilling or unable to resolve the issue by assigning to one priority over the other, it is not for us to rewrite the Constitution by undertaking what they declined to do. It is unnecessary, after nearly two centuries, to establish a priority applicable in all circumstances. Yet it is nonetheless clear that the barriers to prior restraint remain high unless we are to abandon what the Court has said for nearly a quarter of our national existence and implied throughout all of it....

VI

We turn now to the record in this case.... [W]e must examine the evidence before the trial judge when the order was entered to determine (a) the nature and extent of pretrial news coverage; (b) whether other measures would be likely to mitigate the effects of unrestrained pretrial publicity; and (c) how effectively a restraining order would operate to prevent the threatened danger. The precise terms of the restraining order are also important. We must then consider whether the record supports the entry of a prior restraint on publication, one of the most extraordinary remedies known to our jurisprudence.

A

... Our review of the pretrial record persuades us that the trial judge was justified in concluding that there would be intense and pervasive pretrial publicity concerning this case. He could also reasonably conclude, based on common man experience, that publicity might impair the defendant's right to a fair trial. He did not purport to say more, for he found only "a clear and present danger that pre-trial publicity could impinge upon the defendant's right to a fair trial." His conclusion as to the impact of such publicity on prospective jurors was of necessity speculative, dealing as he was with factors unknown and unknowable.

B

We find little in the record that goes to another aspect of our task, determining whether measures short of an order restraining all publication would have insured the defendant a fair trial. Although the entry of the order might be read as a judicial determination that other measures would not suffice, the trial court made no express findings to that effect; the Nebraska Supreme Court referred to the issue only by implication....

Most of the alternatives to prior restraint of publication in these circumstances were discussed with obvious approval in *Sheppard v. Maxwell*: (a) change of trial venue to a place less exposed to the intense publicity that seemed imminent in Lincoln County; (b) postponement of the trial to allow public attention to subside; (c) searching questioning of prospective jurors, as Mr. Chief Justice Marshall used in the *Burr* case, to screen out those with fixed opinions as to guilt or innocence, (d) the use of emphatic and clear instructions on the sworn duty of each juror to decide the issues only on evidence presented in open court. Sequestration of jurors is, of course, always available. Although that measure insulates jurors only after they are sworn, it also enhances the likelihood of dissipating the impact of pretrial publicity and emphasizes the elements of the jurors' oaths.

This Court has outlined other measures short of prior restraints on publication tending to blunt the impact of pretrial publicity. See *Sheppard v. Maxwell*. Professional studies have filled out these suggestions, recommending that trial courts in appropriate cases limit what the contending lawyers, the police, and witnesses may say to anyone.

We have noted earlier that pretrial publicity, even if pervasive and concentrated, cannot be regarded as leading automatically and in every kind of criminal case to an unfair trial....

We have therefore examined this record to determine the probable efficacy of the measures short of prior restraint on the press and speech. There is no finding that alternative measures would not have protected Simants' rights, and the Nebraska Supreme Court did no more than imply that such measures might not be adequate. Moreover, the record is lacking in evidence to support such a finding.

C

We must also assess the probable efficacy of prior restraint on publication as a workable method of protecting Simants' right to a fair trial, and we cannot ignore the reality of the problems of managing and enforcing pretrial restraining orders. The territorial jurisdiction of the issuing court is limited by concepts of sovereignty....

Finally, we note that the events disclosed by the record took place in a community of 850 people. It is reasonable to assume that, without any news accounts being printed or broadcast, rumors would travel swiftly by word of mouth. One can only speculate on the accuracy of such reports, given the generative propensities of rumors; they could well be more damaging than reasonably accurate news accounts. But plainly a whole community cannot be restrained from discussing a subject intimately affecting life within it.

Given these practical problems, it is far from clear that prior restraint on publication would have protected Simants' rights.

D

Finally, another feature of this case leads us to conclude that the restrictive order entered here is not supportable. At the outset the County Court entered a very broad restrictive order, the terms of which are not before us; it then held a preliminary hearing open to the public and the press. There was testimony concerning at least two incriminating statements made by Simants to private persons; the statement—evidently a confession—that he gave to law enforcement officials was also introduced. The State District Court's later order was entered after this public hearing and, as modified by the Nebraska

Supreme Court, enjoined reporting of (1) "[c]onfessions or admissions against interests made by the accused to law enforcement officials"; (2) "[c]onfessions or admissions against interest, oral or written, if any, made by the accused to third parties, excepting any statements, if any, made by the accused to representatives of the news media"; and (3) all "[o]ther information strongly implicative of the accused as the perpetrator of the slayings." To the extent that this order prohibited the reporting of evidence adduced at the open preliminary hearing, it plainly violated settled principles.... [O]nce a public hearing had been held, what transpired there could not be subject to prior restraint.

The third prohibition of the order was defective in another respect as well. As part of a final order, entered after plenary review, this prohibition regarding "implicative" information is too vague and too broad to survive the scrutiny we have given to restraints on First Amendment rights....

E

The record demonstrates, as the Nebraska courts held, that there was indeed a risk that pretrial news accounts, true or false, would have some adverse impact on the attitudes of those who might be called as jurors. But on the record now before us it is not clear that further publicity, unchecked, would so distort the views of potential jurors that twelve could not be found who would, under proper instructions, fulfill their sworn duty to render a just verdict exclusively on the evidence presented in open court. We cannot say on this record that alternatives to a prior restraint on petitioners would not have sufficiently mitigated the adverse effects of pretrial publicity so as to make prior restraint unnecessary. Nor can we conclude that the restraining order actually entered would serve its intended purpose. Reasonable minds can have few doubts about the gravity of the evil pretrial publicity can work, but the probability that it would do so here was not demonstrated with the degree of certainty our cases on prior restraint require.

Of necessity our holding is confined to the record before us. But our conclusion is not simply a result of assessing the adequacy of the showing made in this case; it results in part from the problems inherent in meeting the heavy burden of demonstrating, in advance of trial, that without prior restraint a fair trial will be denied. The practical problems of managing and enforcing restrictive orders will always be present. In this sense, the record now before us is illustrative rather than exceptional. It is significant that when this Court has reversed a state conviction, because of prejudicial publicity, it has carefully noted that some course of action short of prior restraint would have made a critical difference. However difficult it may be, we need not rule out the possibility of showing the kind of threat to fair trial rights that would possess the requisite degree of certainty to justify restraint. This Court has frequently denied that First Amendment rights are absolute and has consistently rejected the proposition that a prior restraint can never be employed.

Our analysis ends as it began, with a confrontation between prior restraint imposed to protect one vital constitutional guarantee and the explicit command of another that the freedom to speak and publish shall not be abridged. We reaffirm that the guarantees of freedom of expression are not an absolute prohibition under all circumstances, but the barriers to prior restraint remain high and the presumption against its use continues intact. We hold that, with respect to the order entered in this case prohibiting reporting or commentary on judicial proceedings held in public, the barriers have not been overcome; to the extent that this order restrained publication of such material, it is clearly invalid. To the extent that it prohibited publication based on information gained from other sources, we conclude that the heavy burden imposed as a condition to securing a prior restraint was not met and the judgment of the Nebraska Supreme Court is therefore *Reversed.*

Mr. Justice WHITE, concurring.

Technically there is no need to go farther than the Court does to dispose of this case, and I join the Court's opinion. I should add, however, that for the reasons which the Court itself canvasses there is grave doubt in my mind whether orders with respect to the press such as were entered in this case would ever be justifiable. It may be the better part of discretion, however, not to announce such a rule in the first case in which the issue has been squarely presented here....

Mr. Justice POWELL, concurring.

Although I join the opinion of the Court, in view of the importance of the case I write to emphasize the unique burden that rests upon the party, whether it be the State or a defendant, who undertakes to show the necessity for prior restraint on pretrial publicity.

In my judgment a prior restraint properly may issue only when it is shown to be necessary to prevent the dissemination of prejudicial publicity that otherwise poses a high likelihood of preventing, directly and irreparably, the impaneling of a jury meeting the Sixth Amendment requirement of impartiality. This requires a showing that (i) there is a clear threat to the fairness of trial, (ii) such a threat is posed by the actual publicity to be restrained, and (iii) no less restrictive alternatives are available. Notwithstanding such a showing, a restraint may not issue unless it also is shown that previous publicity or publicity from unrestrained sources will not render the restraint inefficacious....

Mr. Justice BRENNAN, with whom Mr. Justice STEWART and Mr. Justice MARSHALL join, concurring in the judgment.

... The right to a fair trial by a jury of one's peers is unquestionably one of the most precious and sacred safeguards enshrined in the Bill of Rights. I would hold, however, that resort to prior restraints on the freedom of the press is a constitutionally impermissible method for enforcing that right; judges have at their disposal a broad spectrum of devices for ensuring that fundamental fairness is accorded the accused without necessitating so drastic an incursion on the equally fundamental and salutary constitutional mandate that discussion of public affairs in a free society cannot depend on the preliminary grace of judicial censors....

REPORTING ON
JUDICIAL DISCIPLINE
Landmark Communications, Inc. v. Virginia

States, just like the federal government, often seek to keep information private. When can the media be punished for accurately reporting information contained in government files marked "confidential"? In *Cox Broadcasting Corp. v. Cohn* (1975), the Court held that states may not impose liability on the press for truthful publication of information released to the public in official court records. What about information *about* courts and judges, information that the state wants to keep to itself?

Landmark Communications, Inc. v. Virginia arose after a newspaper was indicted for publishing accurate information about a disciplinary proceeding before a state judicial-ethics commission against a named state judge. A state statute made disclosing this information a criminal offense. The US Supreme Court held that a state may not maintain confidentiality of information through the criminal prosecution of third-party nonparticipants. The Court emphasized that free discussion of governmental affairs is the First Amendment's major purpose.

Later, in *Florida Star v. B.J.F.* (1989), the Court held that there could not be liability for invasion of privacy when there is truthful reporting of information, lawfully obtained from public records, unless there is a state interest of the highest order justifying liability.

435 U.S. 829 (1978).

Mr. Chief Justice BURGER delivered the opinion of the Court.

The question presented on this appeal is whether the Commonwealth of Virginia may subject persons, including newspapers, to criminal sanctions for divulging information regarding proceedings before a state judicial review commission which is authorized to hear complaints as to judges' disability or misconduct, when such proceedings are declared confidential by the State Constitution and statutes.

I

On October 4, 1975, the *Virginian Pilot*, a Landmark newspaper, published an article which accurately reported on a pending inquiry by the Virginia Judicial Inquiry and Review Commission and identified the state judge whose conduct was being investigated. The article reported that "[n]o formal complaint has been filed by the commission against [the judge], indicating either that the five-man panel found insufficient cause for action or that the case is still under review." A month later, on November 5, a grand jury indicted Landmark for violating Va. Code § 2.1-37.13 (1973) by "unlawfully divulg[ing] the identification of a Judge of a Court not of record, which said Judge was the subject of an investigation and hearing" by the Commission....

The case was tried without a jury, and Landmark was found guilty and fined $500 plus the costs of prosecution. The Supreme Court of Virginia affirmed the conviction, with one dissent....

... We noted probable jurisdiction, and we now reverse.

II

At the present time it appears that 47 States, the District of Columbia, and Puerto Rico, have established by constitution, statute, or court rule, some type of judicial inquiry and disciplinary procedures. All of these jurisdictions, with the apparent exception of Puerto Rico, provide for the confidentiality of judicial disciplinary proceedings, although in most the guarantee of confidentiality extends only to the point when a formal complaint is filed with the State Supreme Court or equivalent body.

The substantial uniformity of the existing state plans suggests that confidentiality is perceived as tending to insure the ultimate effectiveness of the judicial review commissions. First, confidentiality is thought to encourage the filing of complaints and the willing participation of relevant witnesses by providing protection against possible retaliation or recrimination. Second, at least until the time when the meritorious can be separated from the frivolous complaints, the confidentiality of the proceedings protects judges from the injury which might result from publication of unexamined and unwarranted complaints. And finally, it is argued, confidence in the judiciary as an institution is maintained by avoiding premature announcement of groundless claims of judicial misconduct or disability since it can be assumed that some frivolous complaints will be made against judicial officers who rarely can satisfy all contending litigants.

In addition to advancing these general interests, the confidentiality requirement can be said to facilitate the work of the commissions in several practical respects. When removal or retirement is justified by the charges, judges are more likely to resign voluntarily or retire without the necessity of a formal proceeding if the publicity that would accompany such a proceeding can thereby be avoided. Of course, if the charges become public at an early stage of the investigation, little would be lost—at least from the judge's perspective—by the commencement of formal proceedings. In the more common situation, where the alleged misconduct is not of the magnitude to warrant removal or even censure, the confidentiality of the proceedings allows the judge to be made aware of minor complaints which may appropriately be called to his attention without public notice.

Acceptance of the collective judgment that confidentiality promotes the effectiveness of this mode of scrutinizing judicial conduct and integrity, however, marks only the beginning of the inquiry. Indeed, Landmark does not challenge the requirement of confidentiality, but instead focuses its attack on the determination of the Virginia Legislature, as construed by the Supreme Court, that the "divulging" or "publishing" of information concerning the work of the Commission by third parties, not themselves involved in the proceedings, should be criminally punishable. Unlike the generalized mandate of confidentiality, the imposition of criminal sanctions for its breach is not a common characteristic of the state plans; indeed only Virginia and Hawaii appear to provide criminal sanctions for disclosure.

III

The narrow and limited question presented, then, is whether the First Amendment permits the criminal punishment of third persons who are strangers to the inquiry, including the news media, for divulging or publishing truthful information regarding confidential proceedings of the Judicial Inquiry and Review Commission. We are not here concerned with the possible applicability of the statute to one who secures the information by illegal means and thereafter divulges it. We do not have before us any constitutional challenge to a State's power to keep the Commission's proceedings confidential or to punish participants for breach of this mandate. Nor does Landmark argue for any constitutionally compelled right of access for the press to those proceedings. Finally, as the Supreme Court of Virginia held, and appellant does not dispute, the challenged statute does not constitute a prior restraint or attempt by the State to censor the news media....

A

In *Mills v. Alabama*, this Court observed: "Whatever differences may exist about interpretations of the First Amendment, there is practically universal agreement that a major purpose of that Amendment was to protect the free discussion of governmental affairs." Although it is assumed that judges will ignore the public clamor or media reports and editorials in reaching their decisions and by tradition will not respond to public commentary, the law gives "[j]udges as persons, or courts as institutions...no greater immunity from criticism than other persons or institutions." *Bridges v. California*. The operations of the courts and the judicial conduct of judges are matters of utmost public concern....

The operation of the Virginia Commission, no less than the operation of the judicial system itself, is a matter of public interest, necessarily engaging the attention of the news media. The article published by Landmark provided accurate factual information about a legislatively authorized inquiry pending before the Judicial Inquiry and Review Commission, and in so doing clearly served those interests in public scrutiny and discussion of governmental affairs which the First Amendment was adopted to protect....

B

... The Commonwealth...focuses on what it perceives to be the pernicious effects of public discussion of Commission proceedings to support its argument. It contends that the public interest is not served by discussion of unfounded allegations of misconduct which defames honest judges and serves only to demean the administration of justice. The functioning of the Commission itself is also claimed to be impeded by premature disclosure of the complainant, witnesses, and the judge under investigation. Criminal sanctions minimize these harmful consequences, according to the Commonwealth, by ensuring that the guarantee of confidentiality is more than an empty promise.

It can be assumed for purposes of decision that confidentiality of Commission proceedings serves legitimate state interests. The question, however, is whether these interests are sufficient to justify the encroachment on First Amendment guarantees which the imposition of criminal sanctions entails with respect to nonparticipants such as Landmark. The Commonwealth has offered little more than assertion and conjecture to support its claim that without criminal sanctions the objectives of the statutory scheme would be seriously undermined. While not dispositive, we note that more than 40 States having similar commissions have not found it necessary to enforce confidentiality by use of criminal sanctions against nonparticipants.

Moreover, neither the Commonwealth's interest in protecting the reputation of its judges, nor its interest in maintaining the institutional integrity of its courts is sufficient to justify the subsequent punishment of speech at issue here, even on the assumption that criminal sanctions do in fact enhance the guarantee of confidentiality. Admittedly, the Commonwealth has an interest in protecting the good repute of its judges, like that of all other public officials. Our prior cases have firmly established, however, that injury to official reputation is an insufficient reason "for repressing speech that would otherwise be free." The remaining interest sought to be protected, the institutional reputation of the courts, is entitled to no greater weight in the constitutional scales. As Mr. Justice Black observed in *Bridges v. California*:

> The assumption that respect for the judiciary can be won by shielding judges from published criticism wrongly appraises the character of American public opinion.... [A]n enforced silence, however limited, solely in the name of preserving the dignity of the bench, would probably engender resentment, suspicion, and contempt much more than it would enhance respect.

Mr. Justice Frankfurter, in his dissent in *Bridges*, agreed that speech cannot be punished when the purpose is simply "to protect the court as a mystical entity or the judges as individuals or as annointed priests set apart from the community and spared the criticism to which in a democracy other public servants are exposed."

The Commonwealth has provided no sufficient reason for disregarding these well-established principles. We find them controlling and, on this record, dispositive.

IV

The Supreme Court of Virginia relied on the clear-and-present-danger test in rejecting Landmark's claim. We question the relevance of that standard here; moreover we cannot accept the mechanical application of the test which led that court to its conclusion. Mr. Justice Holmes' test was never intended "to express a technical legal doctrine or to convey a formula for adjudicating cases." *Pennekamp v. Florida.* Properly applied, the test requires a court to make its own inquiry into the imminence and magnitude of the danger said to flow from the particular utterance and then to balance the character of the evil, as well as its likelihood, against the need for free and unfettered expression. The possibility that other measures will serve the State's interests should also be weighed.

Landmark argued in the Supreme Court of Virginia that "before a state may punish expression, it must prove by 'actual facts' the existence of a clear and present danger to the orderly administration of justice." The court acknowledged that the record before it was devoid of such "actual facts," but went on to hold that such proof was not required when the legislature itself had made the requisite finding "that a clear and present danger to the orderly administration of justice would be created by divulgence of the confidential proceedings of the Commission." This legislative declaration coupled with the stipulated fact that Landmark published the disputed article was regarded by the court as sufficient to justify imposition of criminal sanctions.

Deference to a legislative finding cannot limit judicial inquiry when First Amendment rights are at stake....

A legislature appropriately inquires into and may declare the reasons impelling legislative action but the judicial function commands analysis of whether the specific conduct charged falls within the reach of the statute and if so whether the legislation is consonant with the Constitution. Were it otherwise, the scope of freedom of speech and of the press would be subject to legislative definition and the function of the First Amendment as a check on legislative power would be nullified.

It was thus incumbent upon the Supreme Court of Virginia to go behind the legislative determination and examine for itself "the particular utteranc[e] here in question and the circumstances of [its] publication to determine to what extent the substantive evil of unfair administration of justice was a likely consequence, and whether the degree of likelihood was sufficient to justify [subsequent] punishment." *Bridges v. California.* Our precedents leave little doubt as to the proper outcome of such an inquiry.

In a series of cases raising the question of whether the contempt power could be used to punish out-of-court comments concerning pending cases or grand jury investigations, this Court has consistently rejected the argument that such commentary constituted a clear and present danger to the administration of justice. What emerges from these cases is the "working principle that the substantive evil must be extremely serious and the degree of imminence extremely high before utterances can be punished," *Bridges v. California*, and that a "solidity of evidence," *Pennekamp v. Florida*, is necessary to make the requisite showing of imminence. "The danger must not be remote or even probable; it must immediately imperil." *Craig v. Harney.*

… The threat to the administration of justice posed by the speech and publications in *Bridges, Pennekamp, Craig,* and *Wood* was, if anything, more direct and substantial than the threat posed by Landmark's article. If the clear-and-present-danger test could not be satisfied in the more extreme circumstances of those cases, it would seem to follow that the test cannot be met here. It is true that some risk of injury to the judge under inquiry, to the system of justice, or to the operation of the Judicial Inquiry and Review Commission may be posed by premature disclosure, but the test requires that the danger be "clear and present" and in our view the risk here falls far short of that requirement. Moreover, much of the risk can be eliminated through careful internal procedures to protect the confidentiality of Commission proceedings. In any event, we must conclude as we did in *Wood v. Georgia*, that "[t]he type of 'danger' evidenced by the record is precisely one of the types of activity envisioned by the Founders in presenting the First Amendment for ratification."

Accordingly, the judgment of the Supreme Court of Virginia is reversed, and the case remanded for further proceedings not inconsistent with this opinion.

Reversed and remanded.

PRIOR RESTRAINT AND THE END OF THE WORLD

United States v. Progressive, Inc.

New York Times v. United States established that "national security" would not ordinarily be a basis of injunctions against news media. But the Court did not rule out such restraints for information whose publication would cause direct, catastrophic harm to the nation. The only such injunction so far granted was imposed on a small liberal magazine in Wisconsin that sought to publish directions on how to build a hydrogen bomb. Antinuclear activist Howard Moreland did not make use of secret information; his article, titled "The H-Bomb Secret: How We Got It, Why We're Telling It," made use of public sources, drawing them together into instructions. The magazine stated that its aim was to demonstrate to the American people that this vital information had not been safeguarded and that the danger of nuclear proliferation was greater than the government would admit.

The 1954 Atomic Energy Act included provisions that automatically made all information regarding nuclear weapons a government secret, no matter how it was acquired or created. Accordingly, the government obtained a preliminary injunction from a Federal District Court. The Supreme Court never ruled on the case. When another activist published a letter containing the supposedly secret information, the government dropped the charges as moot.

---

467 F. Supp. 990 (1979).

United States v. Progressive is the only case since *New York Times v. United States* in which a federal court has enjoined a news medium from publishing. Its status as law is debatable, but it serves as the basis for countless "what-if" discussions of the rights and responsibilities of news organizations.

WARREN, J.
MEMORANDUM AND ORDER

On March 9, 1979, this Court, at the request of the government, but after hearing from both parties, issued a temporary restraining order enjoining defendants, their employees, and agents from publishing or otherwise communicating or disclosing in any manner any restricted data contained in the article: "The H-Bomb Secret: How We Got It, Why We're Telling It."...

[A] preliminary injunction hearing was scheduled for one week later, on March 16, 1979....

Under the facts here alleged, the question before this Court involves a clash between allegedly vital security interests of the United States and the competing constitutional doctrine against prior restraint in publication.

In its argument and briefs, plaintiff relies on national security, as enunciated by Congress in The Atomic Energy Act of 1954, as the basis for classification of certain documents. Plaintiff contends that, in certain areas, national preservation and self-interest permit the retention and classification of government secrets. The government argues that its national security interest also permits it to impress classification and censorship upon information originating in the public domain, if when drawn together, synthesized and collated, such information acquires the character of presenting immediate, direct and irreparable harm to the interests of the United States.

Defendants argue that freedom of expression as embodied in the First Amendment is so central to the heart of liberty that prior restraint in any form becomes anathema. They contend that this is particularly true when a nation is not at war and where the prior restraint is based on surmise or conjecture. While acknowledging that freedom of the press is not absolute, they maintain that the publication of the projected article does not rise to the level of immediate, direct and irreparable harm which could justify incursion into First Amendment freedoms....

From the founding days of this nation, the rights to freedom of speech and of the press have held an honored place in our constitutional scheme. The establishment and nurturing of these rights is one of the true achievements of our form of government.

Because of the importance of these rights, any prior restraint on publication comes into court under a heavy presumption against its constitutional validity. *New York Times v. United States.*

However, First Amendment rights are not absolute. They are not boundless.

Justice Frankfurter dissenting in *Bridges v. California* stated it in this fashion: "Free speech is not so absolute or irrational a conception as to imply paralysis of the means for effective protection of all the freedoms secured by the Bill of Rights." In the *Schenck* case, Justice Holmes recognized: "The character of every act depends upon the circumstances in which it is done."

In *Near v. Minnesota*, the Supreme Court specifically recognized an extremely narrow area, involving national security, in which interference with First Amendment rights might be tolerated and a prior restraint on publication might be appropriate. The Court stated: "When a nation is at war many things that might be said in time of peace are such a hindrance to its effort that their utterance will not be endured so long as men fight and that no Court could regard them as protected by any constitutional right." No one would question but that a government might prevent actual obstruction to its recruiting service or the publication of the sailing dates of transports or the number and location of troops.

Thus, it is clear that few things, save grave national security concerns, are sufficient to override First Amendment interests. A court is well admonished to approach any requested prior restraint with a great deal of skepticism.

Juxtaposed against the right to freedom of expression is the government's contention that the national security of this country could be jeopardized by publication of the article.

The Court is convinced that the government has a right to classify certain sensitive documents to protect its national security. The problem is with the scope of the classification system.

Defendants contend that the projected article merely contains data already in the public domain and readily available to any diligent seeker. They say other nations already have the same information or the opportunity to obtain it. How then, they argue, can they be in violation of 42 U.S.C. §§ 2274(b) and 2280 which purport to authorize injunctive relief against one who would disclose restricted data "with reason to believe such data will be utilized to injure the United States or to secure an advantage to any foreign nation..."?

Although the government states that some of the information is in the public domain, it contends that much of the data is not, and that the Morland article contains a core of information that has never before been published.

Furthermore, the government's position is that whether or not specific information is "in the public domain" or has been "declassified" at some point is not determinative. The government states that a court must look at the nature and context of prior disclosures and analyze what the practical impact of the prior disclosures are as contrasted to that of the present revelation.

The government feels that the mere fact that the author, Howard Morland, could prepare an article explaining the technical processes of thermonuclear weapons does not mean that those processes are available to everyone. They lay heavy emphasis on the argument that the danger lies in the exposition of certain concepts never heretofore disclosed in conjunction with one another.

In an impressive affidavit, Dr. Hans A. Bethe...states that sizeable portions of the Morland text should be classified as restricted data because the processes outlined in the manuscript describe the essential design and operation of thermonuclear weapons. He later concludes "that the design and operational concepts described in the manuscript are not expressed or revealed in the public literature nor do I believe they are known to scientists not associated with the government weapons programs."

...After all this, the Court finds concepts within the article that it does not find in the public realm[,] concepts that are vital to the operation of the hydrogen bomb.

Even if some of the information is in the public domain, due recognition must be given to the human skills and expertise involved in writing this article. The author needed sufficient expertise to recognize relevant, as opposed to irrelevant, information and to assimilate the information obtained. The right questions had to be asked or the correct educated guesses had to be made....

Does the article provide a "do-it yourself" guide for the hydrogen bomb? Probably not. A number of affidavits make quite clear that a *sine qua non* to thermonuclear capability is a large, sophisticated industrial capability coupled with a coterie of imaginative, resourceful scientists and technicians. One does not build a hydrogen bomb in the basement. However, the article could possibly provide sufficient information to allow a medium size nation to move faster in developing a hydrogen weapon. It could provide a ticket to by-pass blind alleys.

The Morland piece could accelerate the membership of a candidate nation in the thermonuclear club. Pursuit of blind alleys or failure to grasp seemingly basic concepts have been the cause of many inventive failures....

Although the defendants state that the information contained in the article is relatively easy to obtain, only five countries now have a hydrogen bomb. Yet the United States first successfully exploded the hydrogen bomb some twenty-six years ago.

The point has also been made that it is only a question of time before other countries will have the hydrogen bomb. That may be true. However, there are times in the course of human history when time itself may be very important. This time factor becomes critical when considering mass annihilation weaponry. Witness the failure of Hitler to get his V-1 and V-2 bombs operational quickly enough to materially affect the outcome of World War II.

Defendants have stated that publication of the article will alert the people of this country to the false illusion of security created by the government's futile efforts at secrecy. They believe publication will provide the people with needed information to make informed decisions on an urgent issue of public concern.

However, this Court can find no plausible reason why the public needs to know the technical details about hydrogen bomb construction to carry on an informed debate on this issue. Furthermore, the Court believes that the defendants' position in favor of nuclear non-proliferation would be harmed, not aided, by the publication of this article.

The defendants have also relied on the decision in the *New York Times* case. In that case, the Supreme Court refused to enjoin the *New York Times* and the *Washington Post* from publishing the contents of a classified historical study of United States decision-making in Viet Nam, the so-called "Pentagon Papers."

This case is different in several important respects. In the first place, the study involved in the *New York Times* case contained historical data relating to events that occurred some three to twenty years previously. Secondly, the Supreme Court agreed with the lower court that no cogent reasons were advanced by the government as to why the article affected national security except that publication might cause some embarrassment to the United States....

The Court is of the opinion that the government has shown that the defendants had reason to believe that the data in the article, if published, would injure the United States or give an advantage to a foreign nation. Extensive reading and studying of the documents on file lead to the conclusion that not all the data is available in the public realm in the same fashion, if it is available at all.

What is involved here is information dealing with the most destructive weapon in the history of mankind, information of sufficient destructive potential to nullify the right to free speech and to endanger the right to life itself.

Stripped to its essence then, the question before the Court is a basic confrontation between the First Amendment right to freedom of the press and national security.

Our Founding Fathers believed, as we do, that one is born with certain inalienable rights which, as the Declaration of Independence intones, include the right to life, liberty and the pursuit of happiness. The Constitution, including the Bill of Rights, was enacted to make those rights operable in everyday life.

The Court believes that each of us is born seized of a panoply of basic rights, that we institute governments to secure these rights and that there is a hierarchy of values attached to these rights which is helpful in deciding the clash now before us.

Certain of these rights have an aspect of imperativeness or centrality that make them transcend other rights. Somehow it does not seem that the right to life and the right to not have soldiers quartered in your home can be of equal import in the grand scheme of things. While it may be true in the long-run, as Patrick Henry instructs us, that one would prefer death to life without liberty, nonetheless, in the short-run, one cannot enjoy freedom of speech, freedom to worship or freedom of the press unless one first enjoys the freedom to live.

Faced with a stark choice between upholding the right to continued life and the right to freedom of the press, most jurists would have no difficulty in opting for the chance to continue to breathe and function as they work to achieve perfect freedom of expression.

Is the choice here so stark? Only time can give us a definitive answer. But considering another aspect of this panoply of rights we all have is helpful in answering the question now before us. This aspect is the disparity of the risk involved.

The destruction of various human rights can come about in differing ways and at varying speeds. Freedom of the press can be obliterated overnight by some dictator's imposition of censorship or by the slow nibbling away at a free press through successive bits of repressive legislation enacted by a nation's lawmakers. Yet, even in the most drastic of such situations, it is always possible for a dictator to be overthrown, for a bad law to be repealed or for a judge's error to be subsequently rectified. Only when human life is at stake are such corrections impossible.

The case at bar is so difficult precisely because the consequences of error involve human life itself and on such an awesome scale.

The Secretary of State states that publication will increase thermonuclear proliferation and that this would "irreparably impair the national security of the United States." The Secretary of Defense says that dissemination of the Morland paper will mean a substantial increase in the risk of thermonuclear proliferation and lead to use or threats that would "adversely affect the national security of the United States."

Howard Morland asserts that "if the information in my article were not in the public domain, it should be put there . . . so that ordinary citizens may have informed opinions about nuclear weapons."

Erwin Knoll, the editor of *The Progressive*, states he is "totally convinced that publication of the article will be of substantial benefit to the United States because it will demonstrate that this country's security does not lie in an oppressive and ineffective system of secrecy and classification but in open, honest, and informed public debate about issues which the people must decide."

The Court is faced with the difficult task of weighing and resolving these divergent views.

A mistake in ruling against *The Progressive* will seriously infringe cherished First Amendment rights. If a preliminary injunction is issued, it will constitute the first instance of prior restraint against a publication in this fashion in the history of this country, to this Court's knowledge. Such notoriety is not to be sought. It will curtail defendants' First Amendment rights in a drastic and substantial fashion. It will infringe upon our right to know and to be informed as well.

A mistake in ruling against the United States could pave the way for thermonuclear annihilation for us all. In that event, our right to life is extinguished and the right to publish becomes moot.

In the *Near* case, the Supreme Court recognized that publication of troop movements in time of war would threaten national security and could therefore be restrained. Times have changed significantly since 1931 when *Near* was decided. Now war by foot soldiers has been replaced in large part by war by machines and bombs. No longer need there be any advance warning or any preparation time before a nuclear war could be commenced.

In light of these factors, this Court concludes that publication of the technical information on the hydrogen bomb contained in the article is analogous to publication of troop movements or locations in time of war and falls within the extremely narrow exception to the rule against prior restraint.

Because of this "disparity of risk," because the government has met its heavy burden of showing justification for the imposition of a prior restraint on publication of the objected-to technical portions of the Morland article, and because the Court is unconvinced that suppression of the objected-to technical portions of the Morland article would in any plausible fashion impede the defendants in their laudable crusade to stimulate public knowledge of nuclear armament and bring about enlightened debate on national policy questions, the Court finds that the objected-to portions of the article fall within the narrow area recognized by the Court in *Near v. Minnesota* in which a prior restraint on publication is appropriate.

The government has met its burden under section 2274 of The Atomic Energy Act. In the Court's opinion, it has also met the test enunciated by two Justices in the *New York Times* case, namely grave, direct, immediate and irreparable harm to the United States.

The Court has just determined that if necessary it will at this time assume the awesome responsibility of issuing a preliminary injunction against *The Progressive*'s use of the Morland article in its current form. . . .

"PORNOGRAPHY" AND WOMEN'S RIGHTS

American Booksellers Association, Inc. v. Hudnut

Although legally obscene material may be banned, any American knows that our culture is saturated with hard-core, barely legal pornography, much of which is very degrading to the women it depicts. What is the long-term effect of this pornography industry, and what if anything can government do about it?

In 1983 law professor Catherine MacKinnon and feminist writer Andrea Dworkin drafted an ordinance that defined pornography as the "graphically explicit subordination of women through words and/or pictures." Rather than treating pornography as obscene, the ordinance framed the issue as one of sexual discrimination. The ordinance would have allowed people harmed by pornography to seek damages through a civil lawsuit. At legislative hearings, women testified about the harm they experienced while making pornography, and witnesses of both sexes testified that pornography promotes abuse and violence against women.

The Minneapolis City Council, spurred by the brutal rape of a young girl by a perpetrator emulating scenes from pornography, passed an antipornography ordinance. The ordinance was later vetoed by the mayor, who argued that it violated the First Amendment. The Indianapolis City Council passed a similar ordinance. In *American Booksellers Association, Inc. v. Hudnut*, the US Court of Appeals for the Seventh Circuit struck down the ordinance as a violation of the First Amendment. The US Supreme Court affirmed this decision without oral

771 F.2d 323 (1985).

argument, though three members of the Court, Chief Justice Burger, Justice Rehnquist, and Justice O'Connor, noted that they wished to hear a full appeal.

Before CUDAHY and EASTERBROOK, Circuit Judges, and SWYGERT, Senior Circuit Judge.

EASTERBROOK, Circuit Judge.

Indianapolis enacted an ordinance defining "pornography" as a practice that discriminates against women. "Pornography" is to be redressed through the administrative and judicial methods used for other discrimination. The City's definition of "pornography" is considerably different from "obscenity," which the Supreme Court has held is not protected by the First Amendment.

To be "obscene" under *Miller v. California*, "a publication must, taken as a whole, appeal to the prurient interest, must contain patently offensive depictions or descriptions of specified sexual conduct, and on the whole have no serious literary, artistic, political, or scientific value." Offensiveness must be assessed under the standards of the community. Both offensiveness and an appeal to something other than "normal, healthy sexual desires" are essential elements of "obscenity." *Brockett v. Spokane Arcades, Inc.*

"Pornography" under the ordinance is "the graphic sexually explicit subordination of women, whether in pictures or in words, that also includes one or more of the following:

(1) Women are presented as sexual objects who enjoy pain or humiliation; or

(2) Women are presented as sexual objects who experience sexual pleasure in being raped; or

(3) Women are presented as sexual objects tied up or cut up or mutilated or bruised or physically hurt, or as dismembered or truncated or fragmented or severed into body parts; or

(4) Women are presented as being penetrated by objects or animals; or

(5) Women are presented in scenarios of degradation, injury, abasement, torture, shown as filthy or inferior, bleeding, bruised, or hurt in a context that makes these conditions sexual; or

(6) Women are presented as sexual objects for domination, conquest, violation, exploitation, possession, or use, or through postures or positions of servility or submission or display."

Indianapolis Code § 16-3(q). The statute provides that the "use of men, children, or transsexuals in the place of women in paragraphs (1) through (6) above shall also constitute pornography under this section." . . .

The Indianapolis ordinance does not refer to the prurient interest, to offensiveness, or to the standards of the community. It demands attention to particular depictions, not to the work judged as a whole. It is irrelevant under the ordinance whether the work has literary, artistic, political, or scientific value. The City and many amici point to these omissions as virtues. They maintain that pornography influences attitudes, and the statute is a way to alter the socialization of men and women rather than to vindicate community standards of offensiveness. And as one of the principal drafters of the ordinance has asserted, "if a woman is subjected, why should it matter that the work has other value?" Catharine A. MacKinnon, *Pornography, Civil Rights, and Speech*.

Civil rights groups and feminists have entered this case as amici on both sides. Those supporting the ordinance say that it will play an important role in reducing the tendency of men to view women as sexual objects, a tendency that leads to both unacceptable attitudes and discrimination in the workplace and violence away from it. Those opposing the ordinance point out that much radical feminist literature is explicit and depicts women in ways forbidden by the ordinance and that the ordinance would reopen old battles. It is unclear how Indianapolis would treat works from James Joyce's *Ulysses* to Homer's *Iliad*; both depict women as submissive objects for conquest and domination.

We do not try to balance the arguments for and against an ordinance such as this. The ordinance discriminates on the ground of the content of the speech. Speech treating women in the approved way—in sexual encounters "premised on equality"—is lawful no matter how sexually explicit. Speech treating women in the disapproved way—as submissive in matters sexual or as enjoying humiliation—is unlawful no matter how significant the literary, artistic, or political qualities of the work taken as a whole. The state may not ordain preferred viewpoints in this way. The Constitution forbids the state to declare one perspective right and silence opponents. . . .

III

If there is any fixed star in our constitutional constellation, it is that no official, high or petty, can prescribe what shall be orthodox in politics, nationalism, religion, or other matters of opinion or force citizens to confess by word or act their faith therein.

West Virginia State Board of Education v. Barnette. Under the First Amendment the government must leave to the people the evaluation of ideas. Bald or subtle, an idea is as powerful as the audience allows it to be. A belief may be pernicious—the beliefs of Nazis led to the death of millions, those of the Klan to the repression of millions. A pernicious belief may prevail. Totalitarian governments today rule much of the planet, practicing suppression of billions and spreading dogma that may enslave others. One of the things that separates our society from theirs is our absolute right to propagate opinions that the government finds wrong or even hateful....

Under the ordinance graphic sexually explicit speech is "pornography" or not depending on the perspective the author adopts. Speech that "subordinates" women and also, for example, presents women as enjoying pain, humiliation, or rape, or even simply presents women in "positions of servility or submission or display" is forbidden, no matter how great the literary or political value of the work taken as a whole. Speech that portrays women in positions of equality is lawful, no matter how graphic the sexual content. This is thought control. It establishes an "approved" view of women, of how they may react to sexual encounters, of how the sexes may relate to each other. Those who espouse the approved view may use sexual images; those who do not, may not.

Indianapolis justifies the ordinance on the ground that pornography affects thoughts. Men who see women depicted as subordinate are more likely to treat them so. Pornography is an aspect of dominance. It does not persuade people so much as change them. It works by socializing, by establishing the expected and the permissible. In this view pornography is not an idea; pornography is the injury.

There is much to this perspective. Beliefs are also facts. People often act in accordance with the images and patterns they find around them. People raised in a religion tend to accept the tenets of that religion, often without independent examination. People taught from birth that black people are fit only for slavery rarely rebelled against that creed; beliefs coupled with the self-interest of the masters established a social structure that inflicted great harm while enduring for centuries. Words and images act at the level of the subconscious before they persuade at the level of the conscious. Even the truth has little chance unless a statement fits within the framework of beliefs that may never have been subjected to rational study.

Therefore we accept the premises of this legislation. Depictions of subordination tend to perpetuate subordination. The subordinate status of women in turn leads to affront and lower pay at work, insult and injury at home, battery and rape on the streets....

Yet this simply demonstrates the power of pornography as speech. All of these unhappy effects depend on mental intermediation. Pornography affects how people see the world, their fellows, and social relations. If pornography is what pornography does, so is other speech. Hitler's orations affected how some Germans saw Jews. Communism is a world view, not simply a *Manifesto* by Marx and Engels or a set of speeches. Efforts to suppress communist speech in the United States were based on the belief that the public acceptability of such ideas would increase the likelihood of totalitarian government. Religions affect socialization in the most pervasive way.... Many people believe that the existence of television, apart from the content of specific programs, leads to intellectual laziness, to a penchant for violence, to many other ills. The Alien and Sedition Acts passed during the administration of John Adams rested on a sincerely held belief that disrespect for the government leads to social collapse and revolution—a belief with support in the history of many nations. Most governments of the world act on this empirical regularity, suppressing critical speech. In the United States, however, the strength of the support for this belief is irrelevant. Seditious libel is protected speech unless the danger is not only grave but also imminent.

Racial bigotry, anti-semitism, violence on television, reporters' biases—these and many more influence the culture and shape our socialization. None is directly answerable by more speech, unless that speech too finds its place in the popular culture. Yet all is protected as speech, however insidious. Any other answer leaves the government in control of all of the institutions of culture, the great censor and director of which thoughts are good for us.

Sexual responses often are unthinking responses, and the association of sexual arousal with the subordination of women therefore may have a substantial effect. But almost all cultural stimuli provoke unconscious responses. Religious ceremonies condition their participants. Teachers convey messages by selecting what not to cover; the implicit message about what is off limits or unthinkable may be more powerful than the messages for which they present rational argument. Television scripts contain unarticulated assumptions. People may be conditioned in subtle ways. If the fact that speech plays a role in a process of conditioning were enough to permit governmental regulation, that would be the end of freedom of speech.

It is possible to interpret the claim that the pornography is the harm in a different way. Indianapolis emphasizes the injury that models in pornographic films and pictures may suffer. The record contains materials depicting sexual torture, penetration of women by red-hot irons and the like. These concerns have nothing to do with written materials subject to the statute, and physical injury can occur with or without the "subordination" of women.... [A] state may make injury in the course of producing a film unlawful independent of the viewpoint expressed in the film.

The more immediate point, however, is that the image of pain is not necessarily pain. In *Body Double*, a suspense film directed by Brian DePalma, a woman who has disrobed and presented a sexually explicit display is murdered by an intruder with a drill. The drill runs through the woman's body. The film is sexually explicit and a murder occurs—yet no one believes that the actress suffered pain or died. In *Barbarella* a character played by Jane Fonda is at times displayed in sexually explicit ways and at times shown "bleeding, bruised, [and] hurt in a context that makes these conditions sexual"—and again no one believes that Fonda was actually tortured to make the film. In *Carnal Knowledge* a woman grovels to please the sexual whims of a character played by Jack Nicholson; no one believes that there was a real sexual submission, and the Supreme Court held the film protected by the First Amendment. And this works both ways. The description of women's sexual domination of men in *Lysistrata* was not real dominance. Depictions may affect slavery, war, or sexual roles, but a book about slavery is not itself slavery, or a book about death by poison a murder.

Much of Indianapolis's argument rests on the belief that when speech is "unanswerable," and the metaphor that there is a "marketplace of ideas" does not apply, the First Amendment does not apply either. The metaphor is honored; Milton's *Aeropagitica* and John Stewart Mill's *On Liberty* defend freedom of speech on the ground that the truth will prevail, and many of the most important cases under the First Amendment recite this position. The Framers undoubtedly believed it. As a general matter it is true. But the Constitution does not make the dominance of truth a necessary condition of freedom of speech. To say that it does would be to confuse an outcome of free speech with a necessary condition for the application of the amendment.

A power to limit speech on the ground that truth has not yet prevailed and is not likely to prevail implies the power to declare truth. At some point the government must be able to say (as Indianapolis has said): "We know what the truth is, yet a free exchange of speech has not driven out falsity, so that we must now prohibit falsity." If the government may declare the truth, why wait for the failure of speech? Under the First Amendment, however, there is no such thing as a false idea, so the government may not restrict speech on the ground that in a free exchange truth is not yet dominant.

At any time, some speech is ahead in the game; the more numerous speakers prevail. Supporters of minority candidates may be forever "excluded" from the political process because their candidates never win, because few people believe their positions. This does not mean that freedom of speech has failed.

The Supreme Court has rejected the position that speech must be "effectively answerable" to be protected by the Constitution....

We come, finally, to the argument that pornography is "low value" speech, that it is enough like obscenity that Indianapolis may prohibit it. Some cases hold that speech far removed from politics and other subjects at the core of the Framers' concerns may be subjected to special regulation. These cases do not sustain statutes that select among viewpoints, however....

At all events, "pornography" is not low value speech within the meaning of these cases. Indianapolis seeks to prohibit certain speech because it believes this speech influences social relations and politics on a grand scale, that it controls attitudes at home and in the legislature. This precludes a characterization of the speech as low value. True, pornography and obscenity have sex in common. But Indianapolis left out of its definition any reference to literary, artistic, political, or scientific value. The ordinance applies to graphic sexually explicit subordination in works great and small. The Court sometimes balances the value of speech against the costs of its restriction, but it does this by category of speech and not by the content of particular works. Indianapolis has created an approved point of view and so loses the support of these cases.

Any rationale we could imagine in support of this ordinance could not be limited to sex discrimination. Free speech has been on balance an ally of those seeking change. Governments that want stasis start by restricting speech. Culture is a powerful force of continuity; Indianapolis paints pornography as part of the culture of power. Change in any complex system ultimately depends on the ability of outsiders to challenge accepted views and the reigning institutions. Without a strong guarantee of freedom of speech, there is no effective right to challenge what is....

OFFENSIVE PARODY
Hustler Magazine v. Falwell

The Supreme Court has fashioned careful protection for the media against actions for libel and defamation. But what, if any, notice should the law take when a media outlet deliberately sets out to humiliate and ridicule a prominent American?

In a case made familiar by the 1996 movie *The People vs. Larry Flynt*, Moral Majority founder the Rev. Jerry Falwell sued *Hustler* magazine in 1983 over a vicious ad parody. The parody suggested that Falwell's first sexual experience had been an act of drunken incest committed with his mother in an outhouse, and that Falwell was in the habit of appearing before his church while intoxicated.

By the time the lawsuit was filed, Flynt and his publishing company were no strangers to the US courts or to First Amendment defenses. Flynt had faced obscenity and racketeering charges in Ohio, been sued for libel in Ohio and New Hampshire, and served time for contempt of court. On one occasion, Flynt had appeared in court wearing the American flag as a diaper. Flynt had also been shot and paralyzed by a would-be assassin during an obscenity trial in Georgia. In a deposition given while he was still heavily sedated after the assassination atttempt, Flynt freely admitted that his motive in running the ad parody had been to denigrate and even "assassinate" Falwell's character.

---

485 U.S. 46 (1988).

210

Lower courts quickly dismissed Falwell's claims for libel, because the ad parody could not be taken as making a false statement of fact. However, the trial court allowed Falwell to sue for "intentional infliction of emotional distress," a tort that arises when one person does something outrageous for no other reason than to harm or humiliate another. The jury returned a substantial damage award on this count, and the US Court of Appeals for the Fourth Circuit affirmed. In an opinion that signaled that the new Rehnquist Court would remain committed to a robust view of the First Amendment Speech and Press Clauses, the Court held that such tort actions would chill the robust and even vicious debate that is the mark of American political discourse.

CHIEF JUSTICE REHNQUIST delivered the opinion of the Court.

Petitioner Hustler Magazine, Inc., is a magazine of nationwide circulation. Respondent Jerry Falwell, a nationally known minister who has been active as a commentator on politics and public affairs, sued petitioner and its publisher, petitioner Larry Flynt, to recover damages for invasion of privacy, libel, and intentional infliction of emotional distress....

The inside front cover of the November 1983 issue of *Hustler* magazine featured a "parody" of an advertisement for Campari Liqueur that contained the name and picture of respondent and was entitled "Jerry Falwell talks about his first time." This parody was modeled after actual Campari ads that included interviews with various celebrities about their "first times." Although it was apparent by the end of each interview that this meant the first time they sampled Campari, the ads clearly played on the sexual double entendre of the general subject of "first times." Copying the form and layout of these Campari ads, *Hustler's* editors chose respondent as the featured celebrity and drafted an alleged "interview" with him in which he states that his "first time" was during a drunken incestuous rendezvous with his mother in an outhouse. The *Hustler* parody portrays respondent and his mother as drunk and immoral, and suggests that respondent is a hypocrite who preaches only when he is drunk. In small print at the bottom of the page, the ad contains the disclaimer, "ad parody—not to be taken seriously." The magazine's table of contents also lists the ad as "Fiction; Ad and Personality Parody."

Soon after the November issue of *Hustler* became available to the public, respondent brought this diversity action in the United States District Court for the Western District of Virginia against Hustler Magazine, Inc., Larry C. Flynt, and Flynt Distributing Co., Inc. Respondent stated in his complaint that publication of the ad parody in *Hustler* entitled him to recover damages for libel, invasion of privacy, and intentional infliction of emotional distress. The case proceeded to trial. At the close of the evidence, the District Court granted a directed verdict for petitioners on the invasion of privacy claim. The jury then found against respondent on the libel claim, specifically finding that the ad parody could not "reasonably be understood as describing actual facts about [respondent] or actual events in which [he] participated." The jury ruled for respondent on the intentional infliction of emotional distress claim, however, and stated that he should be awarded $100,000 in compensatory damages, as well as $50,000 each in punitive damages from petitioners....

This case presents us with a novel question involving First Amendment limitations upon a state's authority to protect its citizens from the intentional infliction of emotional distress. We must decide whether a public figure may recover damages for emotional harm caused by the publication of an ad parody offensive to him, and doubtless gross and repugnant in the eyes of most. Respondent would have us find that a state's interest in protecting public figures from emotional distress is sufficient to deny First Amendment protection to speech that is patently offensive and is intended to inflict emotional injury, even when that speech could not reasonably have been interpreted as stating actual facts about the public figure involved. This we decline to do.

At the heart of the First Amendment is the recognition of the funda-mental importance of the free flow of ideas and opinions on matters of public interest and concern.... We have therefore been particularly vigilant to ensure that individual expressions of ideas remain free from governmentally imposed sanctions. The First Amendment recognizes no such thing as a "false" idea....

The sort of robust political debate encouraged by the First Amendment is bound to produce speech that is critical of those who hold public office or those public figures who are "intimately involved in the resolution of impor-tant public questions or, by reason of their fame, shape events in areas of con-cern to society at large." *Associated Press v. Walker* (Warren, C.J., concurring in result). Justice Frankfurter put it succinctly in *Baumgartner v. United States*, when he said that "[o]ne of the prerogatives of American citizenship is the right to criticize public men and measures." Such criticism, inevitably, will not always be reasoned or moderate; public figures as well as public officials will be subject to "vehement, caustic, and sometimes unpleasantly sharp attacks," *New York Times v. Sullivan*....

Of course, this does not mean that *any* speech about a public figure is immune from sanction in the form of damages. Since *New York Times Co. v. Sullivan*, we have consistently ruled that a public figure may hold a speaker liable for the damage to reputation caused by publication of a defamatory falsehood, but only if the statement was made "with knowledge that it was false or with reckless disregard of whether it was false or not." False statements of fact are particularly valueless; they interfere with the truth-seeking function of the marketplace of ideas, and they cause damage to an individual's reputation that cannot easily be repaired by counterspeech, however persuasive or effective.... But even though falsehoods have little value in and of themselves, they are "nevertheless inevitable in free debate," and a rule that would impose strict liability on a publisher for false factual assertions would have an undoubted "chilling" effect on speech relating to public figures that does have constitutional value.... This breathing space is provided by a constitutional rule that allows public figures to recover for libel or defamation only when they can prove *both* that the statement was false and that the statement was made with the requisite level of culpability.

Respondent argues, however, that a different standard should apply in this case because here the state seeks to prevent not reputational damage, but the severe emotional distress suffered by the person who is the subject of an offensive publication.... In respondent's view, and in the view of the Court of Appeals, so long as the utterance was intended to inflict emotional distress, was outrageous, and did in fact inflict serious emotional distress, it is of no constitutional import whether the statement was a fact or an opinion, or whether it was true or false. It is the intent to cause injury that is the gravamen of the tort, and the state's interest in preventing emotional harm simply outweighs whatever interest a speaker may have in speech of this type.

Generally speaking the law does not regard the intent to inflict emotional distress as one which should receive much solicitude, and it is quite understandable that most if not all jurisdictions have chosen to make it civilly culpable where the conduct in question is sufficiently "outrageous." But in the world of debate about public affairs, many things done with motives that are less than admirable are protected by the First Amendment. In *Garrison v. Louisiana*, we held that even when a speaker or writer is motivated by hatred or ill-will his expression was protected by the First Amendment: "Debate on public issues will not be uninhibited if the speaker must run the risk that it will be proved in court that he spoke out of hatred; even if he did speak out of hatred, utterances honestly believed contribute to the free interchange of ideas and the ascertainment of truth." Thus while such a bad motive may be deemed controlling for purposes of tort liability in other areas of the law, we think the First Amendment prohibits such a result in the area of public debate about public figures.

Were we to hold otherwise, there can be little doubt that political cartoonists and satirists would be subjected to damages awards without any showing that their work falsely defamed its subject. Webster's defines a caricature as "the deliberately distorted picturing or imitating of a person, literary style, etc. by exaggerating features or mannerisms for satirical effect." The appeal of the political cartoon or caricature is often based on exploitation of unfortunate physical traits or politically embarrassing events—an exploitation often calculated to injure the feelings of the subject of the portrayal. The art of the cartoonist is often not reasoned or evenhanded, but slashing and one-sided. One cartoonist expressed the nature of the art in these words:

> The political cartoon is a weapon of attack, of scorn and ridicule and satire;
> it is least effective when it tries to pat some politician on the back. It is usu-
> ally as welcome as a bee sting and is always controversial in some quarters.

Despite their sometimes caustic nature, from the early cartoon portraying George Washington as an ass down to the present day, graphic depictions and satirical cartoons have played a prominent role in public and political debate.... Lincoln's tall, gangling posture, Teddy Roosevelt's glasses and teeth, and Franklin D. Roosevelt's jutting jaw and cigarette holder have been memorialized by political cartoons with an effect that could not have been obtained by the photographer or the portrait artist. From the viewpoint of history it is clear that our political discourse would have been considerably poorer without them.

Respondent contends, however, that the caricature in question here was so "outrageous" as to distinguish it from more traditional political cartoons. There is no doubt that the caricature of respondent and his mother published in *Hustler* is at best a distant cousin of the political cartoons described above, and a rather poor relation at that. If it were possible by laying down a principled standard to separate the one from the other, public discourse would probably suffer little or no harm. But we doubt that there is any such standard, and we are quite sure that the pejorative description "outrageous" does not supply one. "Outrageousness" in the area of political and social discourse has an inherent subjectiveness about it which would allow a jury to impose liability on the basis of the jurors' tastes or views, or perhaps on the basis of their dislike of a particular expression. An "outrageousness" standard thus runs afoul of our longstanding refusal to allow damages to be awarded because the speech in question may have an adverse emotional impact on the audience. And, as we stated in *FCC v. Pacifica Foundation*:

> [T]he fact that society may find speech offensive is not a sufficient reason for suppressing it. Indeed, if it is the speaker's opinion that gives offense, that consequence is a reason for according it constitutional protection. For it is a central tenet of the First Amendment that the government must remain neutral in the marketplace of ideas....

Admittedly, these oft-repeated First Amendment principles, like other principles, are subject to limitations.... But the sort of expression involved in this case does not seem to us to be governed by any exception to the general First Amendment principles stated above.

We conclude that public figures and public officials may not recover for the tort of intentional infliction of emotional distress by reason of publications such as the one here at issue without showing in addition that the publication contains a false statement of fact which was made with "actual malice," i.e., with knowledge that the statement was false or with reckless disregard as to whether or not it was true. This is not merely a "blind application" of the *New York Times* standard, it reflects our considered judgment that such a standard is necessary to give adequate "breathing space" to the freedoms protected by the First Amendment.

Here it is clear that respondent Falwell is a "public figure" for purposes of First Amendment law. The jury found against respondent on his libel claim when it decided that the *Hustler* ad parody could not "reasonably be understood as describing actual facts about [respondent] or actual events in which [he] participated." The Court of Appeals interpreted the jury's finding to be that the ad parody "was not reasonably believable," and in accordance with our custom we accept this finding. Respondent is thus relegated to his claim for damages awarded by the jury for the intentional infliction of emotional distress by "outrageous" conduct. But for reasons heretofore stated this claim cannot, consistently with the First Amendment, form a basis for the award of damages when the conduct in question is the publication of a caricature such as the ad parody involved here. The judgment of the Court of Appeals is accordingly *Reversed.*

ACCESS TO CRIMINAL TRIALS
Richmond Newspapers, Inc. v. Virginia

Near v. Minnesota made clear that judges cannot "gag" the media, even in pursuit of the Sixth Amendment's guarantee of a fair trial before an impartial jury. Can a trial judge simply close a criminal trial to everyone, including reporters? In addition to Sixth Amendment issues, the *Richmond Newspapers* case raises the question of when reporters are entitled to access to courts.

In *Gannett v. DePasquale* (1979), decided one year earlier, the Court had held that a trial court could exclude the press from a pretrial proceeding that was considering the admissibility of a confession. But then a trial judge in Virginia went further. With the agreement of both the prosecution and defense, he closed the trial itself to the public. The Supreme Court responded that "absent an overriding interest articulated in findings, the trial of a criminal case must be open to the public." Several cases following *Richmond Newspapers* have reemphasized the importance of the press's access to information. In *Globe Newspaper Co. v. Superior Court* (1982), the Court held that trial courts could not exclude the press and public from hearing the testimony of witnesses regarding sex crimes involving children. Later, in *Press-Enterprise Co. v. Superior Court* (1986), the Court declared unconstitutional a trial court's decision to close a jury selection proceeding. The Court stated that the "presumption of openness may

---

448 U.S. 555 (1980).

be overcome by an overriding interest based on findings that closure is essential to preserve the higher values and narrowly tailored to serve that interest."

The access of the press to the courts, however, derives largely from the long tradition of open trials. Newspapers have from time to time asserted a special right of access to government property or operations not generally open to the public, and the Court has uniformly denied such claims. Media outlets cannot demand access to jails or prisons. Lawsuits demanding unrestricted access to cover combat operations have generally been held moot before trial, as the military operation has ended.

Mr. Chief Justice BURGER announced the judgment of the Court and delivered an opinion, in which Mr. Justice WHITE and Mr. Justice STEVENS joined.

The narrow question presented in this case is whether the right of the public and press to attend criminal trials is guaranteed under the United States Constitution.

I

In March 1976, one Stevenson was indicted for the murder of a hotel manager who had been found stabbed to death on December 2, 1975. Tried promptly in July 1976, Stevenson was convicted of second-degree murder in the Circuit Court of Hanover County, Va. The Virginia Supreme Court reversed the conviction in October 1977, holding that a bloodstained shirt purportedly belonging to Stevenson had been improperly admitted into evidence.

Stevenson was retried in the same court. This second trial ended in a mistrial on May 30, 1978, when a juror asked to be excused after trial had begun and no alternate was available.

A third trial, which began in the same court on June 6, 1978, also ended in a mistrial. It appears that the mistrial may have been declared because a prospective juror had read about Stevenson's previous trials in a newspaper and had told other prospective jurors about the case before the retrial began.

Stevenson was tried in the same court for a fourth time beginning on September 11, 1978. Present in the courtroom when the case was called were appellants Wheeler and McCarthy, reporters for appellant Richmond Newspapers, Inc. Before the trial began, counsel for the defendant moved that it be closed to the public....

The trial judge, who had presided over two of the three previous trials, asked if the prosecution had any objection to clearing the courtroom. The prosecutor stated he had no objection and would leave it to the discretion of the court. Presumably referring to Va. Code §19.2-266 (Supp.1980), the trial judge then announced: "[T]he statute gives me that power specifically and the defendant has made the motion." He then ordered "that the Courtroom be kept clear of all parties except the witnesses when they testify." The record does not show that any objections to the closure order were made by anyone present at the time, including appellants Wheeler and McCarthy.

Later that same day, however, appellants sought a hearing on a motion to vacate the closure order. . . .

The court denied the motion to vacate and ordered the trial to continue the following morning "with the press and public excluded."

What transpired when the closed trial resumed the next day was disclosed in the following manner by an order of the court entered September 12, 1978: ". . . the jury having been excused, the Court doth find the accused NOT GUILTY of murder as charged in the Indictment, and he was allowed to depart."

. . . Appellants then petitioned the Virginia Supreme Court for writs of mandamus and prohibition and filed an appeal from the trial court's closure order. On July 9, 1979, the Virginia Supreme court dismissed the mandamus and prohibition petitions and, finding no reversible error, denied the petition for appeal.

Appellants then sought review in this Court. . . .

II

. . . [H]ere for the first time the Court is asked to decide whether a criminal trial itself may be closed to the public upon the unopposed request of a defendant, without any demonstration that closure is required to protect the defendant's superior right to a fair trial, or that some other overriding consideration requires closure.

B

. . . [T]he historical evidence demonstrates conclusively that at the time when our organic laws were adopted, criminal trials both here and in England had long been presumptively open. This is no quirk of history; rather, it has long been recognized as an indispens[a]ble attribute of an Anglo-American trial. Both Hale in the 17th century and Blackstone in the 18th saw the importance of openness to the proper functioning of a trial; it gave assurance that the proceedings were conducted fairly to all concerned, and it discouraged perjury, the misconduct of participants, and decisions based on secret bias or partiality....

... The early history of open trials in part reflects the widespread acknowledgment, long before there were behavioral scientists, that public trials had significant community therapeutic value. Even without such experts to frame the concept in words, people sensed from experience and observation that, especially in the administration of criminal justice, the means used to achieve justice must have the support derived from public acceptance of both the process and its results.

When a shocking crime occurs, a community reaction of outrage and public protest often follows. Thereafter the open processes of justice serve an important prophylactic purpose, providing an outlet for community concern, hostility, and emotion. Without an awareness that society's responses to criminal conduct are underway, natural human reactions of outrage and protest are frustrated and may manifest themselves in some form of vengeful "self-help," as indeed they did regularly in the activities of vigilante "committees" on our frontiers....

Civilized societies withdraw both from the victim and the vigilante the enforcement of criminal laws, but they cannot erase from people's consciousness the fundamental, natural yearning to see justice done—or even the urge for retribution. The crucial prophylactic aspects of the administration of justice cannot function in the dark.... A result considered untoward may undermine public confidence, and where the trial has been concealed from public view an unexpected outcome can cause a reaction that the system at best has failed and at worst has been corrupted. To work effectively, it is important that society's criminal process "satisfy the appearance of justice," *Offutt v. United States*, and the appearance of justice can best be provided by allowing people to observe it.

Looking back, we see that when the ancient "town meeting" form of trial became too cumbersome, twelve members of the community were delegated to act as its surrogates, but the community did not surrender its right to observe the conduct of trials. The people retained a "right of visitation" which enabled them to satisfy themselves that justice was in fact being done.

People in an open society do not demand infallibility from their institutions, but it is difficult for them to accept what they are prohibited from observing. When a criminal trial is conducted in the open, there is at least an opportunity both for understanding the system in general and its workings in a particular case....

In earlier times, both in England and America, attendance at court was a common mode of "passing the time." With the press, cinema, and electronic media now supplying the representations or reality of the real life drama once available only in the courtroom, attendance at court is no longer a widespread pastime. Yet "[i]t is not unrealistic even in this day to believe that public inclusion affords citizens a form of legal education and hopefully promotes confidence in the fair administration of justice." *State v. Schmit.* Instead of acquiring information about trials by firsthand observation or by word of mouth from those who attended, people now acquire it chiefly through the print and electronic media. In a sense, this validates the media claim of functioning as surrogates for the public. While media representatives enjoy the same right of access as the public, they often are provided special seating and priority of entry so that they may report what people in attendance have seen and heard. This "contribute[s] to public understanding of the rule of law and to comprehension of the functioning of the entire criminal justice system...." *Nebraska Press Ass'n v. Stuart.*

C

From this unbroken, uncontradicted history, supported by reasons as valid today as in centuries past, we are bound to conclude that a presumption of openness inheres in the very nature of a criminal trial under our system of justice....

Despite the history of criminal trials being presumptively open since long before the Constitution, the State presses its contention that neither the Constitution nor the Bill of Rights contains any provision which by its terms guarantees to the public the right to attend criminal trials. Standing alone, this is correct, but there remains the question whether, absent an explicit provision, the Constitution affords protection against exclusion of the public from criminal trials.

III

A

The First Amendment, in conjunction with the Fourteenth, prohibits governments from "abridging the freedom of speech, or of the press; or the right of the people peaceably to assemble, and to petition the Government for a redress of grievances." These expressly guaranteed freedoms share a common core purpose of assuring freedom of communication on matters relating to the functioning of government. Plainly it would be difficult to single out any aspect of government of higher concern and importance to the people than the manner in which criminal trials are conducted; as we have shown, recognition of this pervades the centuries-old history of open trials and the opinions of this Court.

The Bill of Rights was enacted against the backdrop of the long history of trials being presumptively open.... In guaranteeing freedoms such as those of speech and press, the First Amendment can be read as protecting the right of everyone to attend trials so as to give meaning to those explicit guarantees. "[T]he First Amendment goes beyond protection of the press and the self-expression of individuals to prohibit government from limiting the stock of information from which members of the public may draw." *First National Bank of Washington v. Bellotti*. Free speech carries with it some freedom to listen. "In a variety of contexts this Court has referred to a First Amendment right to 'receive information and ideas.'" *Kleindienst v. Mandel*. What this means in the context of trials is that the First Amendment guarantees of speech and press, standing alone, prohibit government from summarily closing courtroom doors which had long been open to the public at the time that Amendment was adopted....

It is not crucial whether we describe this right to attend criminal trials to hear, see, and communicate observations concerning them as a "right of access," or a "right to gather information," for we have recognized that "without some protection for seeking out the news, freedom of the press could be eviscerated." *Branzburg v. Hayes*. The explicit, guaranteed rights to speak and to publish concerning what takes place at a trial would lose much meaning if access to observe the trial could, as it was here, be foreclosed arbitrarily.

B

The right of access to places traditionally open to the public, as criminal trials have long been, may be seen as assured by the amalgam of the First Amendment guarantees of speech and press; and their affinity to the right of assembly is not without relevance.... Subject to the traditional time, place, and manner restrictions, streets, sidewalks, and parks are places traditionally open, where First Amendment rights may be exercised; a trial courtroom also is a public place where the people generally—and representatives of the media—have a right to be present, and where their presence historically has been thought to enhance the integrity and quality of what takes place.

C

The State argues that the Constitution nowhere spells out a guarantee for the right of the public to attend trials, and that accordingly no such right is protected. The possibility that such a contention could be made did not escape the notice of the Constitution's draftsmen; they were concerned that some important rights might be thought disparaged because not specifically guaranteed. It was even argued that because of this danger no Bill of Rights should be adopted....

But arguments such as the State makes have not precluded recognition of important rights not enumerated. Notwithstanding the appropriate caution against reading into the Constitution rights not explicitly defined, the Court has acknowledged that certain unarticulated rights are implicit in enumerated guarantees. For example, the rights of association and of privacy, the right to be presumed innocent, and the right to be judged by a standard of proof beyond a reasonable doubt in a criminal trial, as well as the right to travel, appear nowhere in the Constitution or Bill of Rights. Yet these important but unarticulated rights have nonetheless been found to share constitutional protection in common with explicit guarantees....

We hold that the right to attend criminal trials is implicit in the guarantees of the First Amendment; without the freedom to attend such trials, which people have exercised for centuries, important aspects of freedom of speech and "of the press could be eviscerated." *Branzburg*.

D

Having concluded there was a guaranteed right of the public under the First and Fourteenth Amendments to attend the trial of Stevenson's case, we return to the closure order challenged by appellants.... Absent an overriding interest articulated in findings, the trial of a criminal case must be open to the public. Accordingly, the judgment under review is

Reversed....

Mr. Justice STEVENS, concurring.

This is a watershed case. Until today the Court has accorded virtually absolute protection to the dissemination of information or ideas, but never before has it squarely held that the acquisition of newsworthy matter is entitled to any constitutional protection whatsoever. An additional word of emphasis is therefore appropriate.

... Today, however, for the first time, the Court unequivocally holds that an arbitrary interference with access to important information is an abridgment of the freedoms of speech and of the press protected by the First Amendment....

Mr. Justice BRENNAN, with whom Mr. Justice MARSHALL joins, concurring in the judgment.

... The instant case raises the question whether the First Amendment, of its own force and as applied to the States through the Fourteenth Amendment, secures the public an independent right of access to trial proceedings. Because I believe that the First Amendment—of itself and as applied to the States through the Fourteenth Amendment—secures such a public right of access, I agree with those of my Brethren who hold that, without more, agreement of the trial judge and the parties cannot constitutionally close a trial to the public.

I

While freedom of expression is made inviolate by the First Amendment, and, with only rare and stringent exceptions, may not be suppressed, the First Amendment has not been viewed by the Court in all settings as providing an equally categorical assurance of the correlative freedom of access to information. Yet the Court has not ruled out a public access component to the First Amendment in every circumstance. Read with care and in context, our decisions must therefore be understood as holding only that any privilege of access to governmental information is subject to a degree of restraint dictated by the nature of the information and countervailing interests in security or confidentiality. These cases neither comprehensively nor absolutely deny that public access to information may at times be implied by the First Amendment and the principles which animate it.

The Court's approach in right-of-access cases simply reflects the special nature of a claim of First Amendment right to gather information. Customarily, First Amendment guarantees are interposed to protect communication between speaker and listener. When so employed against prior restraints, free speech protections are almost insurmountable. But the First Amendment embodies more than a commitment to free expression and communicative interchange for their own sakes; it has a *structural* role to play in securing and fostering our republican system of self-government. Implicit in this structural role is not only "the principle that debate on public issues should be uninhibited, robust, and wide-open," *New York Times v. Sullivan*, but also the antecedent assumption that valuable public debate—as well as other civic behavior—must be informed. The structural model links the First Amendment to that process of communication necessary for a democracy to survive, and thus entails solicitude not only for communication itself, but also for the indispensable conditions of meaningful communication....

Mr. Justice REHNQUIST, dissenting.

In the Gilbert and Sullivan operetta "Iolanthe," the Lord Chancellor recites:

> "The Law is the true embodiment
> of everything that's excellent,
> It has no kind of fault or flaw,
> And I, my Lords, embody the Law."

It is difficult not to derive more than a little of this flavor from the various opinions supporting the judgment in this case....

...I do not believe that either the First or Sixth Amendment, as made applicable to the States by the Fourteenth, requires that a State's reasons for denying public access to a trial, where both the prosecuting attorney and the defendant have consented to an order of closure approved by the judge, are subject to any additional constitutional review at our hands. And I most certainly do not believe that the Ninth Amendment confers upon us any such power to review orders of state trial judges closing trials in such situations. . . .

The issue here is not whether the "right" to freedom of the press conferred by the First Amendment to the Constitution overrides the defendant's "right" to a fair trial conferred by other Amendments to the Constitution; it is instead whether any provision in the Constitution may fairly be read to prohibit what the trial judge in the Virginia state-court system did in this case. Being unable to find any such prohibition in the First, Sixth, Ninth, or any other Amendment to the United States Constitution, or in the Constitution itself, I dissent.

PROMISES OF CONFIDENTIALITY AS "CONTRACTS"

Cohen v. Cowles Media

As noted in *Branzburg*, journalists often promise confidentiality to their sources, and the First Amendment affords no protection to those promises. What about when a journalist *breaks* such a promise? May a source sue the reporter or the media outlet for breach of contract? In *Cohen v. Cowles Media*, the Court implied that such promises could give rise to damages under state laws governing contracts.

In 1982 Republican nominee Wheelock Whitney Jr. ran for governor of Minnesota, a race he ultimately lost to Democrat Rudy Perpich. Whitney staffer Dan Cohen offered to the *Minneapolis Star Tribune* and the *St. Paul Pioneer Press Dispatch* damaging information about Marlene Johnson, Perpich's running mate, including her vacated conviction for "petit theft" of $6 worth of sewing supplies and a record of arrest for unlawful assembly arrest in a civil rights protest. The reporters promised Cohen confidentiality, but the newspaper's editors overruled that promise, reasoning that the news value of such a smear effort was greater than that of the police records. The paper published Cohen's name in a series of scathing articles and comics criticizing the "dirty tricks" of Whitney's campaign. As a result, Cohen lost his job at an advertising company and was subsequently fired from his second job as well. Cohen

---

501 U.S. 663 (1991).

brought suit against both Cowles Media Co. and Pioneer Press, owners of the offending newspapers. Cohen was represented by Elliot C. Rothenberg, a former office seeker, who worked the case alone with an old electric typewriter from his home, while the media companies were represented by over four hundred attorneys. Rothenberg had never previously tried a jury case and had never argued an appeal before the Supreme Court. Yet he won an ambiguous victory from the Minnesota Supreme Court, which refused to enforce a "contract" between Cohen and the papers but did suggest that the papers might be liable under the obscure doctrine of "promissory estoppel," which in essence requires a party to keep a promise if the other party has relied on it and has suffered damage. Amicus briefs in support of Cowles Media were filed by, among many others, such behemoths as the New York Times Company and the Associated Press. The Supreme Court held that, because contract law was not targeted at the media, an action for promissory estoppel could proceed.

Justice WHITE delivered the opinion of the Court.

The question before us is whether the First Amendment prohibits a plaintiff from recovering damages, under state promissory estoppel law, for a newspaper's breach of a promise of confidentiality given to the plaintiff in exchange for information. We hold that it does not.

During the closing days of the 1982 Minnesota gubernatorial race, Dan Cohen, an active Republican associated with Wheelock Whitney's Independent-Republican gubernatorial campaign, approached reporters from the *St. Paul Pioneer Press Dispatch* (Pioneer Press) and the *Minneapolis Star and Tribune* (Star Tribune) and offered to provide documents relating to a candidate in the upcoming election. Cohen made clear to the reporters that he would provide the information only if he was given a promise of confidentiality. Reporters from both papers promised to keep Cohen's identity anonymous and Cohen turned over copies of two public court records concerning Marlene Johnson, the Democratic-Farmer-Labor candidate for Lieutenant Governor. The first record indicated that Johnson had been charged in 1969 with three counts of unlawful assembly, and the second that she had been convicted in 1970 of petit theft. Both newspapers interviewed Johnson for her explanation and one reporter tracked down the person who had found the records for Cohen. As it turned out, the unlawful assembly charges arose out of Johnson's participation in a protest of an alleged failure to hire minority workers on municipal construction projects, and the charges were eventually dismissed. The petit theft conviction was for leaving a store without paying for $6 worth of sewing materials. The incident apparently occurred at a time during which Johnson was emotionally distraught, and the conviction was later vacated.

After consultation and debate, the editorial staffs of the two newspapers independently decided to publish Cohen's name as part of their stories concerning Johnson. In their stories, both papers identified Cohen as the source of the court records, indicated his connection to the Whitney campaign, and included denials by Whitney campaign officials of any role in the matter. The same day the stories appeared, Cohen was fired by his employer.

Cohen sued respondents, the publishers of the *Pioneer Press* and *Star Tribune*, in Minnesota state court, alleging fraudulent misrepresentation and breach of contract. The trial court rejected respondents' argument that the First Amendment barred Cohen's lawsuit. A jury returned a verdict in Cohen's favor, awarding him $200,000 in compensatory damages and $500,000 in punitive damages. The Minnesota Court of Appeals, in a split decision, reversed the award of punitive damages after concluding that Cohen had failed to establish a fraud claim, the only claim which would support such an award. However, the court upheld the finding of liability for breach of contract and the $200,000 compensatory damages award.

A divided Minnesota Supreme Court reversed the compensatory damages award. After affirming the Court of Appeals' determination that Cohen had not established a claim for fraudulent misrepresentation, the court considered his breach-of-contract claim and concluded that "a contract cause of action is inappropriate for these particular circumstances." The court then went on to address the question whether Cohen could establish a cause of action under Minnesota law on a promissory estoppel theory. Apparently, a promissory estoppel theory was never tried to the jury, nor briefed nor argued by the parties; it first arose during oral argument in the Minnesota Supreme Court when one of the justices asked a question about equitable estoppel.

In addressing the promissory estoppel question, the court decided that the most problematic element in establishing such a cause of action here was whether injustice could be avoided only by enforcing the promise of confidentiality made to Cohen.... After a brief discussion, the court concluded that "in this case enforcement of the promise of confidentiality under a promissory estoppel theory would violate defendants' First Amendment rights."

We granted certiorari to consider the First Amendment implications of this case.

Respondents rely on the proposition that "if a newspaper lawfully obtains truthful information about a matter of public significance then state officials may not constitutionally punish publication of the information, absent a need to further a state interest of the highest order." . That proposition is unexceptionable, and it has been applied in various cases that have found insufficient the asserted state interests in preventing publication of truthful, lawfully obtained information.

This case, however, is not controlled by this line of cases but, rather, by the equally well-established line of decisions holding that generally applicable laws do not offend the First Amendment simply because their enforcement against the press has incidental effects on its ability to gather and report the news. As the cases relied on by respondents recognize, the truthful information sought to be published must have been lawfully acquired. The press may not with impunity break and enter an office or dwelling to gather news. Neither does the First Amendment relieve a newspaper reporter of the obligation shared by all citizens to respond to a grand jury subpoena and answer questions relevant to a criminal investigation, even though the reporter might be required to reveal a confidential source. *Branzburg v. Hayes.* The press, like others interested in publishing, may not publish copyrighted material without obeying the copyright laws. Similarly, the media must obey the National Labor Relations Act, and the Fair Labor Standards Act; may not restrain trade in violation of the antitrust laws and must pay non-discriminatory taxes. It is, therefore, beyond dispute that "[t]he publisher of a newspaper has no special immunity from the application of general laws. He has no special privilege to invade the rights and liberties of others." *Associated Press v. NLRB.* Accordingly, enforcement of such general laws against the press is not subject to stricter scrutiny than would be applied to enforcement against other persons or organizations.

There can be little doubt that the Minnesota doctrine of promissory estoppel is a law of general applicability. It does not target or single out the press. Rather, insofar as we are advised, the doctrine is generally applicable to the daily transactions of all the citizens of Minnesota. The First Amendment does not forbid its application to the press.

... Here ... Minnesota law simply requires those making promises to keep them. The parties themselves, as in this case, determine the scope of their legal obligations, and any restrictions that may be placed on the publication of truthful information are self-imposed.

Also, it is not at all clear that respondents obtained Cohen's name "lawfully" in this case, at least for purposes of publishing it.... The dissenting opinions suggest that the press should not be subject to any law, including copyright law for example, which in any fashion or to any degree limits or restricts the press' right to report truthful information. The First Amendment does not grant the press such limitless protection.

Nor is Cohen attempting to use a promissory estoppel cause of action to avoid the strict requirements for establishing a libel or defamation claim. As the Minnesota Supreme Court observed here, "Cohen could not sue for defamation because the information disclosed [his name] was true." Cohen is not seeking damages for injury to his reputation or his state of mind. He sought damages in excess of $50,000 for breach of a promise that caused him to lose his job and lowered his earning capacity. Thus, this is not a case like *Hustler Magazine, Inc. v. Falwell*, where we held that the constitutional libel standards apply to a claim alleging that the publication of a parody was a state-law tort of intentional infliction of emotional distress.

Respondents and *amici* argue that permitting Cohen to maintain a cause of action for promissory estoppel will inhibit truthful reporting because news organizations will have legal incentives not to disclose a confidential source's identity even when that person's identity is itself newsworthy. Justice SOUTER makes a similar argument. But if this is the case, it is no more than the incidental, and constitutionally insignificant, consequence of applying to the press a generally applicable law that requires those who make certain kinds of promises to keep them....

Justice BLACKMUN, with whom Justice MARSHALL and Justice SOUTER join, dissenting.

... The majority concludes that this case is not controlled by the decision in *Smith v. Daily Mail Publishing Co.* ... a State may not punish the publication of lawfully obtained, truthful information "absent a need to further a state interest of the highest order." Instead, we are told, the controlling precedent is "the equally well-established line of decisions holding that generally applicable laws do not offend the First Amendment simply because their enforcement against the press has incidental effects on its ability to gather and report the news." I disagree.

I do not read the decision of the Supreme Court of Minnesota to create any exception to, or immunity from, the laws of that State for members of the press. In my view, the court's decision is premised, not on the identity of the speaker, but on the speech itself. Thus, the court found it to be of "critical significance," that "the promise of anonymity arises in the classic First Amendment context of the quintessential public debate in our democratic society, namely, a political source involved in a political campaign." Necessarily, the First Amendment protection afforded respondents would be equally available to nonmedia defendants. The majority's admonition that "'[t]he publisher of a newspaper has no special immunity from the application of general laws,' and its reliance on the cases that support that principle, are therefore misplaced." . . .

Contrary to the majority, I regard our decision in *Hustler Magazine, Inc. v. Falwell*, to be precisely on point. There, we found that the use of a claim of intentional infliction of emotional distress to impose liability for the publication of a satirical critique violated the First Amendment. There was no doubt that Virginia's tort of intentional infliction of emotional distress was "a law of general applicability" unrelated to the suppression of speech. Nonetheless, a unanimous Court found that, when used to penalize the expression of opinion, the law was subject to the strictures of the First Amendment. . . . In so doing, we rejected the argument that Virginia's interest in protecting its citizens from emotional distress was sufficient to remove from First Amendment protection a "patently offensive" expression of opinion.

As in *Hustler*, the operation of Minnesota's doctrine of promissory estoppel in this case cannot be said to have a merely "incidental" burden on speech; the publication of important political speech *is* the claimed violation. Thus, as in *Hustler*, the law may not be enforced to punish the expression of truthful information or opinion. In the instant case, it is undisputed that the publication at issue was true. . . .

To the extent that truthful speech may ever be sanctioned consistent with the First Amendment, it must be in furtherance of a state interest "of the highest order." Because the Minnesota Supreme Court's opinion makes clear that the State's interest in enforcing its promissory estoppel doctrine in this case was far from compelling, I would affirm that court's decision.

I respectfully dissent.

Justice SOUTER, with whom Justice MARSHALL, Justice BLACKMUN, and Justice O'CONNOR join, dissenting.

I agree with Justice BLACKMUN that this case does not fall within the line of authority holding the press to laws of general applicability where commercial activities and relationships, not the content of publication, are at issue....

Nor can I accept the majority's position that we may dispense with balancing because the burden on publication is in a sense "self-imposed" by the newspaper's voluntary promise of confidentiality. This suggests...a conception of First Amendment rights as those of the speaker alone, with a value that may be measured without reference to the importance of the information to public discourse. But freedom of the press is ultimately founded on the value of enhancing such discourse for the sake of a citizenry better informed and thus more prudently self-governed....

The importance of this public interest is integral to the balance that should be struck in this case. There can be no doubt that the fact of Cohen's identity expanded the universe of information relevant to the choice faced by Minnesota voters in that State's 1982 gubernatorial election, the publication of which was thus of the sort quintessentially subject to strict First Amendment protection. The propriety of his leak to respondents could be taken to reflect on his character, which in turn could be taken to reflect on the character of the candidate who had retained him as an adviser. An election could turn on just such a factor; if it should, I am ready to assume that it would be to the greater public good, at least over the long run....

Because I believe the State's interest in enforcing a newspaper's promise of confidentiality insufficient to outweigh the interest in unfettered publication of the information revealed in this case, I respectfully dissent.

FREE SPEECH
ON THE INTERNET

Reno v. American Civil Liberties Union

Soon after Internet service became widely available, citizens, regulators, and media alike recognized that the new technology had the potential to give ordinary citizens a new role in determining dialogue and public debate. As might be expected, government officials found the wide-open new medium profoundly unsettling. In 1996 Congress passed the Communications Decency Act (CDA), which made it a crime to transmit or display material "harmful to minors" on the Internet without affirmative measures to ensure that no minors could see it.

A coalition of plaintiffs, represented by the American Civil Liberties Union, claimed that, by broadly criminalizing an entire class of nonobscene speech, the CDA violated their First Amendment rights to free speech. The government analogized its attempt to control the Internet to the broad regulation of sexual speech on the broadcast media. The Supreme Court agreed that the CDA was overbroad. After the decision in 1996, Congress attempted to limit sexually explicit Internet speech again with the Child Online Protection Act (COPA). The COPA limited its reach to an offense that seemed to draw approval from Justice O'Connor's concurrence: knowingly making sexually explicit communication and purposefully aiming it at minors. In 2004

---

521 U.S. 844 (1997).

the Supreme Court affirmed a temporary injunction against the COPA, on the narrow ground that the government had not shown that there were no less restrictive means (such as software filters) of protecting minors from exposure to sexual material on the Internet (*Ashcroft v. ACLU* [2004]). The Court has, however, approved a federal statute requiring public libraries that receive federal funds to use filtering software on all terminals available to the public (*United States v. American Library Ass'n* [2003]).

JUSTICE STEVENS delivered the opinion of the Court.

At issue is the constitutionality of two statutory provisions enacted to protect minors from "indecent" and "patently offensive" communications on the Internet. Notwithstanding the legitimacy and importance of the congressional goal of protecting children from harmful materials, we agree with the three-judge District Court that the statute abridges "the freedom of speech" protected by the First Amendment....

... [Two provisions in Title V of The Telecommunications Act of 1996, known as the "Communications Decency Act of 1996" (CDA) are being challenged in this case.] They are informally described as the "indecent transmission" provision and the "patently offensive display" provision. The first prohibits the knowing transmission of obscene or indecent messages to any recipient under 18 years of age.... The second provision prohibits the knowing sending or displaying of patently offensive messages in a manner that is available to a person under 18 years of age....

... [T]he Government contends that the CDA is plainly constitutional under three of our prior decisions: (1) *Ginsberg v. New York*; (2) *FCC v. Pacifica Foundation*; and (3) *Renton v. Playtime Theatres*. A close look at these cases, however, raises—rather than relieves—doubts concerning the constitutionality of the CDA.

In *Ginsberg*, we upheld the constitutionality of a New York statute that prohibited selling to minors under 17 years of age material that was considered obscene as to them even if not obscene as to adults.... [But] th[is] statute was narrower than the CDA [in four important ways]. First, we noted in *Ginsberg* that "the prohibition against sales to minors does not bar parents who so desire from purchasing the magazines for their children." Under the CDA, by contrast, neither the parents' consent—nor even their participation—in the communication would avoid the application of the statute. Second, the New York statute applied only to commercial transactions, whereas the CDA contains no such limitation. Third, the New York statute cabined its definition of material that is harmful to minors with the requirement that it be "utterly without redeeming social importance for minors." The CDA fails to provide us with any definition of the term "indecent" and, importantly, omits any requirement that the "patently offensive" material covered by § 223(d) lack serious literary, artistic, political, or scientific value. Fourth, the New York statute defined a minor as a person under the age of 17, whereas the CDA, in applying to all those under 18 years, includes an additional year of those nearest majority.

In *Pacifica*, we upheld a declaratory order of the Federal Communications Commission, holding that the broadcast of a recording of a 12-minute monologue entitled "Filthy Words" that had previously been delivered to a live audience "could have been the subject of administrative sanctions." ...

As with the New York statute at issue in *Ginsberg*, there are significant differences between the order upheld in *Pacifica* and the CDA. First, the order in *Pacifica*, issued by an agency that had been regulating radio stations for decades, targeted a specific broadcast that represented a rather dramatic departure from traditional program content in order to designate when— rather than whether—it would be permissible to air such a program in that particular medium. The CDA's broad categorical prohibitions are not limited to particular times and are not dependent on any evaluation by an agency familiar with the unique characteristics of the Internet. Second, unlike the CDA, the Commission's declaratory order was not punitive; we expressly refused to decide whether the indecent broadcast "would justify a criminal prosecution." Finally, the Commission's order applied to a medium which as a matter of history had "received the most limited First Amendment protection," in large part because warnings could not adequately protect the listener from unexpected program content. The Internet, however, has no comparable history. Moreover, the District Court found that the risk of encountering indecent material by accident is remote because a series of affirmative steps is required to access specific material.

In *Renton*, we upheld a zoning ordinance that kept adult movie theatres out of residential neighborhoods. The ordinance was aimed, not at the content of the films shown in the theaters, but rather at the "secondary effects"— such as crime and deteriorating property values—that these theaters fostered. ... According to the Government, the CDA is constitutional because it constitutes a sort of "cyberzoning" on the Internet. But the CDA applies broadly to the entire universe of cyberspace. And the purpose of the CDA is to protect children from the primary effects of "indecent" and "patently offensive" speech, rather than any "secondary" effect of such speech. Thus, the CDA is a content-based blanket restriction on speech, and, as such, cannot be "properly analyzed as a form of time, place, and manner regulation."

These precedents, then, surely do not require us to uphold the CDA and are fully consistent with the application of the most stringent review of its provisions.

... [S]ome of our cases have recognized special justifications for regulation of the broadcast media that are not applicable to other speakers, see *Red Lion Broadcasting Co. v. FCC*; *Pacifica*. In these cases, the Court relied on the history of extensive government regulation of the broadcast medium.

Those factors are not present in cyberspace. Neither before nor after the enactment of the CDA have the vast democratic forums of the Internet been subject to the type of government supervision and regulation that has attended the broadcast industry. Moreover, the Internet is not as "invasive" as radio or television. The District Court specifically found that "[c]ommunications over the Internet do not 'invade' an individual's home or appear on one's computer screen unbidden. Users seldom encounter content 'by [a]ccident.'" It also found that "almost all sexually explicit images are preceded by warnings as to the content[.]"...

Finally, unlike the conditions that prevailed when Congress first authorized regulation of the broadcast spectrum, the Internet can hardly be considered a "scarce" expressive commodity. It provides relatively unlimited, low-cost capacity for communication of all kinds.... [i]nclud[ing] not only traditional print and news services, but also audio, video, and still images, as well as interactive, real-time dialogue. Through the use of chat rooms, any person with a phone line can become a town crier with a voice that resonates farther than it could from any soapbox. Through the use of Web pages, mail exploders, and newsgroups, the same individual can become a pamphleteer. As the District Court found, "the content on the Internet is as diverse as human thought." We agree with its conclusion that our cases provide no basis for qualifying the level of First Amendment scrutiny that should be applied to this medium....

VI

The vagueness of the CDA is a matter of special concern for two reasons. First, the CDA is a content-based regulation of speech. The vagueness of such a regulation raises special First Amendment concerns because of its obvious chilling effect on free speech. Second, the CDA is a criminal statute. In addition to the opprobrium and stigma of a criminal conviction, the CDA threatens violators with penalties including up to two years in prison for each act of violation. The severity of criminal sanctions may well cause speakers to remain silent rather than communicate even arguably unlawful words, ideas, and images....

The government argues that the statute is no more vague than the obscenity standard this Court established in *Miller v. California*. But that is not so....Having struggled for some time to establish a definition of obscenity, we set forth in *Miller* the test for obscenity that controls to this day:

> (a) whether the average person, applying contemporary community standards would find that the work, taken as a whole, appeals to the prurient interest; (b) whether the work depicts or describes, in a patently offensive way, sexual conduct specifically defined by the applicable state law; and (c) whether the work, taken as a whole, lacks serious literary, artistic, political, or scientific value.

Because the CDA's "patently offensive"...standard is one part of the three-prong *Miller* test, the Government reasons, it cannot be unconstitutionally vague.

The Government's assertion is incorrect as a matter of fact. The second prong of the *Miller* test—the purportedly analogous standard—contains a critical requirement that is omitted from the CDA: that the proscribed material be "specifically defined by the applicable state law." This requirement reduces the vagueness inherent in the open-ended term "patently offensive" as used in the CDA. Moreover, the *Miller* definition is limited to "sexual conduct," whereas the CDA extends also to include (1) "excretory activities" as well as (2) "organs" of both a sexual and excretory nature.

In contrast to *Miller* and our other previous cases, the CDA thus presents a greater threat of censoring speech that, in fact, falls outside the statute's scope. Given the vague contours of the coverage of the statute, it unquestionably silences some speakers whose messages would be entitled to constitutional protection. That danger provides further reason for insisting that the statute not be overly broad. The CDA's burden on protected speech cannot be justified if it could be avoided by a more carefully drafted statute.

VII

... [T]he CDA lacks the precision that the First Amendment requires when a statute regulates the content of speech. In order to deny minors access to potentially harmful speech, the CDA effectively suppresses a large amount of speech that adults have a constitutional right to receive and to address to one another. That burden on adult speech is unacceptable if less restrictive alternatives would be at least as effective in achieving the legitimate purpose that the statute was enacted to serve....

It is true that we have repeatedly recognized the governmental interest in protecting children from harmful materials. But that interest does not justify an unnecessarily broad suppression of speech addressed to adults....

[In addition,] the mere fact that a statutory regulation of speech was enacted for the important purpose of protecting children from exposure to sexually explicit material does not foreclose inquiry into its validity....

In arguing that the CDA does not so diminish adult communication, the Government relies on the incorrect factual premise that prohibiting a transmission whenever it is known that one of its recipients is a minor would not interfere with adult-to-adult communication. The findings of the District Court make clear that this premise is untenable. Given the size of the potential audience for most messages, in the absence of a viable age verification process, the sender must be charged with knowing that one or more minors will likely view it....

The breadth of the CDA's coverage is wholly unprecedented.... [It] is not limited to commercial speech or commercial entities. Its open-ended prohibitions embrace all nonprofit entities and individuals posting indecent messages or displaying them on their own computers in the presence of minors. The general, undefined terms "indecent" and "patently offensive" cover large amounts of nonpornographic material with serious educational or other value. Moreover, the "community standards" criterion as applied to the Internet means that any communication available to a nation-wide audience will be judged by the standards of the community most likely to be offended by the message....

The breadth of this content-based restriction of speech imposes an especially heavy burden on the Government to explain why a less restrictive provision would not be as effective as the CDA. It has not done so. The arguments in this Court have referred to possible alternatives such as requiring that indecent material be "tagged" in a way that facilitates parental control of material coming into their homes, making exceptions for messages with artistic or educational value, providing some tolerance for parental choice, and regulating some portions of the Internet—such as commercial web sites—differently than others, such as chat rooms. Particularly in the light of the absence of any detailed findings by the Congress, or even hearings addressing the special problems of the CDA, we are persuaded that the CDA is not narrowly tailored if that requirement has any meaning at all....

We agree with the District Court's conclusion that the CDA places an unacceptably heavy burden on protected speech, and that the defenses do not constitute the sort of "narrow tailoring" that will save an otherwise patently invalid unconstitutional provision. In *FCC v. Sable Communications*, we remarked that the speech restriction at issue there amounted to "'burning the house to roast the pig.'" The CDA, casting a far darker shadow over free speech, threatens to torch a large segment of the Internet community....

XI

In this Court, though not in the District Court, the government asserts that—in addition to its interest in protecting children—its "[e]qually significant" interest in fostering the growth of the Internet provides an independent basis for upholding the constitutionality of the CDA. The government apparently assumes that the unregulated availability of "indecent" and "patently offensive" material on the Internet is driving countless citizens away from the medium because of the risk of exposing themselves or their children to harmful material.

We find this argument singularly unpersuasive. The dramatic expansion of this new marketplace of ideas contradicts the factual basis of this contention. The record demonstrates that the growth of the Internet has been and continues to be phenomenal. As a matter of constitutional tradition, in the absence of evidence to the contrary, we presume that governmental regulation of the content of speech is more likely to interfere with the free exchange of ideas than to encourage it. The interest in encouraging freedom of expression in a democratic society outweighs any theoretical but unproven benefit of censorship.

For the foregoing reasons, the judgment of the district court is affirmed.

JUSTICE O'CONNOR, with whom THE CHIEF JUSTICE joins, concurring in the judgment in part and dissenting in part.

I write separately to explain why I view the Communications Decency Act of 1996 (CDA) as little more than an attempt by Congress to create "adult zones" on the Internet....

The creation of "adult zones" is by no means a novel concept. States have long denied minors access to certain establishments frequented by adults. States have also denied minors access to speech deemed to be "harmful to minors." The Court has previously sustained such zoning laws, but only if they respect the First Amendment rights of adults and minors. That is to say, a zoning law is valid if (i) it does not unduly restrict adult access to the material; and (ii) minors have no First Amendment right to read or view the banned material. As applied to the Internet as it exists in 1997, the "display" provision and some applications of the "indecency transmission" and "specific person" provisions fail to adhere to the first of these limiting principles by restricting adults' access to protected materials in certain circumstances. Unlike the Court, however, I would invalidate the provisions only in those circumstances.

I

Our cases make clear that a "zoning" law is valid only if adults are still able to obtain the regulated speech....

... [T]he Court has previously only considered laws that operated in the physical world, a world that with two characteristics that make it possible to create "adult zones": geography and identity. A minor can see an adult dance show only if he enters an establishment that provides such entertainment. And should he attempt to do so, the minor will not be able to conceal completely his identity (or, consequently, his age). Thus, the twin characteristics of geography and identity enable the establishment's proprietor to prevent children from entering the establishment, but to let adults inside.

The electronic world is fundamentally different. Because it is no more than the interconnection of electronic pathways, cyberspace allows speakers and listeners to mask their identities....

[I]t is possible to construct barriers in cyberspace and use them to screen for identity, making cyberspace more like the physical world and, consequently, more amenable to zoning laws. This transformation of cyberspace is already underway. Internet speakers have begun to zone cyberspace itself through the use of "gateway" technology. Such technology requires Internet users to enter information about themselves—perhaps an adult identification number or a credit card number—before they can access certain areas of cyberspace, much like a bouncer checks a person's driver's license before admitting him to a nightclub. Internet users who access information have not attempted to zone cyberspace itself, but have tried to limit their own power to access information in cyberspace, much as a parent controls what her children watch on television by installing a lock box. This user-based zoning is accomplished through the use of screening software (such as Cyber Patrol or SurfWatch) or browsers with screening capabilities, both of which search addresses and text for keywords that are associated with "adult" sites and, if the user wishes, blocks access to such sites....

Despite this progress, the transformation of cyberspace is not complete. ...Gateway technology is not ubiquitous in cyberspace, and because without it "there is no means of age verification," cyberspace still remains largely unzoned—and unzoneable. User-based zoning is also in its infancy.

Although the prospects for the eventual zoning of the Internet appear promising,...[g]iven the present state of cyberspace, I agree with the Court that the "display" provision cannot pass muster. Until gateway technology is available throughout cyberspace, and it is not in 1997, a speaker cannot be reasonably assured that the speech he displays will reach only adults because it is impossible to confine speech to an "adult zone." Thus, the only way for a speaker to avoid liability under the CDA is to refrain completely from using indecent speech. But this forced silence impinges on the First Amendment right of adults to make and obtain this speech[.] ...

[However, t]he "indecency transmission" and "specific person" provisions present a closer issue, for they are not unconstitutional in all of their applications. As discussed above, the "indecency transmission" provision makes it a crime to transmit knowingly an indecent message to a person the sender knows is under 18 years of age.

So...both provisions are constitutional as applied to a conversation involving only an adult and one or more minors—e.g., when an adult speaker sends an e-mail knowing the addressee is a minor, or when an adult and minor converse by themselves or with other minors in a chat room. In this context, these provisions are no different from the law we sustained in *Ginsberg*. Restricting what the adult may say to the minors in no way restricts the adult's ability to communicate with other adults. He is not prevented from speaking indecently to other adults in a chat room and he remains free to send indecent e-mails to other adults....

II

Thus, the constitutionality of the CDA as a zoning law hinges on the extent to which it substantially interferes with the First Amendment rights of adults. Because the rights of adults are infringed only by the "display" provision and by the "indecency transmission" and "specific person" provisions as applied to communications involving more than one adult, I would invalidate the CDA only to that extent. Insofar as the "indecency transmission" and "specific person" provisions prohibit the use of indecent speech in communications between an adult and one or more minors, however, they can and should be sustained....

Part III

CONTEMPORARY THOUGHTS

"THE BILL OF RIGHTS"

Hugo L. Black

Former Supreme Court Justice Hugo Black's "Bill of Rights" outlines his view that the Bill of Rights provides absolute guarantees. Black argued that the Fourteenth Amendment "incorporated" all the guarantees of the first eight amendments to the Constitution and thus made them applicable to the states. In this he was opposed by justices like the younger John Marshall Harlan, who believed that the Due Process Clause of the Fourteenth Amendment imposed only the requirements on "ordered liberty" on the states.

One of the most brilliant of twentieth-century justices, Black was also one of the most controversial and colorful as well. Born in 1886 and raised in Alabama, he was elected to the United States Senate in 1926 and served until his appointment to the Court in 1937. Black was a strong progressive and supporter of the New Deal; immediately after his confirmation, news reports revealed that during his Alabama years he had been an active member of the Ku Klux Klan. Despite this clouded background, Black as a justice was respected for his legal acumen and his attention to civil liberties.

"The Bill of Rights" was written at the end of the McCarthy era. In the years immediately before, the US Supreme Court, using the "clear and present danger" test, had affirmed convictions against alleged communists.

New York University Law Review 35 (April 1960): 865–81. Reprinted with permission.

Notably, in the 1951 case of *Dennis v. United States*, the Court upheld a sentence against Communist Party members who allegedly taught and advocated the overthrow of the US government. Years later, Justice Black would explain that he believed there was "no place in the regime of the First Amendment for any 'clear and present danger' test."

In 1961, the year after "The Bill of Rights" was written, Justice Black wrote dissents in seven free speech cases, each decided 5-4. Most upheld judgments against people allegedly associated with the Communist Party.

This article has been edited to focus on his First Amendment discussion, in which he explains his famous "categorical" view of the Amendment's command that "Congress shall make no law ... abridging freedom of speech, or of the press."

... Madison lived in the stirring times between 1750 and 1836, during which the Colonies declared, fought for, and won their independence from England. They then set up a new national government dedicated to Liberty and Justice. Madison's role in creating that government was such a major one that he has since been generally referred to as the Father of our Constitution. He was a most influential member of the Philadelphia Convention that submitted the Constitution to the people of the states; he alone kept a comprehensive report of the daily proceedings of the Convention; he was an active member of the Virginia Convention that adopted the Constitution after a bitter fight; finally, as a member of the First Congress, he offered and sponsored through that body proposals that became the first ten amendments, generally thought of as our Bill of Rights. For these and many other reasons, Madison's words are an authentic source to help us understand the Constitution and its Bill of Rights. In the course of my discussion I shall have occasion to refer to some of the many things Madison said about the meaning of Constitution and the first ten amendments....

What is a bill of rights? In the popular sense it is any document setting forth the liberties of the people. I prefer to think of our Bill of Rights as including all provisions of the original Constitution and amendments that protect individual liberty by barring government from acting in a particular area or from acting except under certain prescribed procedures....

In applying the Bill of Rights to the federal government there is today a sharp difference of views as to how far its provisions should be held to limit the lawmaking power of Congress. How this difference is finally resolved will, in my judgment, have far-reaching consequences upon our liberties. I shall first summarize what those different views are.

Some people regard the prohibitions of the Constitution, even its most unequivocal commands, as mere admonitions which Congress need not always observe. This viewpoint finds many different verbal expressions. For example, it is sometimes said that Congress may abridge a constitutional right if there is a clear and present danger that the free exercise of the right will bring about a substantive evil that Congress has authority to prevent. Or it is said that a right may be abridged where its exercise would cause so much injury to the public that this injury would outweigh the injury to the individual who is deprived of the right. Again, it is sometimes said that the Bill of Rights' guarantees must "compete" for survival against general powers expressly granted to Congress and that the individual's right must, if outweighed by the public interest, be subordinated to the Government's competing interest in denying the right. All of these formulations . . . rest, at least in part, on the premise that there are no "absolute" prohibitions in the Constitution, and that all constitutional problems are questions of reasonableness, proximity, and degree. This view comes close to the English doctrine of legislative omnipotence, qualified only by the possibility of a judicial veto if the Supreme Court finds that a congressional choice between "competing" policies has no reasonable basis.

I cannot accept this approach to the Bill of Rights. It is my belief that there *are* "absolutes" in our Bill of Rights, and that they were put there on purpose by men who knew what words meant, and meant their prohibitions to be "absolutes." The whole history and background of the Constitution and Bill of Rights, as I understand it, belies the assumption or conclusion that our ultimate constitutional freedoms are no more than our English ancestors had when they came to this new land to get new freedoms. The historical and practical purposes of a Bill of Rights, the very use of a written constitution, indigenous to America, the language the Framers used, the kind of three-department government they took pains to set up, all point to the creation of a government which was denied all power to do some things under any and all circumstances, and all power to do other things except precisely in the manner prescribed. . . . I am primarily discussing here whether liberties *admittedly* covered by the Bill of Rights can nevertheless be abridged on the ground that a superior public interest justifies the abridgment. I think the Bill of Rights made its safeguards superior.

Today most Americans seem to have forgotten the ancient evils which forced their ancestors to flee to this new country and to form a government stripped of old powers used to oppress them. But the Americans who supported the Revolution and the adoption of our Constitution knew firsthand the dangers of tyrannical governments. They were familiar with the long existing practice of English persecutions of people wholly because of their religious or political beliefs. They knew that many accused of such offenses had stood, helpless to defend themselves, before biased legislators and judges. ... Unfortunately, our own colonial history also provided ample reasons for people to be afraid to vest too much power in the national government. There had been bills of attainder here; women had been convicted and sentenced to death as "witches"; Quakers, Baptists and various Protestant sects had been persecuted from time to time. Roger Williams left Massachusetts to breathe the free air of new Rhode Island, Catholics were barred from holding office in many places. Test oaths were required in some of the colonies to bar any but Christians from holding office. In New England Quakers suffered death for their faith. Baptists were sent to jail in Virginia for preaching, which caused Madison, while a very young man, to deplore what he called that "diabolical hell-conceived principle of persecution."

In the light of history, therefore, it is not surprising that when our Constitution was adopted without specific provisions to safeguard cherished individual rights from invasion by the legislative, as well as the executive and judicial departments of the national government, a loud and irresistible clamor went up throughout the country. These protests were so strong that the Constitution was ratified by the very narrowest of votes in some of the states. It has been said, and I think correctly, that had there been no general agreement that a supplementary Bill of Rights would be adopted as soon as possible after Congress met, the Constitution would not have been ratified. It seems clear that this widespread demand for a Bill of Rights was due to a common fear of political and religious persecution should the national legislative power be left unrestrained as it was in England.

The form of government which was ordained and established in 1789 contains certain unique features which reflected the Framers' fear of arbitrary government and which clearly indicate an intention absolutely to limit what Congress could do. The first of these features is that our Constitution is written in a single document. Such constitutions are familiar today and it is not always remembered that our country was the first to have one. Certainly

one purpose of a written constitution is to define and therefore more specifically limit government powers. An all-powerful government that can act as it
pleases wants no such constitution—unless to fool the people. England had no
written constitution and this once proved a source of tyranny, as our ancestors well knew. Jefferson said about this departure from the English type of
government: "Our peculiar security is in the possession of a written Constitution. Let us not make it a blank paper by construction."

A second unique feature of our Government is a Constitution supreme
over the legislature. In England, statutes, Magna Charta and later declarations
of rights had for centuries limited the power of the King, but they did not
limit the power of Parliament.... Parliament could change this English "Constitution"; Congress cannot change ours. Ours can only be changed by amendments ratified by three-fourths of the states. It was one of the great achievements of our Constitution that it ended legislative omnipotence here and
placed all departments and agencies of government under one supreme law.

A third feature of our Government expressly designed to limit its powers
was the division of authority into three coordinate branches none of which
was to have supremacy over the others. This separation of powers with the
checks and balances which each branch was given over the others was
designed to prevent any branch, including the legislative, from infringing
individual liberties safeguarded by the Constitution.

Finally, our Constitution was the first to provide a really independent
judiciary. Moreover, as the Supreme Court held in *Marbury v. Madison*...this
judiciary has the power to hold legislative enactments void that are repugnant
to the Constitution and the Bill of Rights. In this country the judiciary was
made independent because it has...the primary responsibility and duty of
giving force and effect to constitutional liberties and limitations upon the
executive and legislative branches. Judges in England were not always independent and they could not hold Parliamentary acts void. Consequently, English courts could not be counted on to protect the liberties of the people
against invasion by the Parliament....

All of the unique features of our Constitution show an underlying purpose to create a new kind of limited government. Central to all of the Framers
of the Bill of Rights was the idea that since government, particularly the
national government newly created, is a powerful institution, its officials—all
of them—must be compelled to exercise their powers within strictly defined
boundaries. As Madison told Congress, the Bill of Rights' limitations point

"sometimes against the abuse of the Executive power, sometimes against the Legislative, and in some cases against the community itself; or in other words, against the majority in favor of the minority." Madison also explained that his proposed amendments were intended "to limit and qualify the powers of Government, by excepting out of the grant of power those cases in which the Government ought not to act, or to act only in a particular mode."

This brings us to the First Amendment. It reads:

> Congress shall make no law respecting an establishment of religion, or pro-hibiting the free exercise thereof; or abridging the freedom of speech, or of the press; or the right of the people peaceably to assemble, and to petition the government for a redress of grievances.

The phrase "Congress shall make no law" is composed of plain words, easily understood. The Framers knew this. The language used by Madison in his proposal was different, but no less emphatic and unequivocal. That proposal is worth reading:

> ... The people shall not be deprived or abridged of their right to speak, to write, or to publish their sentiments; and the freedom of the press, as one of the great bulwarks of liberty, shall be inviolable....

Neither as offered nor as adopted is the language of this Amendment anything less than absolute. Madison was emphatic about this. He told the Congress that under it "The right of freedom of speech is secured; the liberty of the press is expressly declared to be *beyond the reach of this Government....*" (Emphasis added in all quotations.) Some years later Madison wrote that "it would seem scarcely possible to doubt that *no power whatever* over the press was supposed to be delegated by the Constitution, as it originally stood, and that the amendment was intended as a *positive and absolute reservation of it.*" ...

To my way of thinking, at least, the history and language of the Constitution and the Bill of Rights, which I have discussed with you, make it plain that one of the primary purposes of the Constitution with its amendments was to withdraw from the Government all power to act in certain areas— whatever the scope of those areas may be. If I am right in this then there is, at least in those areas, no justification whatever for "balancing" a particular right against some expressly granted power of Congress. If the Constitution with-draws from Government all power over subject matter in an area, such as religion, speech, press, assembly, and petition, there is nothing over which authority may be exerted.

The Framers were well aware that the individual rights they sought to protect might be easily nullified if subordinated to the general powers granted to Congress. One of the reasons for adoption of the Bill of Rights was to prevent just that. Specifically the people feared that the "necessary and proper" clause could be used to project the generally granted Congressional powers into the protected areas of individual rights.... In speaking of the "necessary and proper" clause and its possible effect on freedom of religion [Madison] said, as reported in the *Annals of Congress*:

> Whether the words are necessary or not, he did not mean to say, but they had been required by some of the State Conventions, who seemed to entertain an opinion that under the clause of the Constitution, which gave power to Congress to make all laws *necessary and proper* to carry into execution the Constitution, and the laws made under it, enabled them to make laws of such a nature as might infringe the rights of conscience, and establish a national religion; to prevent these effects he presumed the amendment was intended, and he thought it as well expressed as the nature of the language would admit.

It seems obvious to me that Congress, in exercising its general powers, is expressly forbidden to use means prohibited by the Bill of Rights. Whatever else the phrase "necessary and proper" may mean, it must be that Congress may only adopt such means to carry out its powers as are "proper," that is, not specifically prohibited.

It has also been argued that since freedom of speech, press, and religion in England were narrow freedoms at best, and since there were many English laws infringing those freedoms, our First Amendment should not be thought to bar similar infringements by Congress. Again one needs only to look to the debates in Congress over the First Amendment to find that the First Amendment cannot be treated as a mere codification of English law. Mr. Madison made a clear explanation to Congress that it was the purpose of the First Amendment to grant greater protection than England afforded its citizens. He said:

> In the declaration of rights which that country has established, the truth is, they have gone no farther than to raise a barrier against the power of the Crown; the power of the Legislature is left altogether indefinite. Although I know whenever the great rights, the trial by jury, freedom of the press, or lib-

erty of conscience, come in question in that body, the invasion of them is resisted by able advocates, yet their Magna Charta does not contain any one provision for the security of those rights, respecting which the people of America are most alarmed. The freedom of the press and rights of conscience, those choicest privileges of the people, are unguarded in the British Constitution.

But although the case may be widely different, and it may not be thought necessary to provide limits for the legislative power in that country, yet a different opinion prevails in the United States.

It was the desire to give the people of America greater protection against the powerful Federal Government than the English had had against their government that caused the Framers to put these freedoms of expression, again in the words of Madison, "beyond the reach of this Government."

When closely analyzed the idea that there can be no "absolute" constitutional guarantees in the Bill of Rights is frightening to contemplate even as to individual safeguards in the original Constitution. Take, for instance, the last clause in Article Six that "no religious test shall ever be required" for a person to hold office in the United States. Suppose Congress should find that some religious sect was dangerous because of its foreign affiliations. Such was the belief on which English test oaths rested for a long time and some of the states had test oaths on that assumption at the time, and after, our Constitution was adopted in 1789. Could Congress, or the Supreme Court, or both, put this precious privilege to be free from test oaths on scales, find it outweighed by some other public interest, and therefore make United States officials and employees swear they did not and never had belonged to or associated with a particular religious group suspected of disloyalty? Can Congress, in the name of overbalancing necessity, suspend habeas corpus in peacetime? Are there circumstances under which Congress could, after nothing more than a legislative bill of attainder, take away a man's life, liberty, or property? Hostility of the Framers toward bills of attainder was so great that they took the unusual step of barring such legislative punishments by the States as well as the Federal Government. They wanted to remove any possibility of such proceedings anywhere in this country. This is not strange in view of the fact that they were much closer than we are to the great Act of Attainder by the Irish Parliament, in 1688, which condemned between two and three thousand men, women, and children to exile or death without anything that even resembled a trial.

... The great danger of the judiciary balancing process is that in times of emergency and stress it gives Government the power to do what it thinks necessary to protect itself, regardless of the rights of individuals. If the need is great, the right of Government can always be said to outweigh the rights of the individual. If "balancing" is accepted as the test, it would be hard for any conscientious judge to hold otherwise in times of dire need. And laws adopted in times of dire need are often very hasty and oppressive laws, especially when, as often happens, they are carried over and accepted as normal. Furthermore, the balancing approach to basic individual liberties assumes to legislators and judges more power than either the Framers or I myself believe should be entrusted, without limitation, to any man or any group of men.

It seems to me that the "balancing" approach also disregards all of the unique features of our Constitution which I described earlier. In reality this approach returns us to the state of legislative supremacy which existed in England and which the Framers were so determined to change once and for all. On the one hand, it denies the judiciary its constitutional power to measure acts of Congress by the standards set down in the Bill of Rights. On the other hand, though apparently reducing judicial powers by saying that acts of Congress may be held unconstitutional only when they are found to have no rational legislative basis, this approach really gives the Court, along with Congress, a greater power, that of overriding the plain commands of the Bill of Rights on a finding of weighty public interest. In effect, it changes the direction of our form of government from a government of limited powers to a government in which Congress may do anything that Courts believe to be "reasonable."

Of course the decision to provide a constitutional safeguard for a particular right, such as the fair trial requirements of the Fifth and Sixth Amendments and the right of free speech protection of the First, involves a balancing of conflicting interests. Strict procedures may release guilty men; protecting speech and press may involve dangers to a particular government. I believe, however, that the Framers themselves did this balancing when they wrote the Constitution and the Bill of Rights. They appreciated the risks involved and they decided that certain rights should be guaranteed regardless of these risks. Courts have neither the right nor the power to review this original decision of the Framers and to attempt to make a different evaluation of the importance of the rights granted in the Constitution. Where conflicting values exist in the field of individual liberties protected by the Constitution, that document settles the conflict, and its policy should not be changed without constitutional amendments by the people in the manner provided by the people.

Misuse of government power, particularly in times of stress, has brought suffering to humanity in all ages about which we have authentic history. Some of the world's noblest and finest men have suffered ignominy and death for no crime—unless unorthodoxy is a crime. Even enlightened Athens had its victims such as Socrates. Because of the same kind of bigotry, Jesus, the great Dissenter, was put to death on a wooden cross. The flames of inquisitions all over the world have warned that men endowed with unlimited government power, even earnest men, consecrated to a cause, are dangerous.

For my own part, I believe that our Constitution, with its absolute guarantees of individual rights, is the best hope for the aspirations of freedom which men share everywhere. I cannot agree with those who think of the Bill of Rights as an eighteenth-century straitjacket, unsuited for this age. It is old but not all old things are bad. The evils it guards against are not only old, they are with us now, they exist today. Almost any morning you open your daily paper you can see where some person somewhere in the world is on trial or has just been convicted of supposed disloyalty to a new group controlling the government which has set out to purge its suspected enemies and all those who had dared to be against its successful march to power. Nearly always you see that these political heretics are being tried by military tribunals or some other summary and sure method for disposition of the accused. Now and then we even see the convicted victims as they march to their execution.

Experience all over the world has demonstrated, I fear, that the distance between stable, orderly government and one that has been taken over by force is not so great as we have assumed. Our own free system to live and progress has to have intelligent citizens, citizens who cannot only think and speak and write to influence people, but citizens who are free to do that without fear of governmental censorship or reprisal.

The provisions of the Bill of Rights that safeguard fair legal procedures came about largely to protect the weak and the oppressed from punishment by the strong and the powerful who wanted to stifle the voices of discontent raised in protest against oppression and injustice in public affairs. Nothing that I have read in the Congressional debates on the Bill of Rights indicates that there was any belief that the First Amendment contained any qualifications. The only arguments that tended to look in this direction at all were those that said "that all paper barriers against the power of the community are too weak to be worthy of attention." Suggestions were also made in and out of Congress that a Bill of Rights would be a futile gesture since there would be no way to enforce the safeguards for freedom it provided. Mr. Madison answered this argument in these words:

> If they [the Bill of Rights amendments] are incorporated into the Constitution, independent tribunals of justice will consider themselves in a peculiar manner the guardians of those rights; they will be an impenetrable bulwark against any assumption of power in the Legislative or Executive; they will be naturally led to resist every encroachment upon rights expressly stipulated for in the Constitution by the declaration of rights.

I fail to see how courts can escape this sacred trust.

Since the earliest days philosophers have dreamed of a country where the mind and spirit of man would be free; where there would be no limits to inquiry; where men would be free to explore the unknown and to challenge the most deeply rooted beliefs and principles. Our First Amendment was a bold effort to adopt this principle—to establish a country with no legal restrictions of any kind upon the subjects people could investigate, discuss and deny. The Framers knew, better perhaps than we do today, the risks they were taking. They knew that free speech might be the friend of change and revolution. But they also knew that it is always the deadliest enemy of tyranny. With this knowledge they still believed that the ultimate happiness and security of a nation lies in its ability to explore, to change, to grow and ceaselessly to adapt itself to new knowledge born of inquiry free from any kind of governmental control over the mind and spirit of man. Loyalty comes from love of good government, not fear of a bad one.

The First Amendment is truly the heart of the Bill of Rights. The Framers balanced its freedoms of religion, speech, press, assembly and petition against the needs of a powerful central government, and decided that in those freedoms lies this nation's only true security. They were not afraid for men to be free. We should not be. We should be as confident as Jefferson was when he said in his First Inaugural Address:

> If there be any among us who would wish to dissolve this Union or to change its republican form, let them stand undisturbed as monuments of the safety with which error of opinion may be tolerated where reason is left free to combat it.

FROM *TOWARD A GENERAL THEORY OF THE FIRST AMENDMENT*

Thomas Emerson

A 1931 graduate of Yale Law School, Thomas Emerson was a towering figure in civil liberties and free expression for nearly six decades. It's not too much to say that he virtually created First Amendment theory as an academic subject.

After distinguished stints in private practice and with various offices of the Roosevelt administration, Emerson at thirty-nine returned to Yale, where he would remain for over forty years. In 1966 Emerson published *Toward a General Theory of the First Amendment*, a preliminary version of *The System of Freedom of Expression*, his foundational work. In 1965 he served as co-counsel in *Griswold v. Connecticut*, in which the Supreme Court for the first time recognized a right of privacy within the contours of constitutional due process. He was awarded the American Civil Liberties Union's Medal of Liberty in 1983 for his lifetime of distinguished service, and remained involved in the struggle to uphold the Bill of Rights until his death in 1991.

B. General Principles of First Amendment Interpretation

We come back, then, to the original problem: the formulation of a workable legal doctrine which will take into account the basic factors underlying a sys-

Yale Law Journal 72, no. 5 (April 1963): 877–956. Reprinted with permission.

tem of freedom of expression and which will give effect to the fundamental decision embodied in the *First Amendment* for reconciling freedom of expression with other social values and objectives. Upon the basis of the previous analysis, the essential principles of such a doctrine can be stated as follows:

(1) The root purpose of the First Amendment was to assure an effective system of freedom of expression in a democratic society. Its adoption and its continued acceptance implies that some fundamental decisions with respect to reconciliation have been made, that a certain major balancing of interests has already been performed. These judgments, these prior balancings, are those which necessarily flow from the decision to put into operation a system of free expression, with all the values that such a system is intended to secure, in the realistic context of the actual functioning of society and its legal institutions. It follows from our earlier analysis that the judgments made, stated in the most fundamental and general terms, were that expression must be freely allowed and encouraged; that it may not be restricted either for the direct purpose of controlling it or as a method of obtaining other social objectives; and that the attainment of such other objectives is to be achieved through regulation of action....

(2) The function of the courts is not to reopen this prior balancing but to construct the specific legal doctrines which, within the framework of the basic decision made in adopting the First Amendment, will govern the concrete issues presented in fitting an effective system of freedom of expression into the broader structure of modern society. This problem may appropriately be formalized, as the absolutists do, in terms of defining the key elements in the *First Amendment*, "freedom of expression," "abridge," and "law." These definitions must be functional in character, derived from the basic considerations underlying a system of freedom of expression....

(3) The specific legal doctrines implementing the First Amendment must be framed in the light of the dynamics of a system of freedom of expression. It is not sufficient to formulate theory in the abstract, however refined. The rules must be workable in terms of the realities of maintaining a system in the everyday world. Thus the difficulty of framing precise regulations affecting expression, and the forces that tend to distort and overextend them, must be taken into account. The need of the individual to know with some assurance what his rights are, and of government officials to know with some certainty the limits of their power, require that the legal doctrine be constructed with this object as a major consideration. And the requirement of effective judicial

administration, especially as concerns the functioning of the Supreme Court, is a critical factor.

(4) Construction of a definition of "freedom of expression" centers around two major problems:

(a) The first task is to formulate in detail the distinction between "expression" and "action." As we have seen, the whole theory and practice of freedom of expression—the realization of any of the values it attempts to secure—rests upon this distinction.... The line in many situations is clear. But at many points it becomes obscure. Expression often takes place in a context of action, or is closely linked with it, or is equivalent in its impact. In these mixed cases it is necessary to decide, however artificial the distinction may appear to be, whether the conduct is to be classified as one or the other. This judgment must be guided by consideration of whether the conduct partakes of the essential qualities of expression or action. In the main this is a question of whether the harm attributable to the conduct is immediate and instantaneous, and whether it is irremediable except by punishing and thereby preventing the conduct. A second factor is also significant. This is whether the regulation of the conduct is, as a practical administrative matter, compatible with a workable system of free expression.... In formulating the distinction between expression and action there is thus a certain leeway in which the process of reconciling freedom of expression with other values and objectives can remain flexible. But the crucial point is that the focus of inquiry must be directed toward ascertaining what is expression, and therefore to be given the protection of expression, and what is action, and thus subject to regulation as such.

(b) The second task is to delineate those sectors of social activity which fall outside the area in which, under the basic theory, freedom of expression must be maintained. For reasons which will be elaborated later, these alien sectors include certain aspects of the operations of the military, of communication with foreign countries, and of the activities of children. The problem here is not only to ascertain the areas in which freedom of expression is not intended to operate, at least in its classic form, but to construct rules governing those situations where the area of free expression and the alien area interlock.

(5) Application of the term "abridge" is not difficult in many cases. But a problem arises in certain types of situations. The main ones are where a regulation is not a direct restriction of expression but is designed to accomplish another objective, and the impact upon expression is "secondary" or "indirect"; where the regulation is concerned not with reconciling freedom of

expression with another social objective but operates within the framework of the system itself by attempting to allocate means of communication or facilitate the working of the system; and where the government itself participates in expression. In these situations the formulation of legal doctrine involves construction of a workable definition of "abridge."

(6) The interpretation of the First Amendment in protecting the right of expression against abridgment by private (non-governmental) centers of power revolves around the definition of "law." This problem is essentially the same as that of defining the scope of "state action."

These principles are necessarily general in character....All that is suggested is that they furnish a method of approach which places the specific issues in a functional context, yet one within the capacity of judicial institutions to manage.

V. THE FORMULATION OF LEGAL DOCTRINE IN PARTICULAR AREAS OF FREEDOM OF EXPRESSION

We are now in a position to consider the formulation of specific legal doctrines applicable to the principal areas in which issues of freedom of expression arise in contemporary society....

The major areas fall into five categories: (1) freedom of belief; (2) possible conflict of the right of expression with the other individual interests; (3) possible conflict with other social interests; (4) regulation designed to facilitate the operation of the system; and (5) government participation in the process of expression....

B. RECONCILIATION WITH OTHER INDIVIDUAL INTERESTS

Where more than mere belief is involved, and an idea, opinion or statement is actually communicated to others, the possibility of conflict between freedom of expression and other interests becomes more acute. Here the problem of reconciliation may be more troublesome. It becomes necessary to examine separately the various types of interests at stake and the nature of the possible conflict, and to formulate for specific types of situations the legal doctrines which will best achieve the reconciliation within the basic principles embodied in the First Amendment.

At the outset a fundamental distinction must be made between interests that are individual or private in character, and interests that are social or public.... [T]he difference between a wrong to an individual and a wrong to the community has long been recognized in Anglo-American law. It has crucial significance in framing satisfactory principles to govern a system of freedom of expression.

Utilizing this concept, there are certain types of conflict between freedom of expression and interests that may be considered predominantly private in character. These may involve one or both of two elements. The first is where the injury to the individual is direct and peculiar to him, rather than one suffered in common with others and where society leaves the burden of protecting the interest to the individual himself, either by way of granting him a legal cause of action or by requiring him to raise the issue and support his claim. The second is where the interest is an intimate and personal one, embracing an area of privacy from which both the government and one's neighbors ought to be excluded.

Where conflicts of this nature are involved the problem of reconciliation takes on certain attributes not present where broader social or group interests are at stake. In the first place, the harm to the individual interest is more likely to be direct and immediate in its impact, and irremediable by resource to regulation of the subsequent conduct stimulated by the expression. For this reason communication injuring an individual interest is more readily classifiable as "action" than injury to the general social interest which is capable of protection by control of subsequent overt acts. In the second place, the government as umpire of the conflict can be more objective and impartial. Its function is to decide between two individuals, rather than under the pressures of competing social forces. Hence we need have less concern with the vagueness of the criteria for judgment, the subtlety of questions of proof, the creation of an atmosphere of partisanship or hysteria, or other possible abuses of the governmental process. Moreover, where the individual carries the burden of establishing his case, we face fewer administrative problems. It is likely there will be less resources marshaled to restrict freedom of expression; there is no risk of developing a dangerous apparatus of enforcement; the whole process of reconciliation through governmental action will be more loose, more relaxed, and more consistent with an atmosphere of freedom. Finally, when we are dealing with a question of personal privacy, we are in an area, like that of belief, where the interest involved should receive a paramount measure of protection.

In the light of these generalizations, we are in a position to examine specifically the major points at which freedom of expression may come into conflict with significant private interests.

1. Reputation

Of primary concern in the past has been the problem of reconciling the right to freedom of expression with the right to protection against unfair damage to reputation. A communication by one person may subject another to ridicule, hatred or contempt and thereby seriously injure him in the estimation of his fellows. The competing interest here is partly a material one; the communication may cause damage to business or professional standing or to other interests of property. But the interest is also a broader one, extending to all aspects of the personality. A member of a civilized society should have some measure of protection against unwarranted attack upon his honor, his dignity and his standing in the community.

Reconciliation of the interests at stake in this situation has been effected mainly through methods and doctrines embodied in the civil law of libel and slander. Legal action may be brought by the person injured against the offender to recover damages for statements which caused the injury; but in such a proceeding the truth of the statement made constitutes a defense....

... [M]ore difficult issues arise where the public interest becomes more directly involved, as where the person who considers his reputation impaired is a public official, a candidate for public office, or someone functioning in the public arena, such as a political commentator, an author, or one who otherwise addresses the public. If the damaging statement affects such a person purely in his private and personal capacity, the ordinary principles of libel and slander would obtain. On the other hand, if the alleged defamation relates essentially to the public performance of the person claimed to be injured, the issue is no different from the problem of criminal libel, discussed below. There remains, however, an intermediate category where the alleged defamation is mixed in character, pertaining to both private and public capacities. This occurs, for example, where the honesty of an official in connection with the discharge of his public duties is challenged. The best resolution of such a problem would appear to be through the development of a doctrine of fair comment. Under such a rule, the communication would be protected if it is based upon the facts, or what a reasonable man would accept as the facts, is fair, and is not malicious. This standard of fair comment, if rigorously pressed against unpopular defendants, could cut off much public discussion. Still it may be justified if employed only in private litigation and if the judiciary accepts its obligation to act as a firm defender of the First Amendment interest....

C. RECONCILIATION WITH OTHER SOCIAL INTERESTS

Most of the problems in defining the scope of freedom of expression under the First Amendment concern the reconciliation of that interest with social interests. These issues are vastly more difficult to resolve than those in the private sphere. In this area the state is generally cast less in the role of impartial umpire and more in the role of interested agent, to a considerable extent engaged in making a decision in its own cause. This is because the social interests which compete, or may appear in the short run to compete, with the interest in freedom of expression are ones the state machinery is specifically designed and organized to protect. Maintenance of the social interest in internal order, external security, and the protection of property interests constitutes the day-to-day job of the governmental apparatus. Protection of freedom of expression is more abstract, more remote, less insistent. Furthermore, advancement of the competing social interest is more likely to be the direct concern of the groups which influence and control the government machinery. And the problem of self-control may be even more difficult in a government bureaucracy than in an individual.

...And it must be remembered that the expression which needs protection is normally that which is the unorthodox, the hated and the feared. Most of the powerful pressures of the majority are likely to be ranged against the interest of free expression....

2. Preservation of Internal Order

Broadly speaking, the problem is that exercise of the right of expression may cause, or tend to cause, conduct which violates existing law. The resulting conduct or potential conduct may be violent or nonviolent in character. And it may arise because those to whom the expression is communicated may be persuaded toward unlawful conduct in support of the expression or in opposition to it. But the social interest in maintaining internal order is concerned only with the ensuing unlawful conduct. In this context the expression, in itself and apart from such conduct, is of no social harm. If the theory of freedom of expression means anything, therefore, it requires that social control be directed toward the subsequent action. Hence the appropriate legal doctrine must be derived from the distinction between "expression" and "action." ...

The basic decision made by the Framers that adequate protection can be afforded the interest in internal order through sanctions confined to the illegal action itself applies with even greater force to the problem in our times....

The problem of reconciling freedom of expression with internal order has arisen in two main types of situations. One is where the threat to order is local in nature and relatively isolated. This is the problem of maintaining order in meetings, parades, demonstrations and the like. The other is where the anticipated danger affects the country on the broader scale, arises out of organization activity, and may involve a whole movement. This problem is usually considered one of "national security."

Community attempts to deal with the local problem often give rise to the harder cases. The danger of internal disorder may be more immediate and the relationship of "expression" to "action" more direct. The appropriate response of the community, however, should lie in affording adequate police protection....

As to the broader problem of "national security," the doctrine of drawing the line between "expression" and "action" is even more clearly appropriate. The availability of other legislation protecting society against the use of anti-democratic methods makes such a distinction workable. The increased reliance upon an apparatus of secret police, informers, and other paraphernalia of ideological suppression; and the impact of suppression upon the society generally, render adherence to the basic principle more imperative....

3. Safeguarding External Security

Another major social interest, with which freedom of expression may sometimes be felt to conflict, is the interest of the society in external security. In a broad sense this social interest embraces all relations between the society and other societies or nations. Those aspects of the problem which relate to war and preparation for war, however, have been the subject of most controversy and will be considered first.

In attempting to formulate the legal doctrine by which the interest in freedom of expression must be reconciled with the social interest in carrying on a war or maintaining an effective defense, we start with the general principle already enunciated with respect to internal order—that expression must be protected and only other conduct prohibited. Full and open discussion of matters relating to war and defense are, if anything, more vital to the life of a democracy than in any other area. And the reasons for not attempting to draw a line cutting off expression at any point short of overt action are, generally speaking, equally persuasive in this sphere. Accepting this prior balance, it is clear that full freedom of expression must be allowed with respect to such matters as general opposition to a war, criticism of war or defense policies, and discussion of particular measures whether related to direct military or supporting action.

Nevertheless, in the sphere of war and defense an important factor originating outside the area of free expression must be recognized: military operations cannot be conducted strictly in accordance with democratic principles. A military organization is not constructed along democratic lines and military activity cannot be governed by democratic procedures. To a certain extent, at least, the military sector of a society must function outside the realm of democratic principles, including the principle of freedom of expression. This qualification is in turn qualified by the principle that in a democratic society the military must remain under the ultimate control of civilian authority. Yet at some point the nondemocratic nature of military operations must be recognized; the problem is to fit this sector of society into the basic democratic framework.

Some of the points where conduct in the military sphere falls outside the area of free expression are reasonably clear. Certainly, members of the armed forces, at least when operating in that capacity, can be restricted in their right to open discussion. Similarly, the social interest in external security would justify limitations on the disclosure of military operations in wartime, or certain other forms of military censorship; prohibitions against espionage or the disclosure of military secrets; restrictions on access to military installations; and punishment of direct efforts to create mutiny or insubordination in the armed forces. The problem is to draw the line at that point where the requirements of the military sector end and civilian principles again come into play....

4. Interests Sought to Be Protected by Restrictions on Obscene Publications

There is no clear agreement as to what social interests are sought to be protected by the laws restricting expression on grounds of obscenity. The main justifications advanced for such legislation, however, would seem to fall into the following categories: (1) that the expression has an adverse moral impact, apart from any effect upon overt behavior; (2) that the expression may stimulate or induce subsequent conduct in violation of law; (3) that the expression may produce adverse effects on personality and attitudes which in the long run lead to illegal behavior; (4) that the expression has a shock effect, of an emotionally disturbing nature; and (5) that the expression has especially adverse effects, of the sort described in the previous categories, upon children, who are intellectually and emotionally immature....

If one approaches the problem in the light of the considerations suggested here, it would appear that the first three justifications advanced for the obscenity laws are incompatible with the basic theory of freedom of expression as incorporated in the First Amendment. The fact that expression influences moral beliefs and attitudes, apart from any impact on behavior, is clearly no ground for restriction. Most expression is intended to and does have this result. Similarly, the argument that obscene expression stimulates or induces subsequent illegal conduct, even if true, falls before the fundamental proposition that society must deal with the illegal action directly and may not use restriction of expression as a means of control. Again, many forms of expression would have a similar effect in influencing subsequent conduct. Nor is there anything in the nature of illegal conduct induced by obscene expression which would differentiate it from any other illegal conduct or require application of a different rule. A fortiori, the fact that the expression influences attitudes which in the long run influence behavior is unacceptable as a basis of restriction. Strict adherence to the distinction between "expression" and "action" which underlies the whole theory of freedom of expression is even more important if one takes into consideration the conditions under which obscenity restrictions would operate. No one has yet conceived a formula for defining "obscenity" which can be applied with any precision, and the abuses of all systems of literary censorship are notorious. No general restriction on expression in terms of "obscenity" can, therefore, be reconciled with the First Amendment.

On the other hand, certain aspects of the "shock effect" of erotic expression present different considerations. Where a shock effect is produced by forcing an "obscene" communication upon a person contrary to his wishes, the issue is somewhat similar to that involved in private defamation. The harm is direct, immediate and not controllable by regulating subsequent action. The conduct can realistically be considered an "assault" on the other person, and hence placed within the category of "action." Issues of this sort arise, of course, only in limited situations, such as where the communication is displayed publicly on a billboard, or sent into a private home through the mail. Regulations can be devised to deal with this matter that do not create serious administrative problems....

Different factors come into play, also, where the interest at stake is the effect of erotic expression upon children. The world of children is not strictly part of the adult realm of free expression. The factor of immaturity, and perhaps other considerations, impose different rules. Without attempting here to formulate the principles relevant to freedom of expression for children, it suffices to say that regulations of communication addressed to them need not conform to the requirements of the First Amendment in the same way as those applicable to adults. Serious administrative difficulties arise, of course, in attempting to frame restrictions which affect only children, and do not impinge upon the rights of others. But to the extent that these practical problems can be solved, the First Amendment would not seem to preclude controls over erotic communication addressed to children....

6. Social Interests Sought to Be Protected by Measures Which Also Affect Freedom of Expression

The problems of reconciliation thus far discussed have involved governmental regulations explicitly directed at control of expression. But the expression may be curtailed also by measures which are directed, at least ostensibly, at other forms of activity, but which have a "secondary," "indirect" or "incidental" effect upon expression. Such measures include various types of tax and economic regulations, the imposition of political qualifications for obtaining government employment or other benefits or privileges, the activities of legislative investigating committees, and political restrictions on the rights of aliens. The fact that these forms of government action do not directly prohibit or regulate expression does not mean that they are of less significance in the functioning of a system of free expression....

(a) Taxation and Economic Regulation

Regular tax measures, economic regulations, social welfare legislation and similar provisions may, of course, have some effect upon freedom of expression when applied to persons or organizations engaged in various forms of communication. But where the burden is the same as that borne by others engaged in different forms of activity, the similar impact on expression seems clearly insufficient to constitute an "abridging" of freedom of expression. Hence a general corporate tax, wage and hour or collective bargaining legislation, factory laws and the like are as applicable to a corporation engaged in newspaper publishing as to other business organizations. On the other hand, the use of such measures as a sanction to diminish the volume of expression or control its content would clearly be as impermissible an "abridgment" as direct criminal prohibitions. The line may sometimes be difficult to draw, the more so as the scope of the regulation is narrowed.

Two principles for delineating the bounds of "abridging" may be stated. First, as a general proposition the validity of the measure may be tested by the rule that it must be equally applicable to a substantially larger group than that engaged in expression. Thus a special tax on the press alone, or a tax exemption available only to those with particular political views or associations, would not be permitted. Second, neither the substantive nor procedural provisions of the measure, even though framed in general terms, may place any substantial burden on expression because of their peculiar impact in that area. Thus the enforcement of a tax or corporate registration statute by requiring disclosure of membership in an association, where such disclosure would substantially impair freedom of expression, should be found to violate First Amendment protection....

D. GOVERNMENT ACTION DESIGNED TO FACILITATE OPERATION OF THE SYSTEM

A theory of freedom of expression must deal not only with the powers of the state to restrict the right of expression but also with the obligations of the state to protect it and, in some instances, to encourage it. To use the government itself—the traditional enemy of freedom of expression—as an instrument for promoting freedom of expression and eliminating obstacles to its proper functioning, calls for unprecedented imagination and discipline.

The problems arise in four major areas: (1) traffic controls; (2) purification of the democratic process; (3) protection of the free functioning of the system against undue interference from private (non-governmental) sources; and (4) affirmative measures which the government may take to increase the effective operation of the system by encouraging greater use and diversity of expression....

2. Purification of the Democratic Process

Problems of reconciliation have likewise arisen where the state seeks to impose restrictions upon expression designed to purify the democratic process by eliminating corruption, fraud, misrepresentation, appeals to hatred and similar forms of expression. The chief restrictions of this nature have been corrupt practices legislation, lobbying legislation, registration and disclosure requirements, and group libel laws. The purpose of such measures, at least in theory, is to promote the healthier and more efficient operation of a system of free expression. And the issue posed, again at least in theory, is not the reconciliation of freedom of expression with another kind of interest but the reconciliation of opposing interests within the system of free expression itself. Yet the problems are far more difficult than those arising in connection with the physical ordering of expression. Here the regulation often seeks to deal with the content of expression and, unless carefully circumscribed, is more likely to impair than promote open discussion....

4. Affirmative Measures to Increase the Effective Operation of the System

It is possible here only to point out certain areas in which the problem of governmental encouragement to freedom of expression has arisen, and to suggest tentatively some of the principles which may be applicable in guiding this development....

Development of the mass media of communication in this country raises the most pressing current questions as to the scope of government measures necessary or advisable for maintaining an effective system of free expression. The problem has been clear for some time. More and more control over communication is being centralized in the hands of a small group which owns and operates the mass media. As a result the communication reaching most members of the community conforms to a single pattern; other views are rarely or never heard. Instead of a system of open communication, in which all the facts and a diversity of opinion are available in the market place of ideas, our system approaches a closed one in which only a single point of view with minor variations, can find an outlet.

What can or should be done about this organization of our system of communication? Thus far government action has largely been confined to two areas. One is the use of the anti-trust laws as a deterrent to monopoly. Here no serious problem of principle is involved. Insofar as the anti-trust laws encourage diversity of control and variation in expression they clearly promote freedom of expression. Their impact being upon the majority or predominant views, they are scarcely a threat to minority or unpopular expression. In practice, of course, the anti-trust laws have had little effect upon prevailing trends and hence have not contributed much to the solution of the underlying problem.

The other area of governmental action has been the licensing of radio and television stations, made necessary by physical limitations upon the number of wave lengths. Exercise of this function necessarily involves the development of principles governing the choice of stations to be licensed, including principles relating to the measure of government control over the content of the program. But little progress has been made. The need is to formulate reasonably concrete standards, based upon the underlying principle of public service and diversity. Equally important, it is necessary to develop the institutions and techniques for applying the standard and supervising that application.

(3) A third set of questions concerns what has come to be called "the right to know"—the problem of secrecy in government. Here again the issue is clear. Successful operation of a democratic society, and particularly the functioning of a system of free expression, depends upon members of the society having access to the information necessary for making decisions. But more and more of this essential information is being withheld by the government for reasons of military secrecy, foreign policy, or simple face-saving. This is not an area where the courts, applying First Amendment doctrines, can be of much assistance. But the principle which should be followed by the legislature and executive is plain; the maximum amount of information should be disclosed. Implementation of the principle is difficult and little progress has been made in developing techniques for its realization in practice.

E. GOVERNMENT PARTICIPATION IN POLITICAL EXPRESSION

The function of government has never been confined to regulating the free play of expression by private individuals or groups. The government itself has always participated in the market place of ideas. With the growth of modern industrial society this activity of the government has become ever more pervasive and more significant.

Government activity in the field of expression takes many forms. It includes statements by public officials, publications of all kinds, and the operation of opinion-forming institutions, primarily the system of education. Few limitations have been imposed upon expression by the government, except its own self-restraint, and little thought has been given to the development of principles which should control its action in this field. At this point it is possible only to state certain broad generalizations....

Traditional doctrines of freedom of expression do not provide theories of limitation in these areas. But the need for addressing ourselves to these questions and endeavoring to frame the controlling principles is great.

VI. CONCLUSION

... [W]e may emphasize two of the major conclusions that emerge. One is that the essence of a system of freedom of expression lies in the distinction between expression and action. The whole theory rests upon the general proposition that expression must be free and unrestrained, that the state may not seek to achieve other social objectives through control of expression, and that the attainment of such objectives can and must be secured through regulation of action....

The other conclusion is that conditions in a modern democratic society demand that a deliberate, affirmative, and even aggressive effort be made to support the system of free expression. The natural balance of forces in society today tends to be weighted against individual expression. Only through a positive approach, in which law and judicial institutions play a leading role, can an effective system be maintained.

Our second task [is] to formulate a basic theory and specific legal doctrines which would take into account the underlying factors. Such a theory must start by accepting the prior judgment embodied in the First Amendment. The issue before the court cannot therefore be a de novo balancing of different social values and objectives involved in each case. Rather the issue must be framed in terms of ascertaining the area of expression which it is the purpose of the First Amendment to protect, the kind of governmental action which constitutes an infringement of that area, and the nature of ostensibly private action which nevertheless carries the imprint of government authority to such an extent that it, too, should be considered an exercise of state power. In more formal language these are questions of defining the key terms of the First Amendment: "freedom of expression," "abridge," and "law." The definitions sought must be functional in character, derived from a consideration of the basic elements which shape and determine an effective system of freedom of expression....

It is not to be expected that any reader will be wholly satisfied, or will agree with all of the resolutions proposed for the numerous areas of intense controversy.... But the hope is that they will furnish a rational and acceptable approach for giving significant meaning to the great and vital concept expressed by the First Amendment.

"NEUTRAL PRINCIPLES AND SOME FIRST AMENDMENT PROBLEMS"

Robert H. Bork

The seventh-most cited law review article in the history of American legal scholarship was written by then-Yale Law professor Robert Bork in 1971. In the article, Bork cited what he called inconsistencies of reasoning in decisions of the Warren Court. He used these examples to argue that without transparent "neutral principles" drawn from the Constitution to guide future Courts, the decision in any given case would be determined by the current justices' subjective values. After the publication of this article, Bork served as solicitor general under President Richard Nixon, eventually becoming interim attorney general when Nixon fired both the attorney general and his deputy during the so-called Saturday Night Massacre. Bork, the third-ranking official in the department, obeyed the order to fire Watergate special prosecutor Archibald Cox—an order the other two officials had refused.

While this article has long been hailed by adherents to the theory of "originalism" in constitutional interpretation, it provided ammunition for Bork's opponents after President Ronald Reagan nominated him for the Supreme Court in 1987. Among the decisions assailed in the article was *Griswold v. Connecticut*, the landmark decision that recognized a right of privacy in

Excerpt from Robert H. Bork, "Neutral Principles and Some First Amendment Problems," *Indiana Law Journal* 47 (1971). Reprinted with permission.

the Due Process Clauses of the Fifth and Fourteenth Amendments. *Griswold* held that Connecticut could not make it a criminal offense for married couples to use contraception in the privacy of their homes. Democrats argued that Bork's opposition to even this limited right of privacy suggested that Bork would reverse many of the major privacy, civil rights, and civil liberties decisions of the Warren and Burger Courts. This argument prevailed in the court of public opinion, and the full Senate rejected Bork's nomination.

After the Senate vote, Bork resigned his seat on the Court of Appeals for the District of Columbia Circuit and took up a career as a conservative polemicist. He has authored books such as *The Tempting of America: The Political Seduction of the Law* and *Slouching Toward Gomorrah: Modern Liberalism and American Decline*. In his speeches and writings, Bork has, among other causes, continued to argue for a broad governmental role in regulating and even censoring both print and electronic media.

A persistently disturbing aspect of constitutional law is its lack of theory.... [C]ourts are without effective criteria and, therefore we have come to expect that the nature of the Constitution will change, often quite dramatically, as the personnel of the Supreme Court changes.... [T]hat expectation is inevitable, but it is nevertheless deplorable.

The remarks that follow ... [are] an attempt to establish the necessity for theory and to take the argument of how constitutional doctrine should be evolved by courts a step or two farther....

THE SUPREME COURT AND THE DEMAND FOR PRINCIPLE

... [W]hen is authority legitimate? ... [This issue] arises when any court either exercises or declines to exercise the power to invalidate any act of another branch of government. The Supreme Court is a major power center, and we must ask when its power should be used and when it should be withheld.

Our starting place, inevitably, is Professor Herbert Wechsler's argument that the Court must not be merely a "naked power organ," which means that its decisions must be controlled by principle. "A principled decision," according to Wechsler, "is one that rests on reasons with respect to all the issues in a case, reasons that in their generality and their neutrality transcend any immediate result that is involved." ... Majority tyranny occurs if legislation invades the areas properly left to individual freedom. Minority tyranny occurs if the majority is prevented from ruling where its power is legitimate. Yet, quite obviously, neither the majority nor the minority can be trusted to define the freedom of the other. This dilemma is resolved in constitutional theory, and in popular understanding, by the Supreme Court's power to define both majority and minority freedom through the interpretation of the Constitution....

But this resolution of the dilemma imposes severe requirements upon the Court. For it follows that the Court's power is legitimate only if it has, and can demonstrate in reasoned opinions that it has, a valid theory, derived from the Constitution, of the respective spheres of majority and minority freedom. If it does not have such a theory but merely imposes its own value choices, or worse if it pretends to have a theory but actually follows its own predilections, the Court violates the postulates of the Madisonian model that alone justifies its power....

... [N]o argument that is both coherent and respectable can be made supporting a Supreme Court that "chooses fundamental values" because a Court that makes rather than implements value choices cannot be squared with the presuppositions of a democratic society.... [To illustrate the dangers of neglecting neutral principles, Bork mounted an extended attack on decisions of the Warren court which recognized the right to privacy. Bork's criticism was that those decisions were not built upon a historical or textual foundation in the constitution, but were instead based on an arbitrary value judgment from the Court. Bork asserted that the power to make such judgments belonged entirely to the majority-elected political branches of government, and that it was improper for the Court to resolve a political issue.] ...

We have been talking about neutrality in the *application* of principles. If judges are to avoid imposing their own values upon the rest of us, however, they must be neutral as well in the *definition* and the *derivation* of principles....

It follows, of course, that broad areas of constitutional law ought to be reformulated....

SOME FIRST AMENDMENT PROBLEMS: THE SEARCH FOR THEORY

The law has settled upon no tenable, internally consistent theory of the scope of the constitutional guarantee of free speech.... Constitutional protection should be accorded only to speech that is explicitly political. There is no basis for judicial intervention to protect any other form of expression.... Moreover, within that category of speech we ordinarily call political, there should be no constitutional obstruction to laws making criminal any speech that advocates forcible overthrow of the government or the violation of any law....

The First Amendment states: "Congress shall make no law...abridging the freedom of speech...." Those who take that as an absolute must be reading "speech" to mean any form of verbal communication and "freedom" to mean total absence of governmental restraint.

Any such reading is, of course, impossible.... Is Congress forbidden to prohibit incitement to mutiny aboard a naval vessel engaged in action against an enemy,...or to provide any rules for decorum in federal courtrooms? Are the states forbidden...to punish the shouting of obscenities in the streets?

No one, not the most obsessed absolutist, takes any such position.... Government cannot function if anyone can say anything anywhere at any time. And so we quickly come to the conclusion that lines must be drawn, differentiations made....

...We cannot solve our problems simply by reference to the text or to its history. But we are not without materials for building. The First Amendment indicates that there is something special about speech. We would know that much even without a First Amendment, for the entire structure of the Constitution creates a representative democracy, a form of government that would be meaningless without freedom to discuss government and its policies. Freedom for political speech could and should be inferred even if there were no First Amendment. Further guidance can be gained from the fact that we are looking for a theory fit for enforcement by judges. The principles we seek must, therefore, be neutral in all three meanings of the word: they must be neutrally derived, defined and applied....

...I wish to begin the general discussion of First Amendment theory with consideration of a passage from Justice Brandeis.... His *Whitney* concurrence was Brandeis' first attempt to articulate a comprehensive theory of the constitutional protection of speech, and in that attempt he laid down premises which seem to me correct. But those premises seem also to lead to conclusions which Justice Brandeis would have disowned....

Brandeis [asserted]...that there are four benefits to be derived from speech. These are:

1. The development of the faculties of the individual;
2. The happiness to be derived from engaging in the activity;
3. The provision of a safety valve for society; and,
4. The discovery and spread of political truth.

We may accept these claims as true and as satisfactorily inclusive. When we come to analyze these benefits, however, we discover that in terms of constitutional law they are very different things:

The first two benefits—development of individual faculties and the achievement of pleasure—are or may be found ... in all varieties of speech.... But ... these benefits do not distinguish speech from any other human activity. ... [T]he principled judge ... cannot, on neutral grounds, choose to protect speech that has only these functions more than he protects any other claimed freedom.

The third benefit of speech mentioned by Brandeis—its safety valve function—is different from the first two. It relates not to the gratification of the individual, ... but to the welfare of society. The safety valve function raises only issues of expediency or prudence, and, therefore, raises issues to be determined solely by the legislature or, in some cases, by the executive.... [T]hese decisions ... are indistinguishable from thousands of other managerial judgments governments must make daily.... It seems plain that decisions involving only judgments of expediency are for the political branches and not for the judiciary.

This leaves the fourth function of speech—the "discovery and spread of political truth." This function of speech ... is different from any other form of human activity. But the difference exists only with respect to one kind of speech: explicitly and predominantly political speech. This seems to me the only form of speech that a principled judge can prefer to other claimed freedoms....

Professor Alexander Meiklejohn seems correct when he says: "The First Amendment does not protect a 'freedom to speak.' It protects the freedom of those activities of thought and communication by which we 'govern.' It is concerned, not with a private right, but with a public power, a governmental responsibility." ...

[Professor Harry] Kalven ... states: "[t]he invitation to follow a dialectic progression from public official to government policy to public policy to matters in the public domain, like art, seems to me to be overwhelming." It is an invitation, I wish to suggest, the principled judge must decline.... I agree that there is an analogy between criticism of official behavior and the publication of a novel.... But it is an analogy, not an identity. Other human activities and experiences also form personality,...but no one would...suggest that the First Amendment strikes down regulations of economic activity, control of entry into a trade, laws about sexual behavior, marriage and the like. Yet these activities, in their capacity to create attitudes that ultimately impinge upon the political process, are more like literature and science than literature and science are like political speech.... [T]he protection of the First Amendment must be cut off when it reaches the outer limits of political speech.

Two types of problems may be supposed to arise with respect to this solution. The first is the difficulty of drawing a line between political and non-political speech. The second is that such a line will leave unprotected much speech that is essential to the life of a civilized community. Neither of these problems seems to me to raise crippling difficulties.

The category of protected speech should consist of speech concerned with governmental behavior, policy, or personnel, whether the governmental unit involved is executive, legislative, judicial, or administrative. Explicitly political speech is speech about how we are governed.... It does not cover scientific, educational, commercial or literary expressions as such. A novel may have impact upon attitudes that affect politics, but it would not for that reason receive judicial protection.... Moreover, any conduct may affect political attitudes as much as a novel, and we cannot view the First Amendment as a broad denial of the power of government to regulate conduct. The line drawn must, therefore, lie between the explicitly political and all else....

The other objection—that the political-nonpolitical distinction will leave much valuable speech without constitutional protection—is no more troublesome. The notion that all valuable types of speech must be protected by the First Amendment confuses the constitutionality of laws with their wisdom....

The practical effect of confining constitutional protection to political speech would probably go no further than to introduce regulation or prohibition of pornography. The Court would be freed of the stultifying obligation to apply its self-inflicted criteria....

[C]onstitutionally, art and pornography are on a par with industry and smoke pollution. As Professor Walter Berns says, "[A] thoughtful judge is likely to ask how an artistic judgment that is wholly idiosyncratic can be capable of supporting an objection to the law. The objection, 'I like it,' is sufficiently rebutted by '*we* don't.'" ...

The fourth function of speech, the one that defines and sets apart political speech, is the "discovery and spread of political truth." To understand what the Court should protect, therefore, we must define "political truth." There seem to me three possible meanings to that term:

1. An absolute set of truths that exist independently of Constitution or statute.
2. A set of values that are protected by constitutional provision from the reach of legislative majorities.
3. Within that area of life which the majority is permitted to govern in accordance with the Madisonian model of representative government, whatever result the majority reaches and maintains at the moment.

The judge can have nothing to do with any absolute set of truths existing independently and depending upon God or the nature of the universe. If a judge should claim...to possess a volume of the annotated natural law, we would, quite justifiably, suspect that the source of the revelation was really no more exalted than the judge's viscera. In our system there is no absolute set of truths to which the term "political truth" can refer.

Values protected by the Constitution are one type of political truth. They are, in fact, the highest type since they are placed beyond the reach of simple legislative majorities....

The third meaning of "political truth" extends the category of protected speech. Truth is what the majority thinks it is at any given moment.... "Political truth" in this sense...is what the majority decides it wants today. It may be something entirely different tomorrow....

Speech advocating forcible overthrow of the government contemplates a group less than a majority "seizing control"...when it cannot gain its ends through speech and political activity. Speech advocating violent overthrow is thus not "political speech" as that term must be defined by a Madisonian system of government.... Violent overthrow of government breaks the premises of our system..., yet those premises are the only reasons for protecting political speech. It follows that there is no constitutional reason to protect speech advocating forcible overthrow.

A similar analysis suggests that advocacy of law violation does not qualify as political speech any more than advocacy of forcible overthrow of the government. Advocacy of law violation is a call to set aside the results that political speech has produced.... There should, therefore, be no constitutional protection for any speech advocating the violation of law.

I believe these are the only results that can be reached by a neutral judge who takes his values from the Constitution....

Justice Sanford's opinions for the majorities in *Gitlow* and *Whitney* held essentially that the Court's function in speech cases was the limited but crucial one of determining whether the legislature had defined a category of forbidden speech which might constitutionally be suppressed. The category might be defined by the nature of the speech and need not be limited in other ways. If the category was defined in a permissible way and the defendant's speech or publication fell within the definition, the Court had, it would appear, no other issues to face in order to uphold the conviction.... [T]his would appear to be the correct conclusion....

Justice Holmes' dissent in *Gitlow* and Justice Brandeis' concurrence in *Whitney* insisted the Court must also find that, as Brandeis put it, the "speech would produce, or is intended to produce, a clear and imminent danger of some substantive evil which the state constitutionally may seek to prevent." Neither of them explained why the danger must be "clear and imminent" or, as Holmes had put it in *Schenck*, "clear and present" before a particular instance of speech could be punished. Neither of them made any attempt to answer Justice Sanford's argument on the point....

... The "clear and present danger" requirement, which has had a long and uneven career in our law, is improper not... because it provides a subjective and an inadequate safeguard against the regulation of speech, but rather because it erects a barrier to legislative rule where none should exist. The speech concerned has no political value within a republican system of government....

Modern law has followed the general line and the spirit of Brandeis and Holmes rather than of Sanford, and it has become increasingly severe in its limitation of legislative power. *Brandenburg v. Ohio*...struck down the Ohio criminal syndicalism statute because it punished advocacy of violence, the opinion stating:

> ... *Whitney* [the majority opinion] has been thoroughly discredited by later decisions.... These later decisions have fashioned the principle that the constitutional guarantees of free speech and free press do not permit a State to forbid or proscribe advocacy of the use of force or of law violation except where such advocacy is directed to inciting or producing imminent lawless action and is likely to incite or produce such action.

It is certainly true that Justice Sanford's position in *Whitney* and in *Gitlow* has been completely undercut, or rather abandoned, by later cases, but it is not true that his position has been discredited, or even met, on intellectual grounds. Justice Brandeis failed to accomplish that, and later Justices have not mounted a theoretical case comparable to Brandeis'.

...The Supreme Court's constitutional role appears to be justified only if the Court applies principles that are neutrally derived, defined and applied. And the requirement of neutrality in turn appears to indicate the results I have sketched here.

"OR OF THE PRESS"

Potter Stewart

Justice Potter Stewart served on the Supreme Court from 1958 until 1981, when he was succeeded by Justice Sandra Day O'Connor. A moderate by 1960s standards, Stewart is best remembered for his opinion in *Jacobellis v. Ohio*, in which he said of obscenity, "I know it when I see it."

A firm supporter of First Amendment rights, Justice Stewart argued that "[C]ensorship reflects a society's lack of confidence in itself. It is a hallmark of an authoritarian regime." Though he believed that the executive branch was justified in seeking to keep diplomatic and military information secret, he concurred in *New York Times v. United States*, which allowed the nation's newspapers to print the "Pentagon Papers." In November of 1974, shortly after the resignation of President Nixon, Stewart gave this address at the Yale Law School Sesquicentennial Convocation.

... It was less than a decade ago—during the Vietnam years—that the people of our country began to become aware of the twin phenomena on a national scale of so-called investigative reporting and an adversary press—that is, a press adversary to the Executive Branch of the Federal Government. And only in the two short years that culminated last summer in the resignation of

Yale Law Report 21, no. 2 (Winter 1974–75): 9–11. Reprinted with permission.

a President did we fully realize the enormous power that an investigative and adversary press can exert....

Surprisingly, despite the importance of newspapers in the political and social life of our country the Supreme Court has not until very recently been called upon to delineate their constitutional role in our structure of government.

Our history is filled with struggles over the rights and prerogatives of the press,... [B]ut none of this history made First Amendment law because the Court had earlier held that the Bill of Rights applied only against the Federal Government, not against the individual states.

With the passage of the Fourteenth Amendment, the constitutional framework was modified, and by the 1920's the Court had established that the protections of the First Amendment extend against all government—federal, state, and local.

The next fifty years witnessed a great outpouring of First Amendment litigation, all of which inspired books and articles beyond number. But, with few exceptions, neither these First Amendment cases nor their commentators squarely considered the Constitution's guarantee of a Free Press. Instead, the focus was on its guarantee of free speech. The Court's decisions dealt with the rights of isolated individuals, or of unpopular minority groups, to stand up against governmental power representing an angry or frightened majority. The cases that came to the Court during those years involved the rights of the soapbox orator, the nonconformist pamphleteer, the religious evangelist. The Court was seldom asked to define the rights and privileges, or the responsibilities, of the organized press.

In very recent years cases involving the established press finally have begun to reach the Supreme Court, and they have presented a variety of problems, sometimes arising in complicated factual settings....

It seems to me that the Court's approach to all these cases has uniformly reflected its understanding that the Free Press guarantee is, in essence, a *structural* provision of the Constitution. Most of the other provisions in the Bill of Rights protect specific liberties or specific rights or individuals: freedom of speech, freedom of worship, the right to counsel, the privilege against compulsory self-incrimination, to name a few. In contrast the Free Press Clause extends protection to an institution. The publishing business is, in short, the only organized private business that is given explicit constitutional protection.

The basic understanding is essential, I think, to avoid an elementary error of constitutional law. It is tempting to suggest that freedom of the press means only that newspaper publishers are guaranteed freedom of expression. They *are* guaranteed that freedom, to be sure, but so are we all, because of the Free Speech Clause. If the free press guarantee meant no more than freedom of expression, it would be a constitutional redundancy. Between 1776 and the drafting of our Constitution, many of the state constitutions contained clauses protecting freedom of the press while at the same time recognizing no general freedom of speech. By including both guarantees in the First Amendment, the Founders quite clearly recognized the distinction between the two.

It is also a mistake to suppose that the only purpose of the constitutional guarantee of a free press is to insure that a newspaper will serve as a neutral forum for debate, a "market place for ideas," a kind of Hyde Park corner for the community. A related theory sees the press as a neutral conduit of information between the people and their elected leaders. These theories, in my view, again give insufficient weight to the institutional autonomy of the press that it was the purpose of the Constitution to guarantee.

In setting up the three branches of the Federal Government, the Founders deliberately created an internally competitive system. As Mr. Justice Brandeis once wrote:

> The [Founders'] purpose was, not to avoid friction, but, by means of the inevitable friction incident to the distribution of the governmental powers among three departments, to save the people from autocracy.

The primary purpose of the constitutional guarantee of a free press was a similar one: to create a fourth institution outside the Government as an additional check on the three official branches. Consider the opening words of the Free Press Clause of the Massachusetts Constitution, drafted by John Adams:

> The liberty of the press is essential to the security of the state.

The relevant metaphor, I think, is the metaphor of the Fourth Estate. What Thomas Carlyle wrote about the British Government a century ago has a curiously contemporary ring:

> Burke said there were Three Estates in Parliament; but, in the Reporters' Gallery yonder, there sat a Fourth Estate more important far than they all. It is not a figure of speech or witty saying; it is a literal fact—very momentous to us in these times.

For centuries before our Revolution, the press in England had been licensed, censored, and bedeviled by prosecutions for seditious libel. The British Crown knew that a free press was not just a neutral vehicle for the balanced discussion of diverse ideas. Instead, the free press meant organized, expert scrutiny of government. The press was a conspiracy of the intellect, with the courage of numbers. This formidable check on official power was what the British Crown had feared—and what the American Founders decided to risk.

It is this constitutional understanding, I think, that provides the unifying principle underlying the Supreme Court's recent decisions dealing with the organized press.

Consider first the libel cases. Officials within the three governmental branches are, for all practical purposes, immune from libel and slander suits for statements that they make in the line of duty. This immunity, which has both constitutional and common law origins, aims to insure bold and vigorous prosecution of the public's business. The same basic reasoning applies to the press. By contrast, the Court has never suggested that the constitutional right of free *speech* gives an *individual* any immunity from liability for either libel or slander.

In the cases involving the newspaper reporters' claims that they had a constitutional privilege not to disclose their confidential news sources to a grand jury, the Court rejected the claims by a vote of five to four, or, considering Mr. Justice Powell's concurring opinion, perhaps by a vote of four and a half to four and a half. But if freedom of the press means simply freedom of speech for reporters, this question of a reporter's asserted right to withhold information would have answered itself. None of us—as individuals—has a "free speech" right to refuse to tell a grand jury the identity of someone who has given us information relevant to the grand jury's legitimate inquiry. Only if a reporter is a representative of a protected *institution* does the question become a different one. The members of the Court disagreed in answering the question, but the question did not answer itself.

The cases involving the so-called "right of access" to the press raised the issue whether the First Amendment allows government, or indeed *requires* government, to regulate the press so as to make it a genuinely fair and open "market place for ideas." The Court's answer was "no" to both questions. If a newspaper wants to serve as a neutral market place for debate, that is an objective which it is free to choose. And, within limits, that choice is probably necessary to commercially successful journalism. But it is a choice that government cannot constitutionally impose.

Finally the Pentagon Papers case involved the line between secrecy and openness in the affairs of government. The question, or at least one question, was whether the line is drawn by the Constitution itself. The Justice Department asked the Court to find in the Constitution a basis for prohibiting the publication of allegedly stolen government documents. The Court could find no such prohibition. So far as the Constitution goes, the autonomous press may publish what it knows, and may seek to learn what it can.

But this autonomy cuts both ways. The press is free to do battle against secrecy and deception in government. But the press cannot expect from the Constitution any guarantee that it will succeed. There is no constitutional right to have access to particular government information, or to require openness from the bureaucracy....

The Constitution, in other words, establishes the contest, not its resolution. Congress may provide a resolution, at least in some instances, through carefully drawn legislation. For the rest, we must rely, as so often in our system we must, on the tug and pull of the political forces in American society.

Newspapers, television networks, and magazines have sometimes been outrageously abusive, untruthful, arrogant, and hypocritical. But it hardly follows that elimination of a strong and independent press is the way to eliminate abusiveness, untruth, arrogance, or hypocrisy from government itself....

...Perhaps our liberties might survive without an independent established press. But the Founders doubted it, and, in the year 1974, I think we can all be thankful for their doubts.

"THE MEDIA THAT CITIZENS NEED"

C. Edwin Baker

C. Edwin Baker is Nicholas F. Gallicchio Professor of Law and professor of communication at the University of Pennsylvania and an indefatigable scholar of all aspects of the First Amendment. In "The Media That Citizens Need," Baker examines the appropriate role of the Press Clause in contemporary democratic society. He determines that the role of government regulation of media will depend upon the specific theory of democracy that legislators and courts follow, across a spectrum ranging from "elite democracy," which tends to regard formal legal guarantees and a free market as sufficient conditions for democratic self-government, to "complex democracy," which envisions a multivocal society in which some media institutions work to mobilize popular opinion while others serve to inform it and to provide a common space in which citizens in essence agree on the facts and the nature of the issues confronting society. He provides concrete examples of how the different conceptions compel different results in some of the important Press Clause cases reprinted elsewhere in this volume and concludes that an optimal theory of democracy would allow government a role in ensuring that the structure of news media is not skewed in favor of those forces most successful in the market.

University of Pennsylvania Law Review 147 (1998): 317–408. Reprinted with permission.

Democracy is impossible without a free press. At least courts and commentators tell us so. This consensus, however, floats above crucial, more controversial matters. What type of free press does democracy need and why does democracy need it? Answers to these questions allow the next question. Are existing media in this country adequate? Do they provide for the informational or communication needs of democracy? And if not, in what way do they fail, and what can be done? If there are inadequacies, do they reflect bad decisions made by media professionals, such that the prime need is for better, smarter, tougher editors and reporters or better training in journalism schools? Or do inadequacies reflect, at least in part, deeper structural problems? And if governmental policy correctives are necessary to make matters better, what interventions would promote a more "democratic press"—that is, a press that properly serves a society committed to democracy?

These questions implicate central issues of First Amendment theory. Agreement on two abstractions—that democracy requires a free press and that the First Amendment protects a free press—is relatively easy. But what constitutes "freedom of the press"? That question cannot be answered without understanding the role or purpose of the constitutional guarantee. If the Press Clause is a structural provision designed either to support or to protect a press that adequately serves democracy, how does this premise affect the interpretation of the Press Clause? . . .

IV. CONSTITUTIONAL IMPLICATIONS

Different theories of democracy not only recommend different normative visions of the press but also may lead to different interpretations of the Press Clause. Still, possibly the most important implications of complex democracy, my preferred democratic theory, may appear modest. . . . Here, I wish to explore those implications and consider why they are so limited. . . .

As for the Press Clause, interpretations depend heavily on answers given to two questions. First is the question of the purpose of the Press Clause. I will assume that the constitutional order protects the press because of its crucial contribution to democracy and democratic legitimacy. Freedom of "speech" might be protected as a vital element of individual liberty. The reference to the "press," however, presumably refers to institutionalized structures or legal entities. A discriminatory tax on a newspaper business, for example, raises a constitutional issue even if the law does not specifically tax or target any specific printed "speech." Moreover, unlike individuals, institutions must find their value in their social contribution. The only obvious reason to think that the press merits special protection from democratic processes is to provide for its role in that democratic arrangement. Thus, in order to know what specifically to protect, the interpretation of the Press Clause must, at least implicitly, embody some theory of democracy....

Second is the question of the democratic adequacy of the market. Can the market (and centers of private power) be trusted to provide us with the press that democracy requires or, instead, should the market be expected to fail to perform (or even at times to undermine proper performance of) the tasks assigned by (the favored) democratic theory? If a sufficiently favorable view of the market is justified, prohibiting all media-oriented governmental interventions might best serve democracy. Even a less favorable evaluation of the market might not imply that private power would undermine the press's crucial democratic tasks....

Persuasive critiques of the market's unfortunate effects on the media are legion.... Critics sometimes emphasize an individual owner's or the ownership class's manipulative and ideological control. More often, critics point to predictable distortions resulting from the normal functioning of economic markets. Sometimes it is unclear which is the problem. Did [Rupert] Murdoch cancel the publication of a book on Hong Kong by the conservative Chris Patten for personal or political reasons? Murdoch says it was not commercially motivated. Or, like his 1994 decision to take the BBC off the Chinese broadcasts of his satellite television service, was this a profit-maximizing decision based on not offending the Chinese leadership on which his media expansions in China depended? If the cancellation was a profit-maximizing decision, it is little different than the bottom-line mentality that leads corporate newspapers to eliminate five percent of the newsroom jobs in six years....

Market forces could conceivably cripple the press's performance of the checking function. Competitive, profit-oriented pressures could lead media entities to abandon expensive, investigative journalism and replace it with cheaper, routine beat reporting, or even cheaper "press-release" or wire service journalism. The market could tilt journalism towards stories that are the easiest (that is, the cheapest) to uncover and, even more troubling, the easiest to explain or the most titillating. An effective watchdog would have reported early on about the massive savings and loan scandal, which predictably resulted from deregulation of these financial institutions. The media, however, found that early reporting was simply too difficult or boring.

Nevertheless, the watchdog role is arguably the democratic function least likely to require or benefit from government support. It is arguably best guaranteed by a sense of professionalism that exists among journalists. The watchdog role requires mostly skill, courage, and freedom. Exposés generally make good, profitable news. News entities will have an incentive to devote at least some resources to performing this role. Arguably, there is little that the government could do to add to either the press's willingness or its ability to perform this role.

Not only is intervention needed least, it can be very dangerous. Arguably, the watchdog role is the democratic function most subject to inappropriate, censorious, or "chilling" interventions. The government can unintentionally undermine the capacity for performance by, for example, requiring testimony that identifies a reporter's publicity-shy informants. The watchdog role may be even more vulnerable to purposeful attack. The government can attempt to block performance, as it tried to do by seeking an injunction against publication of the Pentagon Papers. Censorial manipulation of privileges [is] probably more dangerous because [it is] less easily combated. Consider a local government's withdrawal of advertising from a critical newspaper, or the Nixon administration's plans to obstruct a broadcast license renewal after the *Washington Post* exposed alleged Watergate-related misconduct. Government leaders can also attempt to "discipline" reporters by means such as denying them prized interviews, and lower level officials exercise similar power by picking recipients of leaks and background information.

As the history of totalitarian regimes illustrates, the watchdog role is the democratic function with which government leaders have the most overt, systemic, self-interested inclination to undermine. A corrupt or incompetent administration or individual governmental leader has little interest in exposure. In contrast, although they vary in their views of republican issue discussion, pluralist bargaining, or social groups' self-development, they seldom perceive any of these as an overt threat to their status. Of course, even media provision of this content is not safe. Any political group may wish to suppress oppositional media. Suppression could help a dominant political group to retain power or to improve its position in pluralist bargaining. It could also reflect the group's ideological objections to outsiders' values. Still, the watchdog role is most overtly and directly in tension with incumbents' interests, and thus might most require protection. If political branches must be watched, wisdom counsels against granting them power to control the watchdog.

Anyone with confidence in the market's benign effects—and many with less confidence but with a healthy fear of government abuse—will view government intervention as *the* major danger to the performance of the checking function. This suggests sharply limiting governmental authority. A wall of virtually total separation between the government and the press may seem desirable. Thus, elite democrats often interpret the Press Clause to prohibit or strongly disfavor any media-specific regulation, even structural regulation. This partly reflects treating the watchdog role as the press's only really important democratic function. In addition, I suspect that as an empirical matter, many elite democrats, as compared to more participatory democrats, have greater confidence in the market, as well as comparatively greater worries about government.

Participatory democratic theories all place more comprehensive demands on the press. For these more extensive purposes, faith in the market, although still possible, quickly seems naive. As noted, there are overwhelming reasons to predict that markets will fail to provide the media that people want. Markets are even less likely to provide the media that participatory theories identify citizens as needing. Depending on the theory, these needs may include more educational, societal discourse-oriented, advocacy-oriented, mobilizing, or group-constitutive media than people would fully support through their purchases in the market....

Participatory theorists, however, seldom interpret the Constitution as itself mandating the needed interventions. Doctrinally, inadequate press performance is not normally seen as "state action." Although one could see failure of the government to act (or its property and licensing laws that empower some but not other private actors) as the objectionable state action, various considerations counsel against easy reliance on this interpretative strategy. Constitutional adjudication is poorly designed for crafting appropriate structural rules and media subsidies. Participatory theorists can more reasonably argue that the Constitution does not block discretionary legislative authority to intervene with subsidies and noncensorious structural rules— even content-motivated or content-based structural rules—aimed at supporting the press's performance of its democratic roles. This conclusion may be the central constitutional implication of these democratic theories. The conclusion, however, is mostly a nonmandate—restricting the constitutional reach of the Press Clause. Thus, in order to allow needed and appropriate governmental interventions, participatory democratic theories recommend interpreting the Press Clause much more narrowly (in this context) than elitist democratic theory suggests.

Of course, participatory theories do not ignore the press's performance of the checking function. To allow for interventions and to protect against censorious restraints, constitutional doctrine should block government action that has a censorious purpose as either its end or means. In addition, to be consistent with checking function concerns, these theories should favor invalidating government actions that undermine the integrity of the press as an institution, or that burden media entities without a convincing benign explanation.

Thus, my initial claim is that markets and private power are much more likely to frustrate the more ambitious democratic assignments called for by participatory theories than they are to undermine performance of the checking function. If so, the preferred interpretation of the Press Clause would shift depending on the democratic theory adopted....

This analysis, however, moves too quickly. Consideration of several additional issues suggests that different participatory theories may support somewhat different constitutional interpretations.

Can the government provide people other than owners a right to publish in, or broadcast over, privately owned media, especially as to media that are monopolistic or at least limited in number within most communities? Should it do so? Must it? The issue of nonmedia, private speakers' right of access has been controversial. From the perspective of elite democracy, such a right may have little significance. Public access is unlikely to be simultaneously accurate, effective, and necessary for exposing wrongdoing. In cases where the report would be accurate and effective, media entities are likely to make the report on their own if given the information by the group seeking access. The elitist could conclude that the main effect of such laws is to undermine the integrity of the professional watchdog—"editing is what editors are for." Thus, legislation creating such a right should be unconstitutional.

Access rights are even worse from the perspective of the liberal pluralist. These rights can threaten media entities' capacity for partisan mobilization. Balance is a centrist ideology. Except for occasional strategic or rhetorical purposes, it is often the last thing that a mobilizing media needs. A militant black newspaper should not be required to carry the Klan's rebuttal—or vice versa. Thus, the pluralist should join the elite democrat in praising the decision to strike down a law that provides candidates a right to reply to criticism by newspapers.

In contrast, republican democrats most fear lack of inclusiveness (and, maybe, lack of civility). Mandated balance and well-crafted access rights could further inclusive dialogue, which is helpful to a society that needs to reason together about potentially common conceptions of the good. Going beyond support for the fairness doctrine, republicans might even strain to find state action in broadcasting, and then find a station's refusal to accept public issue or editorial advertising to be unconstitutional. Their only worry is whether a lack of editorial management will cause unmoderated dialogue to become too unfocused or unbalanced.

Complex democrats should find merit in the opposing views of both the pluralists and the republicans. Society needs partisan media that are constitutive of groups and that promote group mobilization—and rights of access can undermine such media. Society, however, also needs inclusive collective discourses, a need served by access rights. What society needs most is an empirical question. No abstract answer or even analytic metric on which to base constitutional mandates is available. Hence, the complex democrat should incline toward upholding rights of access created by legislation, especially legislation that leaves some media unaffected, but not incline toward imposing the rights constitutionally.... [T]he complex democrat might favor something like a balance or diversity requirement in legislatively identified core media, which perform a societywide discourse role, but not in media serving pluralist groups.

Thus, on first impression, both the elite democrat and the pluralist democrat, although for different reasons, are likely to oppose mandated access. They would agree with *Miami Herald*...but not *Red Lion.* In contrast, the republican democrat would favor mandated access.... To modify the earlier matrix, and assuming at least some skepticism about the market, this suggests the following formulation:

TENTATIVE FORMULATION

Theories of Democracy	Press Clause Interpretation
Elite Democracy	Hands-off
Pluralist Democracy	Prohibit access rights; allow structural regulations that promote partisan media

Republican Democracy	Allow or mandate access rights; disfavor laws that promote more partisan media
Complex Democracy	Allow, but not mandate, access rights and legislation that promotes partisan media or that makes some media more inclusive
All Democratic Theories	Rule out censorship and legislation or practices aimed at suppressing media

Although this analysis is more fine-grained and precise, it still oversimplifies. The analysis ignores both factual contexts and attitudes towards the judicial role. For example, the Court in *Miami Herald* reasoned that the "choice of material to go into a newspaper ... constitute[s] the exercise of editorial control and judgment," and that the First Amendment does not tolerate "intrusion into the function of editors." The liberal pluralist could approve of the premise, but the republican might reject it. However, the premise that the First Amendment does not allow an intrusion into editorial control was only one of two rationales for the decision. The Court also objected to the fact that the law made access turn on the paper's earlier criticism of the candidate. The Florida statute "exact[ed] a penalty on the basis of the content of the newspaper," which could result in "blunted or reduced" coverage. This deterrence operates like censorship. Recently, the Court faced the argument that *Miami Herald* required invalidating rules which compelled cable systems to carry content (local broadcast stations) that they would prefer to reject. Since these must-carry rules applied regardless of whatever other speech the cable system provided, the Court found that the rules could not have the deterrent effect that was fatal in *Miami Herald*. The intrusion into the "editorial" role apparently did not matter. This sheds a different light on *Miami Herald*. If convinced of the empirical basis of its penalty/deterrence rationale, and this is a big "if," supporters of all theories of democracy should accept the decision....

The liberal pluralist and complex democrat's response rings hollow in at least three situations: first, if the specific media at issue are, and predictably will continue to be, monopolistic within their community; second, if advertisers or other commercial interests effectively impose a nonpartisan, audience-maximizing orientation on these media so that any realistic hope or expectation that these media will become partisan advocates is naive; and third, if legal regulations, such as the fairness doctrine, already preclude this pure partisan role. Under each scenario, the pluralist can conclude that the access right best empowers diverse groups to pursue their aims. The complex democrat can conclude that since these conditions have already made these media entities part of the societywide discourse, they should perform this role as inclusively (and as intelligently) as possible. Thus, given plausible empirical observations, all three participatory democratic theories can accept [Justices] Brennan and Marshall's conclusion that issue-oriented speakers' constitutional rights of nondiscriminatory access should be recognized.

On the other hand, a liberal pluralist or complex democrat judge might demur. Doctrinally, Brennan and Marshall must identify state action—the asserted absence of which is the determinative factor for several Justices. Even given state action, the judge might refuse to create intricate positive rights based on arguable empirical premises. This refusal might reflect less her theory of democracy or her appraisal of the market than her view of the judicial role—a rejection of a type of judicial activism. As these complexities illustrate, even though different democratic theories lead to different programmatic objectives in interpreting the Press Clause, democratic theory will not by itself determine doctrine or specific results.

The capacity of democratic theory to orient, but not determine, interpretations of the Press Clause is seen elsewhere. Media entities have repeatedly invoked the First Amendment in asking courts to grant them access to government facilities or government documents. These requests, typically denied, are usually founded on a claimed right of the people to be informed. The standard view, however, is that the First Amendment provides a right to speak, not a right to the resources that would make speech informed or effective. The argument has fared no better by relying on some special media status under the Press Clause. Even if the press's institutional autonomy requires certain, special constitutional (defensive) rights, these rights do not include affirmative grants of particular resources. As Justice Stewart argued, "The Constitution itself is neither a Freedom of Information Act nor an Official Secrets Act. The Constitution...establishes the contest, not its resolution." Over vigorous dissents, the Court has denied requests for constitutionally based access to documents or facilities except in the context of judicial proceedings. Even here, the Court's initial analysis of courtrooms' openness was based less on a right of access to information and more on a tradition of courtroom trials as places where people could gather information about their government. For First Amendment purposes, this led the Court to analogize the courtroom and trial to streets and parks, rather than to governmentally held informational resources.

Despite these results, the issue divided the Court. It is appropriate to ask whether the disagreements reflect different conceptions of democracy. Arguments for access to information often are based overtly on the importance of information for democracy. Before considering the implications of the different democratic theories, however, I want to make two general observations.

Virtually everyone agrees that sometimes government should restrict access to information. Restrictions often serve individuals' interests in their own privacy, society's interest in military security, the effectiveness of the Federal Reserve Board's actions or law enforcement investigations, and possibly, the quality and frankness of courts' in-chamber discussions. It is also widely agreed that some governmentally generated information should be publicly available. Modern sensibilities find it incredible that reporting on debates held in legislative sessions at one time amounted to contempt of the legislative body. Given the value and legitimacy of both secrecy and information availability—the modern term is "transparency"—line-drawing problems abound. The diverse policy considerations relevant to the lines' placement suggest the possible wisdom of viewing access to information as a legislative issue. Such a legislative issue would be resolved by statutory freedom of information acts, privacy acts, and open meeting laws, or by intelligent executive or agency decisions, rather than as a constitutional matter.

On the other hand, bureaucratic bodies instinctually seem to desire secrecy (except on occasions where their own agenda or their members' egotism favors publicity). They may perceive secrecy as advancing their flexibility, whether or not these gains in flexibility are legitimate. Information could expose their misbehavior, failures, or incompetence. It could also lead to "misguided" criticisms. It forces public officials to defend their actions. For whatever reasons, including partial information or distortions, members of the public often react negatively to information about government actions even though the official believes her action was legitimate, maybe even wise. In any event, deference to the political branches on this issue is often not deference to careful policymaking, but to the self-protective instinct for secrecy. Such deference is problematic. The combination of the occasional real need for secrecy and an organization's systematic tendency to seek excessive secrecy could lead an activist court to formulate constitutional principles to guide a modest degree of judicial supervision over, and serve to restrict, executive and agency discretion. A less activist court, in contrast, might rely on the ability of the press and others seeking access to "coerce" openness by generating negative publicity about those maintaining unwarranted secrecy, or to obtain legislation requiring openness. Even for the more activist court, however, democratic theory could influence the decision to intervene constitutionally—the issue to which I now turn.

Although all democratic theories see value in popular access to information, they vary somewhat in the particular type of information to which they demand access, in the reason for seeking access, and in the centrality of broad access for their conception of democracy. Access to certain information obviously serves the checking function. For instance, I. F. Stone reportedly found plenty of dirt merely by using an informed and careful eye to read publicly available reports and documents. My guess is that the most explosive information will either be made available without the need for a special constitutional right, as I. F. Stone found, or will be information that, absent statutory directives, even an activist judge would not force the government to reveal. Presumptively persuasive arguments will usually support confidentiality. Of course, my empirical guess may be wrong—and is more likely to be wrong as more courts are willing to engage in *in camera* inspections and discover that secrecy is not justified. But, if I am correct, then a constitutional right of access to information may do little to serve the checking function. Moreover, the elite democrat could fear that mandated access will often interfere with and negatively "politicize" expert deliberation. Thus, an elite democrat should find a constitutional right of access to be quite problematic.

All participatory democrats should place greater emphasis on routine access to information. They value access to a much broader range of information than do elite democrats. Each of these participatory theories, however, has a somewhat different interest in the constitutional right. For pluralist democrats, information has largely instrumental or strategic relevance. Interest groups need to know when and where their preformed interests are most at stake and need assertion. Still, the liberal pluralist may conclude that sometimes secrecy will support the bargaining that all sides must rely upon. Arguably normal information disclosure provides most of what the public needs, in which case the pluralist could conclude that a constitutional right is not crucial.

In contrast, a democracy that involves wisely and collectively formulating attitudes, values, and conceptions of a common good—as republicans believe —or conceptions of a subgroup identity—as complex democrats maintain— calls for a broader range of information. Of course, given the centrality of identity and value formation, factual information may be less important for the republican than the pluralist. The republican or complex democrat could agree with Christopher Lasch, who argued that democracy depends on argument and discussion, not information (except to the extent that it is made relevant by, and is the product of, debate). This conclusion led Lasch to argue "that the job of the press is to encourage debate, not to supply the public with information." Still, the republican will be unimpressed with the need for secrecy to promote bargaining. The republican is likely to argue not only that government actions should presumptively be public but also that decisions about these actions should be made only on the basis of publicly available information. The complex democrat is likely to share these views. Even if bargaining is an important part of governing, its legitimacy may depend on its transparency as well as its results, the main concern of the pluralist.

Despite some differences in their concern with access to information, it is less clear how, or even whether, these various democratic theories will differ in their view of a constitutional right. Attitudes about judicial activism may dominate all other considerations. Cutting one way are doubts about the propriety of courts engaging in essentially legislative policymaking under the rubric of constitutional law. Cutting in the other direction is a context in which trust in the judgment of policy-making branches, especially executive agencies, is particularly problematic. These considerations, rather than one's choice among democratic theories, may be the key variable in determining a judge or scholar's attitude toward the legitimacy (and scope) of a constitutional right to information.

The differences among democratic theories have potential constitutional ramifications in other areas. Consider copyright. Copyright overtly limits a later communicator's freedom of speech (or writing). There is, nevertheless, widespread agreement that copyright serves the public by increasing "the harvest of knowledge," as well as furthering various private interests. Likewise, all agree that copyright should not give unlimited rights to an "author," a view reflected in the principle that "facts" and "ideas" are not copyrightable and in the "fair use" privilege. Beyond these areas of agreement, however, people vary in their readiness to find something copyrightable and to find that a subsequent use is a violation. My suggestion is that a person's "readiness" in part reflects the democratic theory to which she is committed.

A broad conception of copyright should pose few problems for the elite democrat and may even serve her ends. As long as copyright does not restrict use of facts and ideas, as it currently does not, a broad right is unlikely to interfere with the checking function. To the extent that a broad right increases the rewards of writing and of journalism, it provides greater incentives for undertaking that work. Likewise, a pluralist democratic theory has little objection to extensive rights. A broad right is unlikely to restrict a group's capacity either to present or to pursue its own exogenously formed interests. In contrast, republican democracy thematizes the salience and openness of cultural dialogue. Both political and cultural dialogue affect the community's conception of itself and the public good. By providing an economic incentive for production and publication, copyright encourages such cultural discussions. But, by restricting creators' or discussants' use of previously copyrighted materials, copyright narrows cultural dialogue. Moreover, if, as Lasch contends, broad participation in discussions is more important than facts—or, to restate the claim, if the democratic value of increased, noncommercial, popular involvement in discussion is greater than the democratic value of the lost media commodities—then a narrower right should be favored. This conclusion, however, is arguable. It depends on both normative judgments (what discourse is valued) and empirical predictions (how different definitions of rights will affect the discourse). Still, a plausible conclusion is that narrowing copyright protection should facilitate diverse public discussion and cultural explorations of common interests more than it dampens commercial incentives to produce useful communications.

Unlike either elite democrats or pluralists, complex democrats agree with republicans that cultural discourses are central to democracy. This may help to explain the variation between those democratic scholars who, when discussing the media, focus solely on nonfiction (with news being the paradigm concern) and those who take a more expansive view of media content that includes fiction, art, and other cultural materials. Democratic elitists and liberal pluralists are more likely to be in the first group and republicans and complex democrats in the second. Moreover, the second group is especially likely to value these discourses when participation is popular and noncommodified, although commodified forms can provide substance to popular discussion and commodification sometimes helps to pay for higher levels of participation....

CONCLUSION

As commentators repeatedly assert, democracy depends on a free press. But different conceptions of democracy are served by different free presses. This insight has direct significance for the practice of journalism. Even the most intelligent and democratically committed journalists, however, write and report within a communications order structured both by law and by the market. Both law and the market can reward but often also can impede desirable journalistic practices. Even more troublesome are the market forces that bankrupt certain types of media entities, sometimes the very media that democracy most needs. The obvious response, even if politically difficult to enact, is legislation favoring, protecting, subsidizing, or even creating the type of media entities or communication practices required by democracy. Because identifying these requirements depends on the specifics of democratic theory, the foregoing analysis should have significant policy relevance for media law and legislative reform.

Finally, there is constitutional law. The press's democratic functions provide the best perspective for understanding the First Amendment guarantee. Elitist democracy and its checking function (a value shared with all other democratic theories) have been most influential in giving the Press Clause doctrinal content that restricts government power. To the extent another theory of democracy is favored—I have implicitly claimed that complex democracy is the soundest theory—that theory may provide further content to the Press Clause. Nevertheless, the primary implication of complex democracy for constitutional interpretation is probably that the Press Clause should be read narrowly. Complex democracy requires a constitutional reading tolerant of structural regulation of the press by government. At any given time, democracy's primary communicative needs inevitably will be disputed. Complex democracy recognizes that the market could be failing, either by providing a media too homogeneous or too pluralistic, or by corrupting the available versions of either or both. These possibilities suggest that the Press Clause should be read to allow the government to promote a press that, in its best judgment, democracy needs but that the market fails to provide.

FROM THE PREFACE TO
EMERGENCE OF
A FREE PRESS
Leonard W. Levy

In 1957 the Fund for the Republic commissioned Leonard Levy to write a brief memorandum on the original understanding of the First Amendment. Levy concluded that, at the time the amendment was framed, American courts recognized the crime of "seditious libel"—criticism of the government that could be punished as a crime even if true. "Freedom of speech," he wrote, then meant only the freedom from "prior restraint"; speakers could be readily punished after the fact. This meant that the Jeffersonians who protested against the Sedition Act were on the wrong side of legal doctrine; Congress had done nothing extraordinary in passing a law punishing dissident editors with fines and prison.

But this was the McCarthy era, and Robert M. Hutchins, head of the fund, wanted a document rebuking the rabid anticommunists who were persecuting liberals and progressives for their views. So he had the pamphlet published without the conclusions about "seditious libel." Levy fought back by expanding his seditious-libel material into *Legacy of Suppression: Freedom of Speech and Press in Early American History*. In its second edition, titled *Emergence of a Free Press*, it remains today the major work in the field. But Levy's conclusions in *Legacy* were subject to fierce critique by other historians. The Supreme

Leonard W. Levy, *Emergence of a Free Press* (New York: Oxford University Press, 1985). Reprinted with permission.

Court repudiated "seditious libel" definitively in *New York Times v. Sullivan.* Nearly two decades later, in *The Legacy Reexamined,* Levy offered a more nuanced view of the history of "seditious libel" in the New World.

The title I chose and the rather strong theme I developed in that book reflected both my shock at discovering the neglected evidence and my indignation at Hutchins and The Fund for attempting to suppress my work. As a result I overdid it. I had a novel position, which I overstated. I summarized my findings as follows in the 1960 preface.

> This book presents a revisionist interpretation of the origins and original understanding of the First Amendment's clause on freedom of speech and press. I have been reluctantly forced to conclude that the generation which adopted the Constitution and the Bill of Rights did not believe in a broad scope for freedom of expression, particularly in the realm of politics.
>
> I find that libertarian theory from the time of Milton to the ratification of the First Amendment substantially accepted the right of the state to suppress seditious libel. I find also that the American experience with freedom of political expression was as slight as the theoretical inheritance was narrow. Indeed, the American legislatures, especially during the colonial period, were far more oppressive than the supposedly tyrannous common-law courts. The evidence drawn particularly from the period 1776 to 1791 indicates that the generation that framed the first state declarations of rights and the First Amendment was hardly as libertarian as we have traditionally assumed. They did not intend to give free rein to criticism of the government that might be deemed seditious libel, although the concept of seditious libel was—and still is—the principal basis of muzzling political dissent. There is even reason to believe that the Bill of Rights was more the chance product of political expediency on all sides than of principled commitment to personal liberties. A broad libertarian theory of freedom of speech and press did not emerge in the United States until the Jeffersonians, when a minority party, were forced to defend themselves against the Federalist Sedition Act of 1798. In power, however, the Jeffersonians were not much more tolerant of their political critics than the Federalists had been.

I was wrong in asserting that the American experience with freedom of political expression was as slight as the conceptual and legal understanding was narrow. Indeed, elsewhere in the 1960 preface I contradicted myself when more accurately stating that the common law did not in fact "actually prevent the widespread discussion of affairs of state by the common people." At several points in the book, but only in passing, I noted the discrepancy between theory and practice. Chapter One, for example, concluded with the observations that an "astonishing degree" of open political discussion existed, considering the legal restraints, and that "the law in the books and the law in life" must be distinguished. At best I was inconsistent. From a far more thorough reading of American newspapers of the eighteenth century I now know that the American experience with a free press was as broad as the theoretical inheritance was narrow.

My original interest lay with law and theory; I had paid little attention to press practices. I had searched the newspapers only for statements on the meaning of freedom of the press and had ignored the nearly epidemic degree of seditious libel that infected American newspapers after Independence. Press criticism of government policies and politicians, on both state and national levels, during the war and in the peaceful years of the 1780s and 1790s, raged as contemptuously and scorchingly as it had against Great Britain in the period between the Stamp Act and the battle of Lexington. Some states gave written constitutional protection to freedom of the press after Independence; others did not. Whether they did or did not, their presses operated as if the law of seditious libel did not exist. To one whose prime concern was law and theory, a legacy of suppression came into focus; to one who looks at newspaper judgments on public men and measures, the revolutionary controversy spurred an expanding legacy of liberty.

If the press freely aspersed on matters of public concern for a generation before 1798, the broad new libertarianism that emerged after the enactment of the Sedition Act formed a continuum linking prior experience with subsequent theory. If a legacy of suppression had existed at all, the realms of law and theory had perpetuated it, not the realm of practice. In effect the concern for freedom of political expression continually evolved, as the American reaction to the Sedition Act illustrated. In England, Fox's Libel Act of 1792, which merely allowed a jury to decide the criminality of a defendant's words, met with popular acclaim and enjoys the historical reputation of having been a libertarian reform. England did not, however, allow a defendant in a criminal libel case to plead truth as a defense until Lord Campbell's Act of 1843. By comparison the Sedition Act of 1798 should resonate as a truly libertarian achievement because it represented the final triumph of the principles of the Zenger case: it emulated Fox's Libel Act and preceded Lord Campbell's by forty-five years, and additionally, it required proof of malice. Its reformist character notwithstanding, the Sedition Act had a notorious reputation in its own time as well as during the subsequent course of American history, showing that Americans respected freedom of political expression far more than theoreticians and legalists had acknowledged before 1798.

I disagree with *Legacy of Suppression* in one other respect. In several places I gave the misleading impression that freedom of the press meant to the Framers merely the absence of prior restraints. Similarly, I sometimes declared that they shared Blackstone's view, as I still deliberately do. Whether referring to that oracle of the common law or to freedom of the press as freedom from prior restraints, I mean, first, that the criminal law held people responsible for abuse of that freedom. Second, I mean not to exhaust the meanings of freedom of the press by identifying it as, at the least, freedom from prior restraint. The Supreme Court was right when declaring in 1936, "It is impossible to concede that by the words 'freedom of the press' the framers of the First Amendment intended to adopt merely the narrow view then reflected by the law of England that such freedom consisted only in immunity from previous censorship; for this abuse had then permanently disappeared from English practice." The test for the criminal abuse of freedom of the press constituted the real problem, not the imposition of subsequent punishment for that abuse. In any case, freedom of the press merely began with its immunity from previous restraints.

Freedom of the press also meant that the press had achieved a special status as an unofficial fourth branch of government, "the Fourth Estate," whose function was to check the three official branches by exposing misdeeds and policies contrary to the public interest. Additionally, freedom of the press had come to mean that the system of popular government could not effectively operate unless the press discharged its obligations to the electorate by judging officeholders and candidates for office. The relationship between the press and the electoral process had become so close that popular government and political parties depended upon the existence of a free press. Some theorists even contended that a free press, by virtue of its watchdog function, also served as the matrix for the perpetuation of all other personal liberties protected by the Bill of Rights.

I am still convinced, however, that the revolutionary generation did not seek to wipe out the core idea of seditious libel, that the government may be criminally assaulted by mere words; that the legislatures were more suppressive than the courts; that the theory of freedom of political expression remained quite narrow until 1798, except for a few aberrant statements; that English libertarian theory was usually in the vanguard of the American; that the Bill of Rights in its immediate history was in large measure a lucky political accident; and that the First Amendment was as much an expression of federalism as of libertarianism. I also still contend that tarring and feathering a Tory editor because of his opinions showed a rather restricted meaning and scope of freedom of the press. Indeed, one may ask whether there was free speech during the revolutionary era if only the speech of freedom was free....

My principal thesis remains unchanged. I still aim to demolish the proposition formerly accepted in both law and history that it was the intent of the American Revolution or the Framers of the First Amendment to abolish the common law of seditious libel. James Madison himself, the "father" of the Constitution and of the Bill of Rights, explicitly argued that proposition, and it has been reiterated in our own time by our greatest judges, as well as by distinguished constitutional scholars.

... They have, however, in Mrs. Malaprop's phrase, "anticipated the past" by succumbing to an impulse to re-create it so that its image may be seen in a manner consistent with our rhetorical tradition of freedom, thereby yielding a message that will instruct the present. The evidence suggests that the proposition is suppositious and unprovable.

We may even have to confront the possibility that the intentions of the Framers were not the most libertarian and their insights on the subject of freedom of expression not the most edifying. But this should be expected because the Framers were nurtured on the crabbed historicism of Coke and the narrow conservatism of Blackstone, as well as Zenger's case. The ways of thought of a lifetime are not easily broken. The Declaration of Independence severed the political connection with England but the American states continued the English common-law system except as explicitly rejected by statute. If the Revolution produced any radical libertarians on the meaning of freedom of speech and press, they were not present at the Constitutional Convention or the First Congress, which drafted the Bill of Rights. Scholars and judges have betrayed a penchant for what John P. Roche called "retrospective symmetry," by giving to present convictions a patriotic lineage and tradition—in this case, the fatherhood of the "Framers." But this is no reason to be distressed. We may miss the comforting assurance of having the past's original intentions coincide with present preferences. Yet the case for civil liberties is so powerfully grounded in political philosophy's wisest principles, as well as the wisest policies drawn from experience, that it need not be anchored to the past. What passed for wisdom in the era of the Framers may very well have passed out of date with the growth of libertarianism in America.

My acknowledgment that the press of the new nation functioned as if the law of criminal libel hardly mattered is not entirely graceful. I refuse to *prove* the existence of unfettered press practices by giving illustrations of savage press criticisms of government policies or vicious character assassinations of American politicians. I am not intent on measuring the degree of freedom that Americans enjoyed. I am interested, to use an analogy, in defining the concept of crime, and therefore do not find crime-rate statistics to be helpful. In our own time, obscenity is still illegal, though we live in a society saturated by it and witness few prosecutions; their paucity does not illumine the meaning of obscenity. So, too, the rarity of prosecutions for seditious libel, and the existence of an unfettered press do not illumine the scope and meaning of freedom of the press or the law on freedom of the press. The argument that freedom of political expression existed as a fact and therefore undermined the old thesis of a legacy of suppression is an odd one in some respects. That argument seems to be on all fours with the proposition that the existence of so many heretics during the reign of Bloody Mary proves there was a great degree of freedom of religion, despite the fires at Smithfield; or, that there was freedom of the press, a century later, because Lilburne, while in prison for his political opinion, was able to smuggle out a series of seditious tracts for publication. More to the point, perhaps, would be the experience of the Jeffersonian press during the Sedition Act period. The fact that the Philadelphia *Aurora* appeared regularly while William Duane, its editor, was under indictment for violation of the Act, strikes me as poor evidence that freedom of the press, as a matter of practice, was really secure at the time. Although the *Aurora* never ceased its scathing comments on the Administration, I believe that the prosecution of its editor for his opinions demonstrated a stunted concept of a free press; and I cannot accept the view that freedom of the press was safe despite the Sedition Act....

I wrote *Legacy of Suppression* and this revision in the unshakable belief that the concept of seditious libel and freedom of the press are incompatible. So long as the press *may* be subjected to government control, whether or not that control is exercised, the press cannot be free—or is not as free as it should be. Freedom of the press cannot thrive as it should if closeted with a time bomb, the concept of seditious libel, ticking away in the law. The number or frequency of detonations does not matter. The Sedition Act of 1798, the Sedition Act of 1918, and the Smith Act of 1940, together with the prosecutions under them, are unendurable. One case is too many....

"RETHINKING PRIOR RESTRAINT"

John Calvin Jeffries Jr.

Among the extraordinary protections for the press fashioned by the Supreme Court is the doctrine of prior restraint—in essence, a legal presumption against prepublication censorship of expression or anything that even smacks of censorship. Although prior restraint is considered a general rule governing free expression rather than a Press Clause doctrine, its contours have clearly been shaped by the justices' awareness of the needs of the institutional media for immediacy and clarity in decision making. In his essay "Rethinking Prior Restraint," John C. Jeffries Jr. argues that the Court's zeal against censorship has led it to the construction of an incoherent set of principles. Jeffries is professor and dean emeritus at the University of Virginia School of Law and a distinguished theorist of constitutional rights and federal jurisdiction. He has been a faculty member at Virginia since 1973, when he returned there after a clerkship with Justice Lewis F. Powell Jr. of the United States Supreme Court. In 1994 he published *Justice Lewis F. Powell Jr.*, the only full-length biography of the most influential member of the Burger Court.

Only once in the history of the Republic has the Supreme Court witnessed a head-on collision between national security and the First Amendment. The

Yale Law Journal 92 (1983): 409–37. Reprinted with permission.

case was *New York Times Co. v. United States*, where the government sought to enjoin publication of classified documents known as the Pentagon Papers. The issue, said the per curiam opinion for the Court, was one of "prior restraint": "Any system of prior restraints of expression comes to this Court bearing a heavy presumption against its constitutional validity." The government therefore faced "a heavy burden of showing justification for the imposition of such a restraint," and its failure to carry that burden meant the denial of injunctive relief.

This sort of talk flows easily from the rhetorical tradition of the First Amendment, but in fact the significance of focusing on prior restraint was not all that clear. . . . Separate concurrences revealed an underlying diversity of opinion. . . .

For two members of the majority . . . the specially disfavored status of prior restraints under the First Amendment seems to have been the actual stuff of decision, and not merely a convenient point of rhetoric. Writing for himself and for Justice Stewart, Justice White announced that his vote rested on "the concededly extraordinary protection against prior restraints enjoyed by the press under our constitutional system." He asserted a constitutional distinction between prior restraint and subsequent punishment and suggested that the government may simply have tried the wrong door:

> Prior restraints require an unusually heavy justification under the First Amendment; but failure by the Government to justify prior restraints does not measure its constitutional entitlement to a conviction for criminal publication. That the Government mistakenly chose to proceed by injunction does not mean that it could not successfully proceed in another way.

Justice White's opinion illustrates the operative significance of the doctrine of prior restraint. The doctrine imposes a special disability on official attempts to suppress speech in advance of publication—a disability that is independent of the scope of constitutional protection against punishment subsequent to publication. In other words, speech that validly could be controlled by subsequent punishment nevertheless would be immune from regulation by prior restraint.

. . . Any instance of speech or expression that would be protected from subsequent punishment is a fortiori secured against prior restraint, and therefore reveals nothing of the independent effect ascribed to that doctrine.

Where the speech in question is in all events guaranteed by the First Amendment, attributing that guarantee to the circumstance of prior restraint is at best irrelevant and often misleading. The testing case is, rather, one in which speech is concededly (or at least arguably) outside the substantive protection of the First Amendment but assertedly within the bar of prior restraints. The position of Justices White and Stewart in *New York Times Co. v. United States* presents just such a case.

My purpose here is to examine the doctrine of prior restraint and to ask what, if any, role it should play in modern adjudication of the First Amendment. The White-Stewart position in *New York Times* is a suitable starting point, both because it presents an analytically clear case of the doctrine at work and because it depicts that doctrine against the background of a professed concern for national security. Focusing on a claim of national security seems to me apt because it is precisely (though not exclusively) in that context that the government is likely to assert a strong justification for imposing prior restraint. Even a weak or highly speculative explanation for the rule of special hostility to prior restraint may well seem persuasive where the government has no good reason to proceed in that manner.... In the field of national security ... virginity matters. The harm that may be expected to flow from revealing a state secret is almost exclusively related to the first publication. Accordingly, the government's interest in acting before publication is greater, and the rationale for a rule of special hostility to this form of regulation is put more sharply in issue.

I.

The history of the doctrine of prior restraint has been recounted elsewhere, and need not be fully related here. Most accounts begin with the English Licensing Act of 1662 and its scheme of official licensing for all printed publications. The Licensing Act was allowed to expire in 1694, apparently not so much from opposition to the principle of the statute as from frustration with the absurdities and inequities of its administration.... A century later, however, freedom from licensing of the press had come to be seen as one of the rights of Englishmen. Hence, the famous passage in which Blackstone equated freedom of the press with a rule against prior restraint:

The liberty of the press is indeed essential to the nature of a free state; but this consists in laying no *previous* restraints upon publications...but if he publishes what is improper, mischievous, or illegal, he must take the consequence of his own temerity.

Two distinct propositions are conjoined in Blackstone's statement....For a long time, the chief import of Blackstone's position lay in what was *not* protected—namely, any "improper, mischievous, or illegal" speech or publication.... Adopted as a construction of the First Amendment, this view would have imposed little or no substantive limit on governmental authority to suppress speech, so long as such suppression was done by subsequent punishment and not by prior restraint....More modern observers usually look to the protective aspect of Blackstone's statement. They commonly cite him to confirm the doctrine of prior restraint as an independent bar to official regulation of speech, one applicable even to speech not otherwise protected under the First Amendment.

...[T]he themes struck in Blackstone's passage on prior restraint recur throughout the later development of the doctrine and continue to shape our habits of thought on the subject. At least two legacies are apparent. First, the doubtful pedigree of First Amendment protection against subsequent punishment created a powerful incentive for advocates of expanded constitutional protection...to describe the restriction at hand as a prior restraint. This characterization was repeatedly urged and not infrequently adopted for matters surprisingly dissimilar from the English scheme of official licensing. In time, exploitation of the latent plasticities of "prior restraint" became a familiar tactical short-cut to expanded substantive coverage of the First Amendment. Second, Blackstone founded the still vigorous tradition that speech should be more protected against prior restraint than against subsequent punishment. And this insistence has been reiterated without regard to whether "more protected" meant "more than not at all" or "more than a great deal."...[A] special bar against prior restraint has come increasingly to be viewed as a good thing, even as the notion of what constitutes a prior restraint has grown progressively more elastic and unstable.

These themes are evident in *Near v. Minnesota*, the Supreme Court's first great encounter with prior restraint, and the subsequent emergence of that case as the doctrine's leading precedent. *Near* involved a very odd statute. It authorized, under the law of public nuisance, judicial abatement of any newspaper or other periodical deemed "malicious, scandalous and defamatory." A defense was provided where the material complained of was both true and published "with good motives and for justifiable ends." . . .

The Court struck down the law as an invalid prior restraint. . . . [Chief Justice Hughes] . . . quoted Blackstone and others in condemnation of prior restraint. Hughes took pains to say that the bar against prior restraint was not absolute, nor was the constitutional protection against subsequent punishment entirely nonexistent. For the Court, however, there was plainly a constitutional difference between the two approaches, and Hughes rested the decision squarely on that ground. . . .

Writing for himself and three other dissenters, Justice Butler disputed the characterization of the statute as a prior restraint. . . :

> The Minnesota statute does not operate as a *previous* restraint on publication. . . . It does not authorize administrative control in advance such as was formerly exercised by the licensers and censors but prescribes a remedy to be enforced by a suit in equity. In this case there was previous publication made in the course of business of regularly producing malicious, scandalous and defamatory periodicals. The business and publications unquestionably constitute an abuse of the right of free press. The statute denounces the things done as a nuisance on the ground . . . that they threaten morals, peace and good order. There is no question of the power of the State to denounce such transgressions. . . .

. . . [T]he implicit assumption seems to have been that unless the law could be treated as a prior restraint, thus falling within the protective part of Blackstone's bifurcation, no settled or familiar basis would exist for holding the statute unconstitutional. And the statute had to be held unconstitutional. Otherwise, it could become a successful prototype for official suppression of hostile comment. . . . In truth, *Near v. Minnesota* involved nothing more or less than a repackaged version of the law of seditious libel, and this the majority rightly refused to countenance. Hence, there was pressure, so typical of this doctrine, to cram the law into the disfavored category of prior restraint, even though it in fact functioned very differently from a scheme of official licensing. . . . Here the decision to suppress was made by a judge (not a bureaucrat), after adversarial (not ex parte) proceedings, to determine the legal character of what had been (and not what might be) published. The only aspect of prior restraint was the incidental fact that the defendants were commanded not to repeat that which they were proved to have done.

The real defect, of course, was the substantive standard for authorizing suppression. The standard of "malicious, scandalous and defamatory" publication that is neither true nor published "with good motives and for justifiable ends" is utterly inconsistent with the fundamental First Amendment principle of free and unfettered political debate....

Now, one may well wonder whether this carping about categorization is not a bit off point. After all, if the *Near* Court reached the right result, does it really matter that it gave the wrong reason? The answer, I think, is that it does matter, at least that it has come to matter as *Near* has become a prominent feature of the First Amendment landscape.... And the course indicated by *Near* is not simply to reject the law of seditious libel.... Instead, *Near* has come to stand for a sort of syllogism about injunctive relief:

Prior restraint of speech is presumptively unconstitutional, even where the speech in question is not otherwise protected.

An injunction is a prior restraint.

Therefore, an injunction against speech is presumptively unconstitutional, even where the speech enjoined is not otherwise protected.

...And despite the continued reliance on this analysis in matters of no little consequence, the Court has yet to explain...what it is about an injunction that justifies this independent rule of constitutional disfavor.

... The most established and coherent line of cases harks back to the original meaning of prior restraint as official licensing.... In each of these cases, the instrument of enforcement was criminal prosecution and punishment. Prior restraint was imposed by conditioning the right to speak on advance approval by a government official. A violation of the law would be shown by proof of failure to obtain the required permit, regardless of whether that permit could constitutionally have been withheld.... Under such schemes, an executive official was empowered to determine, on the basis of ex parte consideration, whether speech should be permitted or suppressed. And, at least where the statutory authorization of such preclearance was not facially invalid, that determination would be binding and enforceable unless and until the would-be speaker obtained a contrary judicial declaration.

Another line of cases picks up the innovation of *Near v. Minnesota* and extends the rule against prior restraint to a wide variety of injunctions against speech and publication. *New York Times Co. v. United States* is the premier example.... In all of these cases, the Court found that the special bar against prior restraint was triggered by issuance of an injunction. In none of them, however, was it clear that the speech in question could validly have been suppressed by subsequent punishment. It is difficult to tell, therefore, whether the doctrine of prior restraint was merely a convenient rhetoric, or whether it was actually applied to protect against injunction speech that would not have been protected against prosecution and punishment. In either event, it seems clear that the mechanism of suppression in the use of injunctions bears little resemblance to that involved in the permit cases.

Finally, the rule against prior restraints has been invoked in a number of situations involving neither permit requirements nor injunctions. These situations are not only unlike both of the established patterns of prior restraint; they are also quite unlike one another. Three cases suffice to illustrate the point. *Grosjean v. American Press Co.* treated as a prior restraint a gross receipts tax on newspapers. *Bantam Books, Inc. v. Sullivan* invoked the same doctrine to strike down the Rhode Island Commission to Encourage Morality in Youth. That body operated as an informal censor by identifying certain books and magazines as objectionable for sale to minors. The Commission, however, had no authority to suppress such publications; it could only recommend criminal prosecution. The statute nevertheless was found to erect a system of prior restraint. And whatever was the common thread linking *Grosjean* to *Bantam Books*, it was also found in *Southeastern Promotions, Ltd. v. Conrad* to apply to a city's refusal to rent a municipal theater for a production of "Hair."...

II.

Even this abbreviated historical review should make plain the essential objection to the doctrine of prior restraint. At least as applied by the courts, the doctrine is fundamentally unintelligible. It purports to assess the constitutionality of government action by distinguishing prior restraint from subsequent punishment, but provides no coherent basis for making that categorization.... The doctrine purports to deal with matters of form rather than of substance, but there is no unity among the forms of government action condemned as prior restraints.

The explanation for this disarray lies in the historic association of "prior restraint" with a declaration of constitutional invalidity and in the consequent impetus to distort doctrine in order to expand protection. Today, such indirection is unnecessary. There is nothing left of the "Blackstonian theory" that the government may do what it will so long as it avoids prior restraint, and hence there is no need to invoke that categorization in order to protect First Amendment freedoms. We are left, therefore, with a doctrine of honored past but contemporary irrelevance—a formulation whose current contribution to the interpretation of the First Amendment is chiefly confusion.

An obvious solution to this problem is to redefine the concept, to restrict the frame of reference to a set of structurally similar situations about which doctrinal generalizations can usefully be made....

A. ADMINISTRATIVE PRECLEARANCE

Of the various things referred to as prior restraint, a system of administrative preclearance is the most plainly objectionable. Under such a system, the lawfulness of speech or publication is made to depend on the prior permission of an executive official. Ordinarily, publication without such permission is punished as a criminal offense, even where the particular speech in question could not constitutionally have been suppressed. Thus, it is the failure to obtain preclearance rather than the character of the speech itself that determines illegality.

Such a scheme has many vices. The administrative apparatus erected to effect preclearance may screen a range of expression far broader than that which otherwise would be brought to official attention. The relative ease and economy of an administrative decision to suppress may make suppression more likely than it would be without a preclearance requirement. Under a system of administrative preclearance, suppression is accomplished "by a single stroke of the pen." At that point the burden falls on the would-be speaker to vindicate his right. Without administrative preclearance, the government's decision to suppress may be constrained by the time and money required to demonstrate in court an appropriate basis for such action. And the fact that those exercising the authority of preclearance operate in the relative informality of administrative action may tend to shield their decisions from effective public scrutiny. Most important, administrative preclearance requires a bureaucracy of censorship. Persons who choose to fill this role may well have psychological tendencies to overstate the need for suppression.

Whether or not this is so, there are powerful institutional pressures to justify one's job, and ultimately one's own importance, by exaggerating the evils which suppression seeks to avoid.... And finally, it may well be that a system of administrative preclearance would be enforced more energetically and efficiently than a system of subsequent punishment. Ultimately, both depend on criminal prosecution, but the issues presented for proof under a preclearance requirement may be significantly more manageable.

These and similar arguments have been detailed by Professor Emerson. They deal with matters of timing, process, and institutional structure rather than with the substantive content of speech, and in my view, they fully justify an attitude of special hostility toward preclearance requirements. All of these concerns, however, are linked to a single factor, a factor ordinarily determinative of the constitutional fate of preclearance requirements. That factor is discretion. Where broad discretion is left in the hands of executive officials—as in a statute authorizing denial of a permit for very general reasons—the vices described above loom very large indeed. Where, on the other hand, executive discretion is tightly controlled—as in a statute requiring issuance of a permit on specified showings—the problems of preclearance seem relatively less troublesome.

The dangers of discretion have been emphasized repeatedly by the Supreme Court. Virtually all of the permit decisions noted earlier identify unconstrained executive discretion over speech and related activities as the chief reason for invalidation. The lesson of numerous older decisions was summarized in *Niemotko v. Maryland*, in which the Court said:

> In those cases this Court condemned statutes and ordinances which required that permits be obtained from local officials as a prerequisite to the use of public places, on the grounds that a license requirement constituted a prior restraint on freedom of speech, press and religion, and, *in the absence of narrowly drawn, reasonable and definite standards for the officials to follow*, must be invalid.

... But what if the criteria for suppression resist narrow, precise, and objective formulation? What if the standard is so general, so vague, or so dependent on questions of degree that substantial discretion inevitably attends its application to particular facts? Obscenity is the classic case. The Supreme Court has held... that obscenity is not protected speech, but it has never succeeded in defining that concept in narrow, precise, and objective terms. No matter how closely an administrator is tied to the constitutional definition of obscenity, the determination that something is obscene necessarily involves judgment and evaluation—in short, the exercise of discretion by an executive official. Where executive discretion cannot effectively be constrained by precise standards for decision, the Court has required that its exercise be closely supervised by judicial authority....

... [T]hese cases seem entirely correct.... Laws that vest such discretion in executive officials should be struck down, even where the discretion has been properly exercised on the facts at hand. The evil of broad preclearance requirements is not limited to the occasional case where the illegality of suppression is fully litigated. It also extends to cases that never reach the courts.... Laws that create a pervasive risk of unconstitutional suppression of protected speech should therefore be invalidated, even where the risk is not immediately realized, as a prophylaxis against the harm that will be done elsewhere.

This, of course, is a familiar argument. It goes under the name of the overbreadth doctrine.... In my view, it provides a more informative frame of reference for examining preclearance requirements than does the invocation of prior restraint.

Simply put, the doctrine asserts that an overbroad regulation of speech or publication may be subject to facial review and invalidation, even though its application in the instant case is constitutionally unobjectionable. Thus, a person whose activity could validly be suppressed under a more narrowly drawn law is allowed to challenge an overbroad law because of its application to others. The bare possibility of unconstitutional application is not enough; the law is unconstitutionally overbroad only if it reaches *substantially* beyond the permissible scope of legislative regulation. Thus, the issue under the overbreadth doctrine is whether a government restriction of speech that is arguably valid as applied to the case at hand should nevertheless be invalidated to avoid the substantial prospect of unconstitutional application elsewhere.

... The reason that the various features of timing, process, and institutional structure noted earlier are thought to render administrative preclearance requirements especially objectionable is precisely that they increase the prospect of unconstitutional application. Put another way, a system of administrative preclearance is likely to render a restriction of speech operatively, if not formally, overbroad. Narrow, precise, and objective standards are one way of constraining discretion; subjecting its exercise to judicial supervision is another. In either event, the goal is to limit the opportunities for unconstitutional suppression of protected speech, regardless of whether that danger arises from an overly broad statement of the substantive standard for suppression or whether it flows from the overly broad administration typical of a preclearance requirement.

B. INJUNCTIONS

The second major type of prior restraint is the injunction.... [D]espite its original reference to official licensing, the doctrine of prior restraint today is understood by many people to mean chiefly a rule of special hostility to injunctions. Of course, to the extent that the speech in question is constitutionally protected against suppression by subsequent punishment, it is also secured against suppression by injunction.... The issue, therefore, is whether injunctions should be constitutionally disfavored even where they are directed against speech not otherwise protected under the First Amendment.

In this connection, it is instructive to note how different from administrative preclearance injunctions really are. Under a regime of injunctions, there is no routine screening of speech and no administrative shortcut to suppression. The government has to shoulder the entire burden of identifying the case for suppression and of demonstrating in court a constitutionally acceptable basis for such action. Moreover, because an injunction must be sought in open court, the character of the government's claims remains subject to public scrutiny and debate. Most important, the decision to suppress is made by a court, not a censor.... [J]udges, unlike professional censors, have no vested interest in the suppression of speech. The institution of the judiciary is peculiarly well suited... to implement the ideals of the First Amendment....

Not only are injunctions unlike administrative preclearance, they are also far more like subsequent punishments than the conventional rhetoric would suggest. In both cases the *threat* of punishment comes before publication; in both cases the *fact* of punishment comes after. The apparent distinction in timing is actually only a shift in the focus of attention. The procedures in an action for criminal contempt—the enforcement phase of the injunctive process—are generally the same as those used in ordinary criminal prosecutions. Proof must be had beyond a reasonable doubt, and the right to trial by jury is guaranteed where the sentence exceeds imprisonment for six months.

On examination, the chief difference between the two schemes turns out to be this: Under a system of injunctions, the adjudication of illegality precedes publication; under a system of criminal prosecution, it comes later. This is a difference, and perhaps for some purposes it matters, but why the timing of the adjudication should affect the scope of First Amendment freedoms is not at all clear. Three related reasons are most frequently advanced.

The first and most common is that an injunction deters speech more effectively than does the threat of criminal prosecution and for that reason should be specially disfavored.... The idea has been variously expressed but never so pithily as in Alexander Bickel's remark that, "A criminal statute chills, prior restraint freezes."... It may be true... that an injunction, because it is particularized, immediate, and concrete, may impinge more forcefully on the consciousness of the individual enjoined than would a more generalized and impersonal threat of criminal prosecution. But that tells only half the story, and the wrong half at that. An injunction may be more effective at stopping the activity at which it is aimed, but it is also more narrowly confined. There is less risk of deterring activities beyond the adjudicated target of suppression.... And many find even an uncertain prospect of criminal conviction and punishment sufficient incentive to steer well clear of arguably proscribed activities. In terms, therefore, of the system of free expression and of the aggregate of arguably protected First Amendment activity that might be inhibited under these regimes, it is anything but clear that injunctions are more costly....

That point is strongly reinforced when one remembers that it is only the possibility of *erroneous* deterrence that should be the subject of concern. To the extent that the activity suppressed, whether by injunction or by criminal prosecution, is outside the protection of the First Amendment and within a legitimate sphere of legislative action, efficient inhibition is a good thing.... In that respect, it seems entirely plausible that the specifically targeted commands of an injunction are actually likely to be *less* threatening to the system of freedom of expression than the inevitably more general proscriptions of a penal statute.

Two additional reasons for regarding injunctions as especially deleterious to speech are really only variations on the theme of efficient deterrence. One is that suppression by criminal prosecution is preferable to suppression by injunction because the latter characteristically delays publication.... The result is a loss in the immediacy of speech, and in some cases an accompanying loss in its value. The other contention is that criminal prosecution is preferable because it allows the disputed material to be published at least once and thus to enter the marketplace of ideas. An injunction, by contrast, is said to prevent the information from ever being made public.

Both of these contentions enjoy wide currency, but neither withstands scrutiny. Both are based on the implicit assumption that the deterrent impact of penal statutes is felt in those cases in which prosecution is brought. Of course, the opposite is true. Every violation of the penal law is, by hypothesis, a case of failed deterrence. Effective deterrence occurs when the violation never takes place. And in some cases, deterrence will be effective. Thus, while an injunction may delay publication for several days, the prospect of penal sanctions may delay publication forever.... There is, in short, no necessary or dependable relation between the form of suppression and any identifiable measure of violence to First Amendment interests.

In my view, there is only one respect in which injunctions plausibly can be claimed to have a First Amendment impact significantly greater than the threat of subsequent punishment. That argument is based on the traditional rule that the legality of an injunction may not be challenged by disobeying its terms. In its most uncompromising form, the traditional approach would declare that the invalidity or even unconstitutionality of a court order would be no defense in a contempt proceeding based on violation of that order....

... For whatever uncertainty may attend the current health of the collateral bar doctrine, its relevance to prior restraint is plain. If... strictly followed *and* if immediate appellate review of judicial orders were not provided, the government might be able temporarily to suppress by injunction speech that could not be suppressed by threat of penal sanctions. That is because persons enjoined from publication would have to forego such action, at least temporarily, in order to preserve their constitutional claims.... Of course, it is an important safeguard against such abuse that the order must be issued by a judge, not a bureaucrat, but the possibility of judicial error or insensitivity to First Amendment freedoms is not so trivial that it may safely be ignored....

The reasons for the collateral bar rule are obvious and not unimportant. They include the preservation of judicial authority and the orderly settlement of disputes.... But it is also clear that, at least in the context of injunctions against speech, the collateral bar rule must be carefully circumscribed....

The first... exception covers the case of an injunction so palpably contrary to authority that it falls under a kind of "plain error" rule.... Existing First Amendment precedents would render "transparently invalid" a vast range of injunctions against speech. Nevertheless, this formulation does not address the truly close case.... The second exception may be more to the point, for it speaks directly to the central problem of the collateral bar rule—

the risk that an injunction against speech, even though ultimately invalidated, will so delay publication as to make the speech untimely and hence valueless for its purpose. The worst case would be an election-eve attempt by the party in power to enjoin publication of politically damaging information. In such circumstances, even the few days necessary to obtain expedited appellate review might prove seriously prejudicial to that system of representative government which the First Amendment, above all else, should be thought to undergird. In my view, therefore, the normal operation of the collateral bar rule can be sustained only so long as expedited appellate review allows an immediate opportunity to test the validity of an injunction against speech and only so long as that opportunity is genuinely effective to allow timely publication should the injunction ultimately be adjudged invalid. In any event, this is, as Professor Blasi put it, only a "controversy over the validity and scope of the collateral bar rule." It should be addressed in those terms and not, in my view, as a remote and usually unarticulated premise underlying a broad and uncritical acceptance of the conventional rhetoric of prior restraint.

The conclusion that I draw from all this is embarrassingly modest. It is not that injunctions are preferable to subsequent punishment.... Nor would I assert that there is never a case in which injunctive relief should be specially disfavored.... My only point is to question the broad and categorical condemnation of injunctions as a form of "prior restraint."

In my view, a rule of special hostility to administrative preclearance is fully justified, but a rule of special hostility to injunctive relief is not. Lumping both together under the name of "prior restraint" obscures rather than clarifies what is at stake in these cases. In the context of administrative preclearance, talking of prior restraint is unhelpful, though not inapt. A more informative frame of reference would be overbreadth, the doctrine that explicitly identifies why preclearance is specially objectionable. In the context of injunctions, however, the traditional doctrine of prior restraint is not merely unhelpful, but positively misleading. It focuses on a constitutionally inconsequential consideration of form and diverts attention away from the critical substantive issues of First Amendment coverage. The result is a two-pronged danger. On the one hand, vindication of First Amendment freedoms in the name of prior restraint may exaggerate the legitimate reach of official competence to suppress by subsequent punishment. On the other hand, insistence on special disfavor for prior restraints outside the realm of substantive protection under the First Amendment may deny to the government an appropriate choice of means to vindicate legitimate interests. In my view, neither risk is justified by any compelling reason to continue prior restraint as a doctrinally independent category of contemporary First Amendment analysis....

"OR OF THE [BLOG]"

Paul Horwitz

Newspapers, broadcast media, and even cable news operations face a stiff challenge from diverse news media on the Internet. The ubiquity and cheapness of publication on the Web has led to a wide variety of news sources available worldwide, ranging from established media Web sites to Web-only publications like slate.com and salon.com to video sites like YouTube. One of the most significant new media in recent years has been the blog (a contraction of "Weblog"), a new literary form that can be as banal as a recital of the blogger's daily doings or as elaborate as any newspaper and magazine. News-oriented bloggers became a significant force during the 2004 and 2006 elections; to cite one example, it was conservative members of the "blogosphere" who forced CBS news to admit that it had inadvertently used apparently forged documents in a report on President Bush's service in the Texas National Guard. In the excerpt below, Professor Paul Horwitz of the University of Alabama reaches back to Justice Stewart's essay, reprinted above, and relates the structural and institutional concerns Stewart discerned in the Press Clause to a changed media universe in which any citizen with ambition and a broadband connection can become a significant force in the twenty-first-century version of journalism. Horwitz himself is a former journalist and holds, in addition to two degrees in law, an MA in journalism from Columbia University.

I. INTRODUCTION

Close to seventy years ago, Chief Justice Hughes, writing for the Supreme Court in *Lovell v. Griffin*, noted that "the liberty of the press is not confined to newspapers and periodicals. It necessarily embraces pamphlets and leaflets... the press in its historic connotation comprehends every sort of publication which affords a vehicle of information and opinion." A mere forty years ago, Mr. Justice Black added that "the Constitution specifically selected the press, which includes not only newspapers, books and magazines, but also humble leaflets and circulars, to play an important role in the discussion of public affairs." Those Justices surely were looking back to our long tradition of "lonely pamphleteers," for they could not possibly have foreseen what was coming down the pike.

I am talking, of course, about the rise of blogs and the blogosphere. We are witnessing an explosion in the number of blogs. While the estimated number of blogs varies greatly, one blog-tracking site boasts that it is currently tracking 23.1 million sites.... Many blogs offer up-to-the-minute reflections on current affairs, and the most popular of these can receive tens of thousands of visits per day. One survey suggests that "by the end of 2004[,] 32 million Americans were blog readers."

Beyond the numbers, we have also witnessed a growth in the importance and influence of blogs. Whether or not their impact has been or will be revolutionary, as some claim, it is certainly true that blogs have assumed a growing role in breaking news, or in calling attention to existing news stories in a way that may have a significant real-world impact. Although blogs are most often thought of as supplements to existing news media, forming a symbiotic relationship with them, the more evangelical proponents of blogs, and detractors of the so-called "mainstream media," have suggested that blogs are in fact displacing traditional forms of gathering and disseminating the news. Only slightly more mildly, Richard Posner has written that blogs pose a "grave challenge to the journalistic establishment."... We might say that the rise of the blog represents the realization of the full promise of the "lonely pamphleteer."

As they mature and are given increasing prominence, blogs are also beginning to face a number of pressing legal questions. What liability should an anonymous poster face for a defamatory comment on a blog, and how easy should it be for a plaintiff to strip that poster of his anonymity? What access should a blogger enjoy to press credentials? Are bloggers entitled to claim either constitutional or statutory privileges to maintain the confidentiality of sources? Should they receive the same exemptions that mainstream media do from election law requirements? Some of these questions directly implicate constitutional rights, while others are founded on statutory privileges; but all of them resound with broader First Amendment concerns.

...In this contribution, I want to think specifically about the relationship between blogs and the Press Clause of the First Amendment....Are blogs part of "the press" for purposes of the Press Clause? Should we think of them in these terms? If we do, what legal consequences does this move carry both for blogs and for the press—and for our understanding of the Press Clause itself?

In a sense, these questions might seem at best quixotic, at worst pointless. It is now widely accepted that the Press Clause is about as useful as the vermiform appendix. As Frederick Schauer writes, "existing First Amendment doctrine renders the Press Clause redundant and thus irrelevant, with the institutional press being treated simply as another speaker." Even those few perquisites that have attached to the press, such as the qualified reporter's privilege, have lost some of the constitutional moorings that lower courts were willing to give them in the wake of the Court's confused ruling in *Branzburg v. Hayes*. In a recent article, David Anderson has suggested that "the demise of the press as a legally preferred institution," whether constitutionally or under statute, "is quite possible and perhaps even probable." If any heavy lifting in the protection of blogs is likely to be done, either by the Constitution or by legislative grace, why turn to this unfortunate redundancy of a constitutional provision?

I think there are good reasons to do so. Thirty years after Justice Stewart provocatively suggested that "the publishing business is ... the only organized private business that is given explicit constitutional protection," we have arrived at a moment in which the lines between old and new media are so blurred that the very idea of "established news media" may seem antique. But this article will suggest that the second-class status of the Press Clause should again nevertheless be open to reexamination.

Thinking about this question in light of the rise of the blog raises a number of important issues. The objections that were advanced in reaction to the initial push by Justice Stewart and others to give some meaning to the Press Clause included, most prominently, the view that it was just too difficult to define the press, and that according the press special privileges would be an unpardonable act of constitutional elitism. If only some people get to be "the press," how can we determine who is entitled to claim that mantle, and how can we justify granting them special privileges? On the other hand, if anyone can now be "the press," won't any "special" protections simply be watered down to nothing? These are still difficult questions, and it is not clear how the addition of blogs to the mix affects the analysis. But they are worth asking at this moment, both because of broader developments in constitutional theory and doctrine, and because the rise of blogs may spark new thoughts about this old debate. The Press Clause may yet have important things to tell us about our understanding of the Constitution and its relationship to the real world of speech....

II. "FREE PRESS" AND "OPEN PRESS"

...Much has been written on the question of what, precisely, the Press Clause was meant to do, and whether it actually signaled that the framers of the Constitution intended to provide any meaningful independent protection for the press. It is possible that the Press Clause singled out the press by name only because it had been subjected to official restrictions that were unique to that medium and inapplicable to individual speakers. Or perhaps the Framers simply used the terms interchangeably, with little thought for any distinct meaning the Speech and Press Clauses might hold.

Those arguments might not suffice to settle the question. I think they do not. In the final analysis, as Professor Nimmer wrote, "It is what [the Framers] *said*, and not necessarily what they meant, that in the last analysis may be determinative"—and what they said was that speech and press merited separate consideration. Still, looking at the historical understanding and development of "the press" may help us think more clearly about the purposes and uses of the Press Clause today.

Recent work in this area may, in fact, shed some new light on the ways we think about the Press Clause in the age of the blog. Drawing on the historical work of Robert W. T. Martin, some scholars have discerned *two* traditions at work in the history of law and the press in America. One is the idea of a "free press"—the idea that "the press should be free of state intervention so as to engage in criticism of government and thereby defend public liberty." The press in this conception should operate as an independent, autonomous institution carrying out a "watchdog" function as a monitor of government. This is essentially the model Justice Stewart drew on when he argued that the Press Clause was meant "to create a fourth institution outside the government as an additional check on the three official branches."

The other tradition is that of the "open press." This is the idea that "all individuals have a right to disseminate their viewpoints for general consideration." On this view, a free press means nothing more than that "all people should have the opportunity to articulate their views for popular consideration." The press is not an expert and autonomous watchdog scrutinizing government action. Rather, it is simply a vehicle for the dissemination of ideas and a forum for "uninhibited, robust and wide-open" debate.

These competing conceptions of "the press" may cash out in different and interesting ways. Understanding the Press Clause from the perspective of the "free press" model leads to a more specific and specialized understanding of the role of the press within the Press Clause. It suggests, as Justice Stewart wrote, that the clause safeguards a uniquely structural role for the press as a monitor of the conduct of public officials. This conception of the Press Clause could serve as the source of a richer, more positive set of protections for the press. To the extent the press serves a structural role as a check on the "official branches" of government, it is but a small step—though not an inevitable one—to argue that the Press Clause provides some degree of privileges and immunities for the press. At the same time, the free press model raises the definitional concerns I have already noted, and gives rise to the charge that the Constitution should create no privileged institutions. Moreover, to the extent that the free press model is based squarely on the press's function as a watchdog of government, it offers little direct basis for institutional protection of the press when it discusses issues other than public affairs, such as sports or entertainment....

The "open press" model avoids these problems. It is less likely to be limited in orientation to press discussions of public affairs; and because the model "conveys the right to free expression to individuals, rather than to an institution," it does not face the same problems of definition or elitism. At the same time, the open press model does not do the same degree of work that the free press model potentially could. To the extent that the free press model simply acknowledges the right of "all individuals" to "disseminate their viewpoints," it is unlikely to say anything about reporters' privileges, press access, or any other positive rights of the press. The open press model thus does seem to invite the charge of earlier writers on the Press Clause that it risks becoming redundant in light of the protections already offered by the Speech Clause. Indeed, the open press model may at times even be suggestive of additional limits on the press: if one generalizes from the view that the open press model historically entailed the willingness of publishers to offer up to the public any views that were presented to them, then the open press model lends support to the view, rejected thus far by the Court, that newspapers ought to be required to make their pages available to a broad range of contending views, just as broadcasters may constitutionally be required to do so.

A good deal of evidence suggests that citizens in the founding era would have understood the "press" protected by the Press Clause according to something like the open press model. If by the free press model we mean something like the model of an "organized, expert" body capable of conducting "scrutiny of government," then few if any of the newspapers extant during the pre-Revolutionary and Revolutionary periods met these criteria.... The development of an understanding of "the press" more closely aligned with our own modern understanding of journalism—reasonably expert, autonomous, disinterested, governed by professional norms and dedicated to its watchdog function—would not occur until the 1830s, at the earliest, and perhaps as late as the early 20th century.

...But we must be careful not to overstate this conclusion. While the early American press little resembled the professional watchdog described in Justice Stewart's article, the Revolutionary and post-Revolutionary eras did see the increasing development of norms of journalistic autonomy and the rise of newspaper editors who were "becoming seriously engaged in political reporting and in presenting to [their] readership, the citizenry, a systematic account of government." Even at the outset of this nation's constitutionalization of press freedom, in other words, the concept of a free and institutional press serving a watchdog function, with all that this concept entails, was in the air....

...In their current state, many blogs resemble in many respects the passionate, partisan, largely amateur, and often anonymous collection of printers and writers who were at work during the founding era, and who were memorialized in the Press Clause. To the extent the blogosphere resembles the press of the founding era, it may then be natural to suggest that our thoughts concerning the constitutional status of and protection for blogs should stem as much from the Press Clause as from the Speech Clause. Moreover, we can protect blogs under an open press model of the Press Clause without incurring at least some of the risks that this model entails. In particular, the nature of blogs obviates the concern that an open press model may fuel calls for forced access to another's "press." Given the inexpensive nature of blogging, we can ensure a diversity of views without having to treat any blog as a public good that may be forced to offer space to individuals with contrary views.

Thus, blogs find a natural home in the open press model of the Press Clause. We should hesitate before settling on this model, however, for two related reasons. First, as I have already suggested, if the open press model is largely about the protection of "uninhibited, robust and wide-open" debate, then the Press Clause does not do anything that the Speech Clause does not already do; we are back to the redundancy problem.

Second, however mixed the success of the advocates of a free press model of the Press Clause may have been, we should not be too swift to trade in that understanding of the Press Clause, with its more vigorous protection for the newsgathering process, for a model that sacrifices that vigor for the sake of the universality of the right. The institutional press captured in the free press model, and in Justice Stewart's argument for the Press Clause as a structural guarantee, continues to fulfill important functions in our society....

III. BLOGS, "THE PRESS," AND "JOURNALISM": A FUNCTIONAL APPROACH

... The usual understanding of "expert scrutiny of government," and of the watchdog model more generally, is that it involves, not a *status*, but an *activity*: it involves skilled newsgathering, interviewing, ferreting out of facts, investigative reporting—in short, that set of activities we call "journalism." If that is so, we should not think of the constitutional status of blogs in terms of a contest between blogs and the mainstream media. Rather, we might think about the Press Clause, or various statutes that protect the press, as offering protection to certain functions that may be performed by either blogs or the established institutional press. We could think in terms of constitutional or non-constitutional protection for the function of journalism.

This way of thinking about the Press Clause assumes that some form of heightened protection ought to be available for individuals or institutions when they engage in activities that meet some definition of the practice of journalism. For example, we might say that an individual who "is involved in a process that is intended to generate and disseminate truthful information to the public on a regular basis" is a journalist, and ought to be able to claim whatever protections the Press Clause provides for that process, or whatever non-constitutional sources of protection the legislatures or common law provide for the newsgathering process. Or we might conclude that any person may claim some set of privileges where he or she is engaged in investigative reporting, gathering news, and doing so with the present intention to disseminate the news to the public.

In a variety of ways, this functional approach to the understanding of those protections afforded to "the press," whether by the Constitution or by various statutes, is already a common feature in the law.... For example, a number of courts have taken a functional approach when examining claims of constitutional or statutory qualified privilege by a variety of individuals: a person who gathered information for personal use and later decided to use that information to write a book, an investigative reporter who deliberately set out to gather information for a book, and the producer of taped commentaries for a 900 number controlled by the World Championship Wrestling organization. Legal academics have proposed a slew of similar approaches. And, of course, the states that have adopted statutory reporters' privileges have relied, at least in part, on functional definitions when drafting those statutory protections. To these shield statutes we could also add a variety of federal and state statutes dealing with questions of press access to information or to government proceedings, freedom from intrusive searches, and other privileges or immunities. But a functional understanding of the press is also present in the law in ways that may be less apparent. Thus, Randall Bezanson has argued persuasively that many courts, when examining the contours of constitutional protection for the press in libel cases, have asked whether the press actor was exercising editorial judgment, defined as the "independent choice of information and opinion of current value, directed to public need, and born of non-self-interested purposes."

Depending on how one defines the function of journalism, this functional understanding of the Press Clause could obviously protect blogs as well as the more established and recognized press.... It now seems safe to say, not that all blogs are a form of journalism, or that blogging is never journalism, but that "some Weblogs are doing journalism, at least part of the time." At the very least, when a blogger engages in fact-gathering for purposes of public dissemination of newsworthy information, that blogger can be seen as having engaged in an act of journalism that is worthy of some constitutional or statutory protection.

A functional understanding of the Press Clause, or of the myriad statutory protections that fulfill the potential of the Press Clause, thus would provide a measure of protection to blogs when they are actively engaged in those core activities that we think of as constituting journalism. The medium by which that journalism is disseminated to the public matters far less than the fact that an individual has deliberately gathered and disseminated newsworthy facts.

Some observations about this approach are in order. First, it should be noted that a number of current statutory protections for journalism partake of institutional elements that would leave blogs unprotected even if they were engaged in journalism. For example, California's shield law requires the person claiming the protection of the law to be "connected with or employed upon a newspaper, magazine, or other periodical publication, or by a press association or wire service"; and New York's statute provides protection only to regular employees of news organizations or those who are "otherwise professionally affiliated for gain or livelihood" with news organizations.... [A] functional approach certainly recommends that states reexamine their shield laws with bloggers in mind, focusing on function rather than affiliation.

Second, I have assumed that the functional approach is most relevant for positive claims that a blogger should be entitled to the same privileges or immunities—the right not to be compelled to reveal one's sources, the right to resist searches, the right of access to government records or proceedings, and so forth—that the traditional press have, in one way or another, been able to claim. As such, I have assumed a fairly narrow compass for the functional approach. This approach would thus offer little protection for the primary activity of most blogs (and many newspapers, for that matter)—"shaping, filtering, commenting, contextualizing, and disseminating...the news reports that others have produced." That does not mean that such blogs are simply left out in the cold; they may still rely on the protections offered by the Speech Clause. But it does suggest that a functional approach would only protect *some* of the functions performed by blogs or the established press.

Is the functional approach, then, a better way of understanding both the Press Clause and the role of blogs within the Press Clause? One might think so. Certainly this approach would protect much of what is at the core of journalism: not merely first-person observation, but the gathering of facts from a variety of sources for the purposes of public dissemination of important information. And because it is available to anyone who engages in the function of journalism, and not simply those individuals who are employed by recognized and established news media, this approach gets rid of any concerns about elitism.

Nevertheless, we should not be wholly satisfied with this approach. First, the functional approach may avoid one definitional problem—are blogs journalism?—only to replace it with other, equally difficult definitional questions: What *is* journalism, exactly? ... Once we decide that certain journalistic functions merit heightened protection, whether under the Press Clause or under a statute, then a definitional problem is simply inevitable. ... [I]t is safe to say that adding blogs to the mix complicates the situation considerably. Furthermore, because blogs rarely involve the kinds of internal controls that govern in the newsroom—in particular, the restraining force of professional norms of reporting, the presence of layers of editors, the time for reflection provided by (usually) non-instantaneous communication, and the simple cost of establishing a newspaper or other news medium—there may be more reasons to worry that bloggers will invoke the legal protections offered to journalists for purely opportunistic reasons.

These objections should not carry *too* much weight. If one believes that the newsgathering function merits added protection, the definitional problems and the threat of opportunism must simply be counted as part of the inevitable but necessary cost of seeing those additional protections into being. Nevertheless, even if one sets these objections aside, something still seems lacking in the functional approach. Focusing on function alone hardly seems to capture all the ways in which the news media, old or new, contribute to our social discourse. It seems a thin conception of the ways in which mainstream media form a part of the fabric of our social life simply to suggest that they add some store of new facts to what we knew already. It does not describe, in Professor Balkin's words, the ways in which old media form part of the ongoing conversation that makes up our "democratic culture." And if that is true of conventional media, it is doubly true of blogs, whose value consists primarily of their role as "*participatory* media," and which have quickly established their own unique role in our cultural conversation. A functional approach to the role of the blogosphere within the Press Clause does not seem to engage its real role, which is only secondarily about "journalism" and far more about its status as a "miniature public sphere of its own."...

IV. STEWART REDUX: A NEW INSTITUTIONAL APPROACH

So I return to the inspiration for the title of this contribution: Justice Stewart's provocative suggestion that we think of the Press Clause as "a *structural* provision of the Constitution" that protects "the institutional autonomy of the press." We might conclude after thirty years that Stewart's institutional vision of the Press Clause is a non-starter. The Supreme Court certainly has never signed on to anything like a fully fledged version of Stewart's description of the Press Clause... there may be more life in it than one would expect.

...Under an institutional approach to the First Amendment, it is not out of the question that blogs, despite their evident variety, can and should find some degree of protection in the Press Clause as an autonomous "press" institution in their own right.

In making this argument, I leave much open for future discussion. It is certainly not clear at this point what the precise scope and nature of the protection blogs might enjoy under an institutional approach to the Press Clause would be; and it is not necessarily the case that blogs ought to enjoy precisely the same degree of protection that the established news media would enjoy in their own right under an institutional approach to the Press Clause. Instead, I will argue that the established press and the blogosphere should each be protected largely according to the internal norms—evolving norms, in the case of the blogosphere—that govern each of these "First Amendment institutions."

We might start by stepping back from the Press Clause and thinking about First Amendment doctrine more generally. Frederick Schauer has argued persuasively that the current state of the doctrine might be characterized as one of institutional agnosticism. The Supreme Court's general reluctance to invest the Press Clause with any content that might suggest press speakers have different rights than individual speakers is but one example....

There are some good arguments in favor of an institutionally agnostic approach. But the cost of this approach is that the Court is obliged to force the complex real world in which speech occurs onto the Procrustean bed of its First Amendment doctrine, to draw myriad exceptions, or simply to distort the existing doctrine....

...Rather than build First Amendment doctrine from the top down, crafting general rules that apply imperfectly across a range of situations, the courts might begin with the recognition that a "number of existing social institutions"—such as the press, universities, religious associations, libraries, and perhaps others—"serve functions that the First Amendment deems especially important." Building on this foundation, the courts could "construct First Amendment doctrine in response to the actual functions and practices" of those institutions that merit recognition as "First Amendment institutions."

Under this approach, the Court would identify those institutions that merit recognition as First Amendment institutions. Those institutions would then be granted significant presumptive autonomy to act, and the courts would defer substantially to actions taken by those institutions within their respective spheres of autonomy. The courts might go further still, and recognize instances in which the social value served by some First Amendment institution counsels privileges or immunities, such as some degree of protection for reporters' ability to maintain the confidentiality of their sources, that might not be available to other speakers. The courts might, in short, value First Amendment institutions as *institutions*, and accord them substantial autonomy to act within that institutional framework.

To argue for an institutional approach to the First Amendment is not the equivalent of an argument in favor of an absolute constitutional immunity for First Amendment institutions. That a First Amendment institution might have substantial autonomy to act does not mean it would not be obliged to act within "constitutionally prescribed limits." This approach does entail granting a substantial degree of self-governance to those institutions that play a substantial role in contributing to the world of public discourse that the First Amendment aims to promote and preserve. But my point is precisely that these institutions are already substantially *self*-governing institutions: they operate in accordance with an often detailed and highly constraining set of *internal* norms that govern the bounds of appropriate behavior within different First Amendment institutions.

An institutional approach thus simply suggests that courts should, in the first instance, defer to those institutions' capacity for self-governance rather than attempt to impose an ill-fitting doctrinal framework based on the idea that one set of First Amendment rules can and should apply to the radically different social institutions in which speech takes place. To the extent it is necessary to build some set of "constitutionally prescribed limits" around the behavior of those institutions, the courts should build from the bottom up, taking their cue from the norms and practices of the institution in question and from the social values served by that institution. Thus, the court might ask of a First Amendment institution's action in a particular case, not whether it comports with some universal First Amendment rule, but whether it falls within the boundaries of behavior broadly consistent with the norms and practices of that institution, and whether those norms and practices serve the First Amendment values that are advanced by the role of that institution within the broader society....

...In various ways, the Court already acknowledges the unique value of a variety of traditional speech institutions, the press not least among them. This tendency is perhaps most apparent in the cases involving the law of government speech, in which the Court has shaped its doctrine according to whether the government speaker is acting as a library, a journalist, or an arts funder. It is also evident in the Court's hesitant but clear recognition that universities operate under principles of academic freedom.... It is also arguable that these cases can be seen as part of a broader trend on the current Court of recognizing and protecting the autonomy of a variety of intermediary institutions that serve a vital social and structural role in our society.

If we think of the First Amendment in institutional terms, the Press Clause is obviously the most natural, most textually rooted place to find some form of institutional autonomy for what we might label the conventional working press. Here, too, we may see some traces of institutionally oriented thinking in the Supreme Court's treatment of the press. Although it is true that the Court has refused to explicitly grant the press any institutional autonomy, underneath the surface the picture is a little different.... The Court has repeatedly suggested that in evaluating cases involving the press, it will erect a sphere of autonomy around the press's performance of some of its key functions, such as editing. Finally, although the protections of *New York Times v. Sullivan* and its progeny may also apply to non-media speakers, it is clear that the constitutional rules governing defamation actions involving public figures or matters of public concern were crafted with the press in mind. In sum, in a variety of ways, the Court's treatment of issues involving the press has both informed and, more importantly, been informed by a series of norms and principles that emerge from the nature of the press as an institution....

...Blogs can be thought of as a kind of emerging First Amendment institution. More particularly, they can be viewed as an especially visible and well-crystallized example of a broader developing speech institution: the unique environment that is public discourse in cyberspace. Once we think of blogs as a First Amendment institution, we might ask whether the Press Clause, recognizing the blogosphere as a unique form of "press," could accord the blogosphere a similar form of institutional autonomy, and create some breathing space for the formation and evolution of this new institutional form of public discourse.

Conceiving of blogs as a type of First Amendment institution, entitled to substantial autonomy as an institution, raises some difficult questions about the scope of autonomy blogs should enjoy. In particular, notwithstanding the disdain for the professionalized print and broadcast press that is so common in the blogosphere, there are good reasons to believe that the institutional structure of the established news media makes them better suited for some degree of legally granted, constitutionally grounded institutional autonomy than blogs might be. The established news media typically operate subject to a set of ethical and professional norms, made explicit in a host of ethical codes and, more importantly, absorbed by individual journalists in a deeply embedded sense of professional identity that shapes and constrains their actions.... In addition, mainstream news media are subject to a variety of constraints that emerge from the editing process and the simple fact of their corporate and hierarchical structure. Blogs, on the other hand, are written by individuals or small groups, and postings are typically transmitted without editing and often without much reflection on the part of the blogger. Nor are many bloggers enamored of the idea of a bloggers' code of ethics.

To raise these questions does not mean that blogs should not receive any institutional protection under the Press Clause, however. Rather, these questions simply lead to the conclusion that an institutionally differentiated First Amendment would naturally suggest: that an institutional approach to blogs under the Press Clause should attempt to draw the contours of blogs' institutional autonomy in a way that is appropriate to *blogs as an institution*. On this view, it would be an error to characterize blogs as "a new form of journalism," and attempt to draw institutional protections that simply ape whatever institutional protections the conventional press are entitled to. Instead, we should ask what protections are necessary given the purpose, value, and nature of blogs as an institution.

If we consider blogs from this institutional perspective, the first thing that is apparent is that blogs form a *collective* institution. Although it may make sense to think of newspapers as singular, if similar, entities, it makes less sense to think of blogs as isolated speech instruments. We might say, grandiosely, that there are no blogs—there is only the blogosphere. Blogging ultimately is a collective enterprise, and must be understood as part of the distinctly collective and participatory public discourse that is speech in cyberspace.

Once blogs are viewed collectively rather than individually, there is much to be said for the idea that blogs *do* enjoy the kind of institutional framework that makes it less dangerous for courts to cede a considerable degree of autonomy to them. Typically, we rely on newspapers to correct their own errors; we thus emphasize, through libel law, the importance of newspapers' acting according to the proper institutional norms: reporting and editing without actual malice, and with the sound exercise of editorial judgment. Blogs' correction practices are not singular but collective: errors are exposed and corrected through the exposure of mistakes and the airing of corrective views on many, many other blogs. Furthermore, whatever bloggers may say about not wanting a code of ethics to be imposed on them, it should be apparent to anyone who has engaged in sustained blogging that an organic set of norms and practices *has* evolved, and continues to evolve, in the blogosphere. Bloggers already seek to conform to a wide variety of relevant norms: norms in favor of linking to other sites; norms in favor of linking to the newspaper article or other source that forms the subject of, and that supports (or refutes) the arguments made by, the blogger in a given post; norms in favor of correcting or disputing errors that have been pointed out by others; and norms in favor of allowing commenters, who also serve as error-correcting agents. Corresponding to these norms is an evolving set of norms that govern readers' expectations on the blogosphere: norms that suggest that certain sites may be more trustworthy than others, and that assertions made on any one site ought not be completely credited unless and until they have been verified elsewhere.

In sum, the norms developing in and around the blogosphere—both bloggers' norms and readers' norms—suggest the development of an institutional framework that may collectively do much of the verification, correction, and trust-establishing work that established news media institutions do individually. These conclusions lead us to some tentative thoughts about what an institutional First Amendment approach to blogs under the Press Clause might look like. Certainly it would entail the same assumption I have urged should govern the treatment of the established press under the Press Clause: that they should be given substantial institutional autonomy by the courts. But the shape of that autonomy, built from the ground up based on what we know of social discourse in the blogosphere, might be different.

For example, with respect to defamation law, it might make sense to shape legal doctrine in a way that recognizes the collective environment in which speech and the correction of errors takes place in the blogosphere. I do not mean by this that individual blogs would be utterly immune from liability for defamation simply because of the fact that errors might be corrected elsewhere in the blogosphere. We might, for instance, give greater or lesser immunity to individual blogs depending on how much they actually make use of this collective error-correcting mechanism: the degree to which they link to the sources they cite, the degree to which they track back to other sites, the degree to which they allow commentary, the degree to which they respond to others' efforts to correct them, the degree to which they actually acknowledge and correct errors, and so forth.

It is not clear how arguments for more affirmative rights, such as rights of access or rights against the compelled disclosure of sources, should fare under an institutional First Amendment treatment of blogs. It is obviously impossible to grant press credentials to every blog that might request them, for example. But it is also the case that most blogs still rely on original reporting supplied primarily by the established news media. So it might be the case that an individual's claim of constitutional access rights under the Press Clause would fail on *institutional* grounds. For similar reasons, it is not clear how we should treat bloggers' claims of a constitutionally grounded privilege of nondisclosure of sources. But the age of the blogger-journalist is still young, and we should look to the norms and practices that develop in considering this question over the long term.

Would an institutional understanding of blogs' place under the Press Clause offer any payoff for blogs, or for our understanding of First Amendment doctrine? I think it would. To be sure, much of the law that would result from an explicitly institutional approach to the First Amendment and blogs would resemble existing First Amendment doctrine. That has less to do, however, with the sufficiency of existing doctrine, and more to do with the fact that the existing doctrine already contorts itself in an effort to respond to the nature and value of different speech institutions. An institutional approach would simply permit courts to do explicitly, transparently, and self-consciously what they already do implicitly and clumsily.

Moreover, because an institutionally differentiated understanding of the role of blogs would not simply attempt to import the law of the established press wholesale into this very different medium, it would ease the fear that if everyone is treated as "the press," any rights granted under the Press Clause will be so diluted as to be meaningless. Rather, it would be clear that the Press Clause protects more than one institution, and that the content of the rights pertaining to each must vary according to the nature and practices of each institution. Thinking of blogs on an institutional level would also encourage courts to pay attention to such issues as blogs' treatment under the election laws and how they should be treated for purposes of taxation, keeping in mind both the commonalities and differences between blogs *and* the established press.

Most importantly, an institutional approach to the treatment of blogs under the Press Clause would encourage courts to more self-consciously consider blogs in *context*: to give blogs substantial autonomy to act, while monitoring the development of norms of behavior in the blogosphere and encouraging blogs to develop rules of conduct that deter the worst of the social ills that might emerge from the blogosphere. It would encourage courts to develop a constitutional law of blogging that allows the relevant legal norms to emerge from those cultural norms that the blogs develop themselves. In this way, our constitutional law, whether with respect to blogs or with respect to the press, universities, and other First Amendment institutions, will be the product of an organic dialogue about legal, constitutional, and cultural norms both inside and outside of the courts....

APPENDICES

CONSTITUTION OF THE UNITED STATES OF AMERICA

We, the people of the United States, in order to form a more perfect union, establish justice, insure domestic tranquility, provide for the common defense, promote the general welfare, and secure the blessings of liberty to ourselves and our posterity, do ordain and establish this Constitution for the United States of America.

ARTICLE I

Section I

1. All legislative powers herein granted shall be vested in a Congress of the United States, which shall consist of a Senate and House of Representatives.

Section II

1. The House of Representatives shall be composed of members chosen every second year by the people of the several States; and the electors in each

State shall have the qualifications requisite for electors of the most numerous branch of the State Legislature.

2. No person shall be a Representative who shall not have attained to the age of twenty-five years, and been seven years a citizen of the United States, and who shall not, when elected, be an inhabitant of that State in which he shall be chosen.

3. Representatives and direct taxes shall be apportioned among the several States which may be included within this Union, according to their respective numbers, which shall be determined by adding to the whole number of free persons, including those bound to service for a term of years, and excluding Indians not taxed, three-fifths of all other persons. The actual enumeration shall be made within three years after the first meeting of the Congress of the United States, and within every subsequent term of ten years, in such manner as they shall by law direct. The number of Representatives shall not exceed one for every thirty thousand, but each State shall have at least one Representative; and until such enumeration shall be made, the State of New Hampshire shall be entitled to choose three; Massachusetts, eight; Rhode Island and Providence Plantations, one; Connecticut, five; New York, six; New Jersey, four; Pennsylvania, eight; Delaware, one; Maryland, six; Virginia, ten; North Carolina, five; South Carolina, five, and Georgia, three.

4. When vacancies happen in the representation from any State, the executive authority thereof shall issue writs of election to fill such vacancies.

5. The House of Representatives shall choose their speaker and other officers; and shall have the sole power of impeachment.

Section III

1. The Senate of the United States shall be composed of two Senators from each State, chosen by the Legislature thereof for six years; and each Senator shall have one vote.

2. Immediately after they shall be assembled in consequence of the first election, they shall be divided as equally as may be into three classes. The

seats of the Senators of the first class shall be vacated at the expiration of the second year, of the second class at the expiration of the fourth year, and of the third class at the expiration of the sixth year, so that one third may be chosen every second year; and if vacancies happen by resignation, or otherwise, during the recess of the Legislature of any State, the executive thereof may make temporary appointments until the next meeting of the Legislature, which shall then fill such vacancies.

3. No person shall be a Senator who shall not have attained to the age of thirty years, and been nine years a citizen of the United States, and who shall not, when elected, be an inhabitant of that State for which he shall be chosen.

4. The Vice-President of the United States shall be President of the Senate, but shall have no vote unless they be equally divided.

5. The Senate shall choose their other officers, and also a President pro tempore, in the absence of the Vice-President, or when he shall exercise the office of President of the United States.

6. The Senate shall have the sole power to try all impeachments. When sitting for that purpose, they shall all be on oath or affirmation. When the President of the United States is tried, the chief-justice shall preside: and no person shall be convicted without the concurrence of two thirds of the members present.

7. Judgment in cases of impeachment shall not extend further than to removal from office, and disqualification to hold and enjoy any office of honor, trust, or profit under the United States; but the party convicted shall nevertheless be liable and subject to indictment, trial, judgment, and punishment, according to law.

Section IV

1. The times, places and manner of holding elections for Senators and Representatives shall be prescribed in each State by the Legislature thereof; but the Congress may at any time by law make of alter such regulations, except as to the place of choosing Senators.

Section V

1. Each House shall be the judge of the election, returns, and qualifications of its own members, and a majority of each shall constitute a quorum to do business; but a smaller number may adjourn from day to day, and may be authorized to compel the attendance of absent members, in such manner and under such penalties as each House may provide.

2. Each House may determine the rule of its proceedings, punish its members for disorderly behavior, and, with the concurrence of two thirds, expel a member.

3. Each House shall keep a journal of its proceedings, and from time to time publish the same, excepting such parts as may in their judgment require secrecy; and the yeas and nays of the members of either House on any questions shall, at the desire of one fifth of those present, be entered on the journal.

4. Neither House, during the session of Congress, shall, without the consent of the other, adjourn for more than three days, nor to any other place than that in which the two houses shall be sitting.

Section VI

1. The Senators and Representatives shall receive a compensation for their services, to be ascertained by law, and paid out of the treasury of the United States. They shall, in all cases, except treason, felony, and breach of the peace, be privileged from arrest during their attendance at the sessions of their respective houses, and in going to and returning from same; and for any speech or debate in either house, they shall not be questioned in any other place.

2. No Senator or Representative shall, during the time for which he was elected, be appointed to any civil office under the authority of the United States which shall have been created, or the emoluments whereof shall have been increased during such time; and no person holding any office under the United States shall be a member of either House during his continuance in office.

Section VII

1. All bills for raising revenue shall originate in the House of Representatives, but the Senate may propose or concur with amendments, as on other bills.

2. Every bill which shall have passed the House of Representatives and the Senate shall, before it become a law, be presented to the President of the United States; if he approve, he shall sign it, but if not, he shall return it, with his objections, to that House in which it shall have originated, who shall enter the objections at large on their journal, and proceed to reconsider it. If after such reconsideration two thirds of that House shall agree to pass the bill, it shall be sent, together with the objections, to the other House, by which it shall likewise be reconsidered; and if approved by two thirds of that House it shall become a law. But in all such cases the votes of both Houses shall be determined by yeas and nays, and the names of the persons voting for and against the bill shall be entered on the journal of each House respectively. If any bill shall not be returned by the President within ten days (Sundays excepted) after it shall have been presented to him, the same shall be a law in like manner as if he had signed it, unless the Congress by their adjournment, prevent its return; in which case it shall not be a law.

3. Every order, resolution, or vote to which the concurrence of the Senate and House of Representatives may be necessary (except on a question of adjournment) shall be presented to the President of the United States; and before the same shall take effect shall be approved by him, or being disapproved by him, shall be repassed by two thirds of the Senate and the House of Representatives, according to the rules and limitations prescribed in the case of a bill.

Section VIII

1. The Congress shall have power to lay and collect taxes, duties, imposts, and excises, to pay the debts and provide for the common defense and general welfare of the United States; but all duties, imposts, and excises shall be uniform throughout the United States.

2. To borrow money on the credit of the United States.

3. To regulate commerce with foreign nations, and among the several States, and with the Indian tribes.

4. To establish an uniform rule of naturalization and uniform laws on the subject of bankruptcies throughout the United States.

5. To coin money, regulate the value thereof, and of foreign coin, and fix the standard of weights and measures.

6. To provide for the punishment of counterfeiting the securities and current coin of the United States.

7. To establish post offices and post roads.

8. To promote the progress of science and useful arts, by securing for limited times to authors and inventors the exclusive rights to their respective writings and discoveries.

9. To constitute tribunals inferior to the Supreme Court.

10. To define and punish piracies and felonies committed on the high seas, and offenses against the law of nations.

11. To declare war, grant letters of marque and reprisal, and make rules concerning captures on land and water.

12. To raise and support armies, but no appropriation of money to that use shall be for a longer term than two years.

13. To provide and maintain a navy.

14. To make rules for the government and regulation of the land and naval forces.

15. To provide for calling forth the militia to execute the laws of the Union, suppress insurrections, and repel invasions.

16. To provide for organizing, arming, and disciplining the militia, and for governing such part of them as may be employed in the service of the United States, reserving to the States respectively the appointment of the officers, and the authority of training the militia according to the discipline prescribed by Congress.

17. To exercise exclusive legislation in all cases whatsoever over such district (not exceeding ten miles square) as may, by cession of particular States and the acceptance of Congress, become the seat of Government of the United States, and to exercise like authority over all places purchased by the consent of the Legislature of the State in which the same shall be, for the erection of forts, magazines, arsenals, dry docks, and other needful buildings.

18. To make all laws which shall be necessary and proper for carrying into execution the foregoing powers, and all other powers vested by this Constitution in the Government of the United States, or in any department or officer thereof.

Section IX

1. The migration or importation of such persons as any of the States now existing shall think proper to admit shall not be prohibited by the Congress prior to the year one thousand eight hundred and eight, but a tax or duty may be imposed on such importation, not exceeding ten dollars for each person.

2. The privilege of the writ of habeas corpus shall not be suspended, unless when in cases of rebellion or invasion the public safety may require it.

3. No bill of attainder or ex post facto law shall be passed.

4. No capitation or other direct tax shall be laid, unless in proportion to the census or enumeration hereinbefore directed to be taken.

5. No tax or duty shall be laid on articles exported from any State.

6. No preference shall be given by any regulation of commerce or revenue to the ports of one State over those of another, nor shall vessels bound to or from one State be obliged to enter, clear, or pay duties in another.

7. No money shall be drawn from the Treasury but in consequence of appropriations made by law; and a regular statement and account of the receipts and expenditures of all public money shall be published from time to time.

8. No title of nobility shall be granted by the United States. And no person holding any office of profit or trust under them shall, without the consent of the Congress, accept of any present, emolument, office, or title of any kind whatever from any king, prince, or foreign state.

Section X

1. No state shall enter into any treaty, alliance, or confederation, grant letters of marque and reprisal, coin money, emit bills of credit, make anything but gold and silver coin a tender in payment of debts, pass any bill of attainder, ex post facto law, or law impairing the obligation of contracts, or grant any title of nobility.

2. No State shall, without the consent of the Congress, lay any impost or duties on imports or exports, except what may be absolutely necessary for executing its inspection laws, and the net produce of all duties and imposts, laid by any State on imports or exports, shall be for the use of the Treasury of the United States; and all such laws shall be subject to the revision and control of the Congress.

3. No State shall, without the consent of Congress, lay any duty of tonnage, keep troops or ships of war in time of peace, enter into any agreement or compact with another State, or with a foreign power, or engage in war, unless actually invaded, or in such imminent danger as will not admit of delay.

ARTICLE II

Section I

1. The Executive power shall be vested in a President of the United States of America. He shall hold his office during the term of four years, and, together with the Vice-President, chosen for the same term, be elected as follows:

2. Each State shall appoint, in such manner as the Legislature thereof may direct, a number of electors, equal to the whole number of Senators and Representatives to which the State may be entitled in the Congress; but no Senator or Representative or person holding an office of trust or profit under the United States shall be appointed an elector.

3. [The electors shall meet in their respective States and vote by ballot for two persons, of whom one at least shall not be an inhabitant of the same State with themselves. And they shall make a list of all the persons voted for, and of the number of votes for each, which list they shall sign and certify and transmit, sealed, to the seat of the government of the United States, directed to the President of the Senate. The President of the Senate shall, in the presence of the Senate and House of Representatives, open all the certificates, and the votes shall then be counted. The person having the greatest number of votes shall be the President, if such number be a majority of the whole number of electors appointed, and if there be more than one who have such majority, and have an equal number of votes, then the House of Representatives shall immediately choose by ballot one of them for President; and if no person have a majority, then from the five highest on the list the said House shall in like manner choose the President. But in choosing the President, the vote shall be taken by States, the representation from each State having one vote. A quorum, for this purpose, shall consist of a member or members from two thirds of the States, and a majority of all the States shall be necessary to a choice. In every case, after the choice of the President, the person having the greatest number of votes of the electors shall be the Vice-President. But if there should remain two or more who have equal votes, the Senate shall choose from them by ballot the Vice-President.]*

---

*This clause is superseded by Article XII.

4. The Congress may determine the time of choosing the electors and the day on which they shall give their votes, which day shall be the same throughout the United States.

5. No person except a natural born citizen, or a citizen of the United States at the time of the adoption of this Constitution, shall be eligible to the office of President; neither shall any person be eligible to that office who shall not have attained to the age of thirty-five years and been fourteen years a resident within the United States.

6. In case of the removal of the President from office, or of his death, resignation, or inability to discharge the powers and duties of the said office, the same shall devolve on the Vice-President, and the Congress may by law provide for the case of removal, death, resignation, or inability, both of the President and Vice-President, declaring what officer shall then act as President, and such officer shall act accordingly until the disability be removed or a President shall be elected.

7. The President shall, at stated times, receive for his services a compensation, which shall neither be increased nor diminished during the period for which he shall have been elected, and he shall not receive within that period any other emolument from the United States, or any of them.

8. Before he enter on the execution of his office he shall take the following oath or affirmation: "I do solemnly swear (or affirm) that I will faithfully execute the office of President of the United States, and will, to the best of my ability, preserve, protect, and defend the Constitution of the United States."

Section II

1. The President shall be Commander-in-Chief of the Army and Navy of the United States, and of the militia of the several States when called into the actual service of the United States; he may require the opinion, in writing, of the principal officer in each of the executive departments upon any subject relating to the duties of their respective offices, and he shall have power to grant reprieves and pardons for offenses against the United States except in cases of impeachment.

2. He shall have power, by and with the advice and consent of the Senate, to make treaties, provided two thirds of the Senators present concur; and he shall nominate, and by and with the advice and consent of the Senate shall appoint ambassadors, other public ministers and consuls, judges of the Supreme Court, and all other officers of the United States whose appointments are not herein otherwise provided for, and which shall be established by law; but the Congress may by law vest the appointment of such inferior officers as they think proper in the President alone, in the courts of law, or in the heads of departments.

3. The President shall have power to fill up all vacancies that may happen during the recess of the Senate by granting commissions, which shall expire at the end of their next session.

Section III

He shall from time to time give to the Congress information of the state of the Union, and recommend to their consideration such measure as he shall judge necessary and expedient; he may, on extraordinary occasions, convene both Houses, or either of them, and in case of disagreement between them with respect to the time of adjournment, he may adjourn them to such time as he shall think proper; he shall receive ambassadors and other public ministers; he shall take care that the laws be faithfully executed, and shall commission all the officers of the United States.

Section IV

The President, Vice-President, and all civil officers of the United States shall be removed from office on impeachment for and conviction of treason, bribery, or other high crimes and misdemeanors.

ARTICLE III

Section I

The judicial power of the United States shall be vested in one Supreme Court, and in such inferior courts as the Congress may from time to time ordain and establish. The judges, both of the Supreme and inferior courts, shall hold their offices during good behavior, and shall at stated times receive for their services a compensation which shall not be diminished during their continuance in office.

Section II

1. The judicial power shall extend to all cases in law and equity arising under this Constitution, the laws of the United States, and treaties made, or which shall be made, under their authority; to all cases affecting ambassadors, other public ministers, and consuls; to all cases of admiralty and maritime jurisdiction; to controversies to which the United States shall be a party; to controversies between two or more States, between a State and citizens of another State, between citizens of different States, between citizens of the same State claiming lands under grants of different States, and between a State, or the citizens thereof, and foreign States, citizens, or subjects.

2. In all cases affecting ambassadors, other public ministers, and consuls, and those in which a State shall be party, the Supreme Court shall have original jurisdiction. In all the other cases before mentioned the Supreme Court shall have appellate jurisdiction both as to law and fact, with such exceptions and under such regulations as the Congress shall make.

3. The trial of all crimes, except in cases of impeachment, shall be by jury, and such trial shall be held in the State where the said crimes shall have been committed; but when not committed within any State the trial shall be at such place or places as the Congress may by law have directed.

Section III

1. Treason against the United States shall consist only in levying war against them, or in adhering to their enemies, giving them aid and comfort. No person shall be convicted of treason unless on the testimony of two witnesses to the same overt act, or on confession in open court.

2. The Congress shall have power to declare the punishment of treason, but no attainder of treason shall work corruption of blood or forfeiture except during the life of the person attained.

ARTICLE IV

Section I

Full faith and credit shall be given in each State to the public acts, records, and judicial preceedings of every other State. And the Congress may by general laws prescribe the manner in which such acts, records and proceedings shall be proved, and the effect thereof.

Section II

1. The citizens of each State shall be entitled to all privileges and immunities of citizens in the several States.

2. A person charged in any State with treason, felony, or other crime, who shall flee from justice, and be found in another State, shall on demand of the Executive authority of the State from which he fled, be delivered up, to be removed to the State having jurisdiction of the crime.

3. No person held to service or labor in one State, under the laws thereof, escaping into another shall, in consequence of any law or regulation therein, be discharged from such service or labor, but shall be delivered up on claim of the party to whom such service or labor may be due.

Section III

1. New States may be admitted by the Congress into this Union; but no new State shall be formed or erected within the jurisdiction of any other State, nor any State be formed by the junction of two or more States, or parts of States, without the consent of the Legislatures of the States concerned, as well as of the Congress.

2. The Congress shall have power to dispose of and make all needful rules and regulations respecting the territory or other property belonging to the United States; and nothing in this Constitution shall be so construed as to prejudice any claims of the United States, or of any particular State.

Section IV

The United States shall guarantee to every State in this Union a republican form of government, and shall protect each of them against invasion, and, on application of the Legislature, or of the Executive (when the Legislature cannot be convened), against domestic violence.

ARTICLE V

The Congress, whenever two thirds of both Houses shall deem it necessary, shall propose amendments to this Constitution, or, on the application of the Legislatures of two thirds of the several States, shall call a convention for proposing amendments, which, in either case, shall be valid to all intents and purposes, as part of this Constitution, when ratified by the Legislatures of three fourths of the several States, or by conventions in three fourths thereof, as the one or the other mode of ratification may be proposed by the Congress; provided that no amendment which may be made prior to the year one thousand eight hundred and eight shall in any manner affect the first and fourth clauses in the Ninth Section of the First Article; and that no State, without its consent, shall be deprived of its equal suffrage in the Senate.

ARTICLE VI

1. All debts contracted and engagements entered into before the adoption of this Constitution shall be as valid against the United States under this Constitution as under the Confederation.

2. This Constitution and the laws of the United States which shall be made in pursuance thereof and all treaties made, or which shall be made, under the authority of the United States, shall be the supreme law of the land, and the judges in every State shall be bound thereby, anything in the Constitution of laws of any State to the contrary notwithstanding.

3. The Senators and Representatives before mentioned, and the members of the several State Legislatures, and all executive and judicial officers, both of the United States and of the several States, shall be bound by oath or affirmation to support this Constitution; but no religious test shall ever be

required as a qualification to any office or public trust under the United States.

ARTICLE VII

The ratification of the Conventions of nine States shall be sufficient for the establishment of this Constitution between the States so ratifying the same.

THE AMENDMENTS
TO THE CONSTITUTION*

The Conventions of a number of the States having, at the time of adopting the Constitution, expressed a desire, in order to prevent misconstruction or abuse of its powers, that further declaratory and restrictive clauses should be added, and as extending the ground of public confidence in the Government will best insure the beneficent ends of its institution;

Resolved, by the Senate and House of Representatives of the United States of America, in Congress assembled, two-thirds of both Houses concurring, that the following articles be proposed to the Legislatures of the several States, as amendments to the Constitution of the United States; all or any of which articles, when ratified by three-fourths of the said Legislatures, to be valid to all intents and purposes as part of the said Constitution, namely:

AMENDMENT I

Congress shall make no law respecting an establishment of religion, or prohibiting the free exercise thereof; or abridging the freedom of speech, or of the press; or the right of the people peaceably to assemble, and to petition the Government for a redress of grievances.

---

*The Bill of Rights consists of the first ten amendments to the Constitution.

AMENDMENT II

A well regulated Militia, being necessary to the security of a free State, the right of the people to keep and bear Arms, shall not be infringed.

AMENDMENT III

No Soldier shall, in time of peace be quartered in any house, without the consent of the Owner, nor in time of war, but in a manner to be prescribed by law.

AMENDMENT IV

The right of the people to be secure in their persons, houses, papers, and effects, against unreasonable searches and seizures, shall not be violated, and no Warrants shall issue, but upon probable cause, supported by Oath or affirmation, and particularly describing the place to be searched, and the persons or things to be seized.

AMENDMENT V

No person shall be held to answer for a capital, or otherwise infamous crime, unless on a presentment or indictment of a Grand Jury, except in cases arising in the land or naval forces, or in the Militia, when in actual service in time of War or public danger; nor shall any person be subject for the same offense to be twice put in jeopardy of life or limb; nor shall be compelled in any criminal case to be a witness against himself, nor be deprived of life, liberty, or property, without due process of law; nor shall private property be taken for public use, without just compensation.

AMENDMENT VI

In all criminal prosecutions, the accused shall enjoy the right to a speedy and public trial, by an impartial jury of the State and district wherein the crime shall have been committed, which district shall have been previously ascertained by law, and to be informed of the nature and cause of the accusation; to be confronted with the witnesses against him; to have compulsory process for obtaining witnesses in his favor, and to have the Assistance of Counsel for his defence.

AMENDMENT VII

In Suits at common law, where the value in controversy shall exceed twenty dollars, the right of trial by jury shall be preserved, and no fact tried by a jury, shall be otherwise re-examined in any Court of the United States, than according to the rules of the common law.

AMENDMENT VIII

Excessive bail shall not be required, nor excessive fines imposed, nor cruel and unusual punishments inflicted.

AMENDMENT IX

The enumeration in the Constitution, of certain rights, shall not be construed to deny or disparage others retained by the people.

AMENDMENT X

The powers not delegated to the United States by the Constitution, nor prohibited by it to the States, are reserved to the States respectively, or to the people.

AMENDMENT XI

The Judicial power of the United States shall not be construed to extend to any suit in law or equity, commenced or prosecuted against one of the United States by Citizens of another State, or by Citizens or Subjects of any Foreign State.

AMENDMENT XII

The Electors shall meet in their respective states, and vote by ballot for President and Vice-President, one of whom, at least, shall not be an inhabitant of the same state with themselves; they shall name in their ballots the person voted for as President, and in distinct ballots the person voted for as Vice-President, and they shall make distinct lists of all persons voted for as President, and of all persons voted for as Vice-President and of the number of votes for each, which lists they shall sign and certify, and transmit sealed to the seat of the government of the United States, directed to the President of the Senate; The President of the Senate shall, in the presence of the Senate and House of Representatives, open all the certificates and the votes shall then be counted; The person having the greatest Number of votes for President, shall be the President, if such number be a majority of the whole number of Electors appointed; and if no person have such majority, then from the persons having the highest numbers not exceeding three on the list of those voted for as President, the House of Representatives shall choose immediately, by ballot, the President. But in choosing the President, the votes shall be taken by states, the representation from each state having one vote; a quorum for this purpose shall consist of a member or members from two-thirds of the states, and a majority of all the states shall be necessary to a choice. And if the House of Representatives shall not choose a President whenever the right of choice shall devolve upon them, before the fourth day of March next following, then the Vice-President shall act as President, as in the case of the death or other constitutional disability of the President. The person having the greatest number of votes as Vice-President, shall be the Vice-President, if such number be a majority of the whole number of Electors appointed, and if no person have a majority, then from the two highest numbers on the list, the Senate shall choose the Vice-President; a quorum for the purpose shall consist of two-thirds of the whole number of Senators, and a majority of the whole number shall be necessary to a choice. But no person constitutionally ineligible to the office of President shall be eligible to that of Vice-President of the United States.

Amendment XIII

1. Neither slavery nor involuntary servitude, except as a punishment for crime whereof the party shall have been duly convicted, shall exist within the United States, or any place subject to their jurisdiction.
2. Congress shall have power to enforce this article by appropriate legislation.

Amendment XIV

1. All persons born or naturalized in the United States, and subject to the jurisdiction thereof, are citizens of the United States and of the State wherein they reside. No State shall make or enforce any law which shall abridge the privileges or immunities of citizens of the United States; nor shall any State deprive any person of life, liberty, or property, without due process of law; nor deny to any person within its jurisdiction the equal protection of the laws.

2. Representatives shall be apportioned among the several States according to their respective numbers, counting the whole number of persons in each State, excluding Indians not taxed. But when the right to vote at any election for the choice of electors for President and Vice-President of the United States, Representatives in Congress, the Executive and Judicial officers of a State, or the members of the Legislature thereof, is denied to any of the male inhabitants of such State, being twenty-one years of age, and citizens of the United States, or in any way abridged, except for participation in rebellion, or other crime, the basis of representation therein shall be reduced in the proportion which the number of such male citizens shall bear to the whole number of male citizens twenty-one years of age in such State.

3. No person shall be a Senator or Representative in Congress, or elector of President and Vice-President, or hold any office, civil or military, under the United States, or under any State, who, having previously taken an oath, as a member of Congress, or as an officer of the United States, or as a member of any State legislature, or as an executive or judicial officer of any State, to support the Constitution of the United States, shall have engaged in insurrection or rebellion against the same, or given aid or comfort to the enemies thereof. But Congress may by a vote of two-thirds of each House, remove such disability.

4. The validity of the public debt of the United States, authorized by law, including debts incurred for payment of pensions and bounties for services in suppressing insurrection or rebellion, shall not be questioned. But neither the United States nor any State shall assume or pay any debt or obligation incurred in aid of insurrection or rebellion against the United States, or any claim for the loss or emancipation of any slave; but all such debts, obligations and claims shall be held illegal and void.

5. The Congress shall have power to enforce, by appropriate legislation, the provisions of this article.

Amendment XV

1. The right of citizens of the United States to vote shall not be denied or abridged by the United States or by any State on account of race, color, or previous condition of servitude.

2. The Congress shall have power to enforce this article by appropriate legislation.

Amendment XVI

The Congress shall have power to lay and collect taxes on incomes, from whatever source derived, without apportionment among the several States, and without regard to any census or enumeration.

Amendment XVII

The Senate of the United States shall be composed of two Senators from each State, elected by the people thereof, for six years; and each Senator shall have one vote. The electors in each State shall have the qualifications requisite for electors of the most numerous branch of the State legislatures. When vacancies happen in the representation of any State in the Senate, the executive authority of such State shall issue writs of election to fill such vacancies: Provided, That the legislature of any State may empower the executive thereof to make temporary appointments until the people fill the vacancies by election as the legislature may direct. This amendment shall not be so construed as to affect the election or term of any Senator chosen before it becomes valid as part of the Constitution.

Amendment XVIII

1. After one year from the ratification of this article the manufacture, sale, or transportation of intoxicating liquors within, the importation thereof into, or the exportation thereof from the United States and all territory subject to the jurisdiction thereof for beverage purposes is hereby prohibited.

2. The Congress and the several States shall have concurrent power to enforce this article by appropriate legislation.

3. This article shall be inoperative unless it shall have been ratified as an

amendment to the Constitution by the legislatures of the several States, as provided in the Constitution, within seven years from the date of the submission hereof to the States by the Congress.

AMENDMENT XIX

The right of citizens of the United States to vote shall not be denied or abridged by the United States or by any State on account of sex. Congress shall have power to enforce this article by appropriate legislation.

AMENDMENT XX

1. The terms of the President and Vice President shall end at noon on the 20th day of January, and the terms of Senators and Representatives at noon on the 3d day of January, of the years in which such terms would have ended if this article had not been ratified; and the terms of their successors shall then begin.

2. The Congress shall assemble at least once in every year, and such meeting shall begin at noon on the 3d day of January, unless they shall by law appoint a different day.

3. If, at the time fixed for the beginning of the term of the President, the President elect shall have died, the Vice President elect shall become President. If a President shall not have been chosen before the time fixed for the beginning of his term, or if the President elect shall have failed to qualify, then the Vice President elect shall act as President until a President shall have qualified; and the Congress may by law provide for the case wherein neither a President elect nor a Vice President elect shall have qualified, declaring who shall then act as President, or the manner in which one who is to act shall be selected, and such person shall act accordingly until a President or Vice President shall have qualified.

4. The Congress may by law provide for the case of the death of any of the persons from whom the House of Representatives may choose a President whenever the right of choice shall have devolved upon them, and for the case of the death of any of the persons from whom the Senate may choose a Vice President whenever the right of choice shall have devolved upon them.

5. Sections 1 and 2 shall take effect on the 15th day of October following the ratification of this article.

6. This article shall be inoperative unless it shall have been ratified as an amendment to the Constitution by the legislatures of three-fourths of the several States within seven years from the date of its submission.

AMENDMENT XXI

1. The eighteenth article of amendment to the Constitution of the United States is hereby repealed.

2. The transportation or importation into any State, Territory, or possession of the United States for delivery or use therein of intoxicating liquors, in violation of the laws thereof, is hereby prohibited.

3. The article shall be inoperative unless it shall have been ratified as an amendment to the Constitution by conventions in the several States, as provided in the Constitution, within seven years from the date of the submission hereof to the States by the Congress.

AMENDMENT XXII

1. No person shall be elected to the office of the President more than twice, and no person who has held the office of President, or acted as President, for more than two years of a term to which some other person was elected President shall be elected to the office of the President more than once. But this Article shall not apply to any person holding the office of President, when this Article was proposed by the Congress, and shall not prevent any person who may be holding the office of President, or acting as President, during the term within which this Article becomes operative from holding the office of President or acting as President during the remainder of such term.

2. This article shall be inoperative unless it shall have been ratified as an amendment to the Constitution by the legislatures of three-fourths of the several States within seven years from the date of its submission to the States by the Congress.

AMENDMENT XXIII

1. The District constituting the seat of Government of the United States shall appoint in such manner as the Congress may direct: A number of electors of President and Vice President equal to the whole number of Senators

and Representatives in Congress to which the District would be entitled if it were a State, but in no event more than the least populous State; they shall be in addition to those appointed by the States, but they shall be considered, for the purposes of the election of President and Vice President, to be electors appointed by a State; and they shall meet in the District and perform such duties as provided by the twelfth article of amendment.

2. The Congress shall have power to enforce this article by appropriate legislation.

Amendment XXIV

1. The right of citizens of the United States to vote in any primary or other election for President or Vice President, for electors for President or Vice President, or for Senator or Representative in Congress, shall not be denied or abridged by the United States or any State by reason of failure to pay any poll tax or other tax.

2. The Congress shall have power to enforce this article by appropriate legislation.

Amendment XXV

1. In case of the removal of the President from office or of his death or resignation, the Vice President shall become President.

2. Whenever there is a vacancy in the office of the Vice President, the President shall nominate a Vice President who shall take office upon confirmation by a majority vote of both Houses of Congress.

3. Whenever the President transmits to the President pro tempore of the Senate and the Speaker of the House of Representatives his written declaration that he is unable to discharge the powers and duties of his office, and until he transmits to them a written declaration to the contrary, such powers and duties shall be discharged by the Vice President as Acting President.

4. Whenever the Vice President and a majority of either the principal officers of the executive departments or of such other body as Congress may by law provide, transmit to the President pro tempore of the Senate and the Speaker of the House of Representatives their written declaration that the President is unable to discharge the powers and duties of his office, the Vice President shall immediately assume the powers and duties of the office as

Acting President. Thereafter, when the President transmits to the President pro tempore of the Senate and the Speaker of the House of Representatives his written declaration that no inability exists, he shall resume the powers and duties of his office unless the Vice President and a majority of either the principal officers of the executive department or of such other body as Congress may by law provide, transmit within four days to the President pro tempore of the Senate and the Speaker of the House of Representatives their written declaration that the President is unable to discharge the powers and duties of his office. Thereupon Congress shall decide the issue, assembling within forty eight hours for that purpose if not in session. If the Congress, within twenty one days after receipt of the latter written declaration, or, if Congress is not in session, within twenty one days after Congress is required to assemble, determines by two thirds vote of both Houses that the President is unable to discharge the powers and duties of his office, the Vice President shall continue to discharge the same as Acting President; otherwise, the President shall resume the powers and duties of his office.

Amendment XXVI

1. The right of citizens of the United States, who are eighteen years of age or older, to vote shall not be denied or abridged by the United States or by any State on account of age.

2. The Congress shall have power to enforce this article by appropriate legislation.

Amendment XXVII

No law, varying the compensation for the services of the Senators and Representatives, shall take effect, until an election of Representatives shall have intervened.